MARTIN BUBER

Prophet of Religious Secularism

MARTIN BUBER

Prophet of Religious Secularism

—

*The Criticism of Institutional Religion
in the Writings of Martin Buber*

by

DONALD J. MOORE

THE JEWISH PUBLICATION SOCIETY OF AMERICA

Philadelphia

To my brothers

of the Society of Jesus

and to all who are striving

for real community among men

ACKNOWLEDGMENTS

Among the many who have assisted me in numerous ways during the writing and editing of this book and to whom I am deeply indebted, I wish to acknowledge in particular Prof. Maurice Friedman who initiated me into the thought of Martin Buber and who encouraged me to undertake this work, and Prof. Charles Robert of the University of Strasbourg whose gentle prodding, criticism, and support helped so much to bring this work to completion; also my deep thanks to Carol Marie Bandini who read and criticized each chapter as it was written, and to Ms. Cathie Sclafani and Ms. Frances Kestler who so generously typed the original manuscript.

Grateful acknowledgment is also made to the following publishers for permission to use copyrighted material from the sources listed:

From A BELIEVING HUMANISM by Martin Buber. Copyright © 1967 by Simon & Schuster, Inc. Reprinted by permission of Simon & Schuster.

From BETWEEN MAN AND MAN by Martin Buber. First published by Routledge & Kegan Paul, Ltd. Reprinted by permission of The Macmillan Company and Routledge & Kegan Paul, Ltd.

From DANIEL by Martin Buber. Translated by Maurice Friedman. Copyright © 1964 by Holt, Rinehart and Winston, Inc. Reprinted by permission of Holt, Rinehart and Winston, Inc.

From ECLIPSE OF GOD by Martin Buber. Copyright © 1952 by Harper and Brothers. Reprinted by permission of Harper & Row, Publishers.

From GOOD AND EVIL by Martin Buber. Copyright 1952, 1953 by Martin Buber. Reprinted by permission of Charles Scribner's Sons and Routledge & Kegan Paul, Ltd.

From HASIDISM AND MODERN MAN by Martin Buber. Copyright © 1958 by Martin Buber. Reprinted by permission of the publisher, Horizon Press, and Rafael Buber.

From I AND THOU, 2d edition, by Martin Buber. Translated by Ronald Gregor Smith. Copyright © 1958 by Charles Scribner's Sons. Reprinted by permission of Charles Scribner's Sons and T. & T. Clark, Ltd.

CONTENTS

FOREWORD

by Maurice Friedman

When my book *Martin Buber: The Life of Dialogue* was published in 1955,* it was the first comprehensive and systematic study of Buber's thought in any language. Two years before, despite the strong recommendations of readers and editors, the board of the University of Chicago Press had turned *The Life of Dialogue* down because they had never heard of Martin Buber. Only the intervention of Sir Herbert Read, who persuaded Routledge & Kegan Paul to commit itself to a British edition, made possible an American copublication and, by the same token, the first book in English on Buber's life and thought. In the twenty years since then most of Buber's own works have appeared in English, and all of them, except the important collection *Pointing the Way,* are still available in paperback. Buber himself has become one of the best-known thinkers and figures of the twentieth century. In this same period a whole spate of books about Buber have been published in England and America, some more scholarly† and some more popular, some more concerned with Buber's thought and some with his life, most by a single author but some, like *The Philosophy of Martin*

*Buber called this book "the classic study of my thought" and tried for years to arrange for its publication in German and Hebrew translation. The second, somewhat revised and expanded edition of *Martin Buber: The Life of Dialogue* was published as a Harper's Torchbooks (paperback) in 1960 and is still in print.

†The most scholarly, most thorough, and most important single book on Buber to appear since my own *Life of Dialogue* is Grete Schaeder, *The Hebrew Humanism of Martin Buber* (Detroit: Wayne State University Press, 1973), translated from the German original. Dr. Schaeder is at present completing a three-volume German edition of Buber's correspondence under the title *Buber Briefwechsel* (Heidelberg: Verlag Lambert Schneider), two volumes of which have already been published, the last to appear shortly.

Buber,* by many authors, some by Catholics, some by Protestants, and some by Jews.

Father Donald J. Moore's *Martin Buber: Prophet of Religious Secularism* had its inception in a course on Buber's philosophy of religion that I taught at Union Theological Seminary, New York City, in the summer of 1965 and grew by stages through a Ph.D. dissertation for the University of Strasbourg to its present form. It represents ten years of study, growth, and thought so integrally united that I am proud to have played a role in starting it on its road.

That one of the stages on this road was a doctoral dissertation for a great French university might mislead the reader into anticipating still another scholarly tome. Nothing could be further from the truth. Even in its dissertation form it was a remarkably nonacademic presentation, and as it appears today it is still less so. Indeed, though Father Moore had read everything available on Buber in English and French, he did not know either German or Hebrew and made no claim to a definitive scholarly interpretation. The importance of his book lies elsewhere. One of the virtues of *Martin Buber: Prophet of Religious Secularism* is that it makes Buber's thought available to the average intelligent layman. Father Moore's excellent understanding of Buber's thought from within enables him to present relatively difficult matters with remarkable clarity and simplicity. The major headings of the book, the many subheads, and his tactful sense of how to group the subheads together under the chapter are all very helpful.

But there are two other reasons why this is an important book. The first is that it represents a whole new stage in the Jewish-Christian ecumenical dialogue since the first period of Buber's influence. During this early period, as I demonstrate at length in my chapter "Buber and Christianity" in *The Life of Dialogue*, although Buber's influence on Christian thought was revolutionary, it was mostly christianized in the process of be-

---

*Edited by Paul Arthur Schilpp and Maurice Friedman, this volume of *The Library of Living Philosophers* contains Buber's now-famous "Autobiographical Fragments" (separately published by Open Court under the title *Meetings*), thirty essays by distinguished scholars and philosophers the world over, Buber's "Replies to My Critics," and a comprehensive bibliography of Buber's publications in all languages prepared by Maurice Friedman.

ing taken over, so that many of its salient features were lost. For example, Buber's I-Thou relationship became a Thou-I relationship for many neoorthodox theologians, who wished to cling to the sundering of God and man through original sin and the total dependency of man on God's grace through faith in Christ. For many, it became a choice *between* I-Thou and I-It, rather than the alternation of the two, as Buber held. For others, only Christ could have an I-Thou relationship with God, whereas ordinary men were largely condemned to I-It. For still others, Christ was the Thou rather than the imageless God to whom Buber points. Finally, far more attention was paid by Christian theologians to the I-Thou relationship between man and God and far less to that between man and man—and the integral unity of the two for Buber tended to be lost sight of. Even the biblical-sounding language of "Thou" in Ronald Gregor Smith's beautiful translation of *I and Thou* misled many into thinking of Buber solely in theological terms rather than in the interhuman and anthropological terms which were central for him.

If this trend is beginning to be corrected and a new and more authentic Buber renaissance is under way, as the lead article in the London *Times Literary Supplement* for December 28, 1973, suggests may be the case, it is because men like Father Moore, instead of appropriating Buber for Christianity, have allowed themselves to enter into an open, mutual dialogue with this prophet of the "narrow ridge" and let their own Christianity be modified by it. Father Moore does not seek to "baptize" Buber, like the young seminarian who, after talking with me for three hours, plaintively said in parting, "Buber is so good. How is it that he is not a Christian?" Instead, Father Moore recognizes that Buber enables us to see more clearly "that in many areas genuine Christianity is in basic agreement with genuine Judaism" and that "we who call ourselves Christian would be much more faithful to our task and to our vocation if we could follow, each in his own way, the spirit of Buber." "Perhaps," Moore concludes, "Martin Buber should be called a man of universal religion, for he was indeed a man of God." Even this would be misleading if one did not understand Buber's universalism precisely as that of the life of dialogue. If Buber did not use his Judaism to shut himself away from men of other faiths, neither did he have to leave the ground of his Judaism to meet openhearted men and women of other religions. "I can stand in the doorway of my ancestral house," Buber wrote, "and speak into the street. The word that is uttered there will not go astray."

The first significant way in which the dialogue with Buber has helped to modify Christianity is in the post–Vatican II climate in which Christians, including a great many pious Catholics, have not only moved into serious dialogue with Judaism but have also questioned some of the forms, dogmas, and institutions of their own church without seeing themselves thereby as in any sense *outside* the church. An example of this attitude is Father Moore's memorable statement on personal responsibility, a position which is all the more striking since he is a member of the Society of Jesus, a religious order of men well known for its stress on obedience:

> Real faith imposes an awesome responsibility on the believer: I must assume before God personal responsibility for the whole of my life. I must answer before God for *this* hour; nothing can relieve me of this responsibility; no one can provide the response I must give to the present situation which confronts me. No individual, no institution, no authority, no law can answer for me; *I must not let them.* For the man of faith there can be no substitute for personal responsibility: I stand before God at each hour responsible for the whole of my life.

Another way in which the appreciation of Buber has come of age in our day is the recognition that the "death of God" theologies and above all the impact of Dietrich Bonhoeffer, far from dating Buber, have served to bring into focus his lifelong concern with "religious secularism." Religious secularism, to Buber, is that claim for the hallowing of the everyday and the sanctifying of the profane which stands in uncompromising opposition to every tendency to make of religion a separate upper story of spirituality with no binding force in our lives. "Religion," Buber once wrote, "is the great enemy of mankind." By "religion" Buber meant the tendency of every organized religion throughout history to promote and sanction a dualism that obscures the face of God and leaves our ordinary lives unhallowed and unhallowable. Buber never attacked organized religion as such, but neither did he support it as such. It had to submit to the criterion of its place within the dialectic of the movement toward meeting with the eternal Thou and the movement away from it. Therefore, it would be seriously misleading if we were to take Father Moore's emphasis on the need for continuity and renewal of religious tradition in Buber's thought as synonymous with an unqualified affirmation by Buber of the need for *organized* religion. If Buber was not a "religious anarchist," as Gershom Scholem has characterized him in his one-sided attack on Buber's interpretation of Hasidism, neither can anything Buber says about the need for "law" or about each religion being a separate house in an exile which only God can overcome justify turning Buber into an advocate of organized religion in general.

What Buber does say repeatedly is that structure is necessary as well as spontaneity—not just any structure, but structure that makes spontaneity possible, planning that leaves room for surprises. For Buber, the *mitzvah*, or command of God, can never be divorced from the address of the particular hour and the particular situation and turned into a universally valid prescription or law. Here, as elsewhere in Buber's thought, it is not I-Thou *or* I-It which is the basic choice but the healthy alternation between I-Thou and I-It. It is this alternation that allows every It to be taken again into the meeting with the Thou, every structure to be brought again and again into the meeting between person and person, community and community, people and God, mortal I and "eternal Thou."

MAURICE FRIEDMAN

Del Mar, California
June 1974

PREFACE

"Next to being the children of God our greatest privilege is being the brothers of each other."[1] These words of Martin Buber, given at his first conference after his arrival in the United States in 1951, illustrate so well the basic theme of his life; they illustrate, too, what I would like to think is the basic theme of this work. If there is a single insight which dominated Buber's writings, it is precisely this: men cannot say Thou to God unless they also say Thou to one another; and men cannot truly say Thou to one another unless in some way they also say Thou to God.

In preparing this study of the thought of Martin Buber, my purpose has not been so much to criticize and to analyze as to listen and to learn. I believe that this is the only way to read the works of Buber. This man who was such an advocate of dialogue continues to dialogue with us through his writings. It is a dialogue akin to that which Buber himself described in his postscript to *I and Thou*, a dialogue of the spirit.[2] If we make an object of Buber's writings, if we read them primarily in order to analyze and criticize, then we have already distorted their meaning; we have muted the voice that speaks to us through these works. We must be open, and we must listen.

Listening is difficult for man today. We are living in confused and confusing times, in a world that is changing so rapidly that it often leaves man bewildered and riddled with doubt; he finds it difficult to recognize the role he is called upon to play in the world. There is an increasing spirit of alienation and estrangement. Dialogue has become difficult and unappealing; it is almost nonexistent between generations, between races, between nations. There are some who have too narrow a concept of dialogue, not realizing the awesome responsibility that dialogue imposes upon each person in the area of concrete action; there are others who insist more and more on replacing dialogue by action and protest, as if this alone can bring about that type of life and community that we call human. Unless action springs from dialogue, it is without direction and meaning; unless dialogue leads to action, it is truncated and inauthentic; unless protest recognizes the central importance of dialogue, it becomes all too often negative and destructive.

This confusion and doubt, this protest and lack of trust that permeates society is also reflected in institutional religion, and especially in the life of the Christian Church. It is not surprising that a church which is trying with renewed effort to find its place in the world shares also in these struggles of man. "The joys and hopes, the griefs and anxieties of the men of this age, especially those who are poor or in any way afflicted, these too are the joys and hopes, the griefs and anxieties of the followers of Christ."[3] The confusion, the restlessness, the doubts that afflict mankind find their counterpart in the confusion, the restlessness, the doubts that strike at the hearts of so many believers. The fruit of this is often discouragement and frustration, and this in turn produces a spirit of anger and revolt, a revolt aimed primarily at the institutional church as it now exists.

Amid this growing sensitivity to the shortcomings of institutional religion, many believers feel that they can live authentic human lives and, seemingly, authentic religious lives apart from any church or religious institution. The Christian of this type believes that the church is no longer relevant to our age, that it no longer speaks to the heart of living man.

It is in this context that I would like to consider Martin Buber's critique of organized religion. I am convinced that all that goes by the name of religion today has much to gain from the insights of Buber. Buber has taken the language and concepts of the Bible, filtered through the experience of his own life of faith, and expressed them in a way accessible to all men. For Buber, religion is rooted in everyday life; indeed, life is viewed as a continual dialogue between man and God. There is no division of the sacred from the secular. It is in the lived concrete, here and now, that man encounters the living God. For this reason religion cannot be isolated into any one segment of life; it permeates every aspect of human life. Buber speaks to man's everyday experience of life; his language touches the heart of living man; he speaks of religion in terms that can be grasped by every man. Martin Buber speaks to the needs of religion today; he helps give direction to religion for the morrow.

In a memorial service held in New York City on July 13, 1965, thirty days after Buber's death, there was applied to him the talmudic saying "When a wise man dies, all are related to him." The wise man addresses himself to all men; when this scholar and man of God passed away, the loss was everyman's. Few men of the spirit have left so profound an impression on the best thinking of their time as has Martin Buber; few men have emphasized and witnessed so profoundly to the need of man for a personal relationship with God and with his fellowmen. The memorial service continued:

> In the book of Daniel it is written . . . "And they that are wise shall shine as the brightness of the firmament, and they that turn many to righteousness, as the stars, for ever and ever."
> Stars, dead for ages, continue to send forth their light. So, too, with *hakham shemet,* "the wise man who dies." His wisdom will continue to enlighten *leolam vaed,* "for ever and ever."[4]

In this present crisis of faith and religion that agonizes the hearts of so many men, it might be well to ponder anew the wisdom and religious insights of Martin Buber, and hopefully in this pondering to meet the person who, in his wisdom and writings, shines as the brightness of the firmament, "for ever and ever."

D. J. M.

Fordham University
Bronx N.Y.
July 1974

MARTIN BUBER

A Biographical Portrait

The bare biographical data of Martin Buber's life can be summed up very briefly. He was born in Vienna in 1878, but at a very early age, because of the separation of his parents, he was taken to the home of his paternal grandparents in Lemberg, Galicia, Austria, where he was reared until the age of fourteen. At that time he moved to his father's estate in eastern Galicia. He began his university studies in philosophy and the history of art at Vienna, continued them briefly at Leipzig, and received his Ph.D. from the University of Berlin in 1904.

It was about this time that Buber recognized the importance of Hasidism for his own personal life. He was reading a saying by Rabbi Israel ben Eliezer, the founder of Hasidism, on the fervor and inward renewal of the pious man, and he recognized in himself the Hasidic soul. As a result of this he gave up most of his other activity and spent the next five years in isolation studying the texts of Hasidism. Only when he emerged from this isolation was he ready to begin his real life work as a writer, speaker, and teacher.[1]

He was one of the founders, in 1902, of the German Jewish publishing house, Jüdischer Verlag. In the two years prior to World War I Buber became increasingly interested in social problems, an interest that sprang in part from his long-abiding concern with Zionism and from the general demand of his milieu for more rootedness and community. In 1913 he helped to sponsor a conference in Berlin to work for the establishment of a Jewish college in Germany, which he hoped would have an influence beyond Jewish circles for the advancement of a general cultural and religious renewal. In 1914 Buber met in Potsdam with Gustav Landauer, Florence Christian Rang, Theodor Daeubler and other prominent figures in European life to form a cultural group to work in behalf of international unity. The outbreak of World War I put an end to these efforts.[2]

In 1916 Buber founded *Der Jude,* a periodical which he edited until 1924 and which became under his leadership one of the best-known organs of Judaism in Germany. From 1926 to 1930 he published, along with the Catholic Joseph Wittig and the Protestant Viktor von Weizsäcker, *Die Kreatur,* a periodical concerned with the social and pedagogical problems of religion. During this period, from 1923 to 1933, he taught Jewish philosophy of religion and the history of religions at the University of Frankfurt. Much of his time during these years was also given to his monumental translation of the Hebrew Bible into German, accomplished for the most part with the collaboration of Franz Rosenzweig. From 1933 to 1938 Buber was outstanding in his efforts in behalf of German Jews in their resistance to Nazi anti-Semitism.

In 1938 he left Germany for Palestine, where he was professor of social philosophy at the Hebrew University until 1951. After his retirement Buber continued for two more years as director of the government-sponsored Institute for Adult Education.[3] He died in Jerusalem in 1965 at the age of eighty-seven.

Obviously this simple outline tells us very little about the man, his characteristics, his personality. However, certain personal reminiscences of Buber were collected from his writings and published under the title "Autobiographical Fragments."[4] Three of these fragments in particular help us to understand the real humanity of Martin Buber.

THE NEED TO BE PRESENT

The first of these personal reflections, written in 1929, is called "A Conversion."[5] It recounts the story of a young man who came seeking Buber's advice, failed to find what he sought, and apparently died soon after in tragic circumstances. Buber realized too late that he was never truly present to this young man; he never really listened to him. It was an experience which was to have a profound effect on Buber's philosophy of dialogue. The encounter was simple enough. Late one morning, after a period of "religious enthusiasm," Buber was visited by an unknown young man. He treated the visitor in a friendly manner, as he had treated countless other students who sought his advice. But he realized later that he was not present in spirit and had failed to guess the questions that were never asked. After the young man's death, Buber was informed of the content of these questions: "I learned that he had come to me not casually, but borne by destiny, not for a chat but for a decision. He had come to me, he had come in this hour. What do we expect when we are in despair and yet go to a man? Surely a presence by means of which we are told that nevertheless there is meaning."[6]

Buber uses this story to illustrate his "conversion" from the attitude toward religion and things religious as something apart from ordinary life, as something which "lifted you out," as an experience of an otherness which did not fit into the context of this life.[7] Religion now became "just *everything*, simply all that is lived in its possibility of dialogue." Buber now realized that there was no fulfillment save in the fullness of claim and responsibility offered in the present moment. It is always in the present moment that "I am claimed and may respond in responsibility, and know who speaks and demands a response." He concludes this brief memoir:

> As when you pray you do not thereby remove yourself from this life of yours . . . so too . . . when you are called upon from above, required, chosen, empowered, sent, you with this your mortal bit of life are referred to, this moment is not extracted from it, it rests on what has been and beckons to the remainder which has still to be lived, you are not swallowed up in a fulness without obligation, you are willed for the life of communion.[8]

Besides the significance which Buber himself explicitly attaches to this experience, we may point out also the importance of "the meeting," of "presence," which plays such a vital role in all his mature thought. The young man who sought Buber's help had the right to expect a presence which says there is meaning. And the call from above which enters our life does not withdraw us from reality, but sends us forth to a "life of communion." Here, certainly, we begin to understand the real person of Martin Buber, a man who throughout his life was to exemplify this meaningful presence to others, and who saw in the life of communion the only real life for man; for him there could be no authentic human life except in meeting, in presence, in communion; when we begin to realize the supreme importance of each present moment, then we will begin to live.

THE DANGER OF TALK ABOUT GOD

The second of these personal reminiscences of Buber was written in 1932 and entitled "Report on Two Talks."[9] It is important because it gives us an indication of the approach to God which governed the greater part of his life.

The first of the two talks occurred after a series of three lecture-discussions in an unidentified German city. At the end of the series Buber had a special discussion session for the workers who attended. In this group there stood a man whose face Buber came back to again and again because he gave such a strong impression of one who "listened as one who really wished to hear."

> What was notable about him was that he heard and pondered, in a manner as slow as it was impressive. Finally, he opened his lips as well. "I have had the experience," he explained slowly and impressively ... "that I do not need this hypothesis 'God' in order to be quite at home in the world."[10]

Buber was struck by the man's objection, and felt himself obliged to ponder before replying to him. "It came to me that I must shatter the security of his *Weltanschauung*, through which he thought of a 'world' in which one 'felt at home.'" Buber then proceeded to point out the difference between the "world of the senses" and the "scientific" world. Were there not three different worlds—of objects, of subjects, of phenomena? Was not some being needed to give this "world" its foundation? "When I was through a stern silence ruled in the now twilit room. Then the man with the shepherd's face raised his heavy lids, which had been lowered the whole time, and said slowly and impressively, 'You are right.'"[11]

And what was Buber's reaction?

> I sat in front of him dismayed. What had I done? I had led the man to the threshold beyond which there sat enthroned ... the God of the Philosophers. Had I wished for that? Had I not rather wished to lead him to the other, ... the God of Abraham, Isaac, and Jacob, Him to whom one can say Thou?
> It grew dusk, it was late. On the next day I had to depart. I could not remain, as I now ought to do; I could not enter into the factory where the man worked, become his comrade, live with him, win his trust through real life-relationship, help him to walk

with me the way of the creature who *accepts* the creation. I could only return his gaze.[12]

Thus ends the account of the first of these two talks. But in reality the conversation had no end; from Buber's point of view no conclusion had been reached. He had failed because he had led this worker to accept the God of the philosophers, to accept a new world outlook which included this God; God had become for this man Something to fit into a system; he had simply substituted one weltanschauung without God for another that contained God. But a God who is contained in a systematic world view is not the God of Abraham, Isaac, and Jacob; such a God has become an object among other objects; He is no God at all. This is the danger always present when one talks *about* God. And so the conversation ended in failure and dismay.

THE NEED TO ADDRESS GOD

The second of these two talks took place some time later in the home of an elderly, scholarly man, where Buber was staying as a guest. Buber read to him the galley proofs of a statement of faith that he was about to publish. There was a brief silence as Buber finished, and then this noble old man began to speak, at first with hesitance and then with growing passion, criticizing the frequent use of the word "God" in Buber's statement of faith. He argued that frequent speaking about God only demeans the meaning one wants to convey. He ended: "When I hear the highest called 'God' it sometimes seems almost blasphemous."[13]

The two men sat in silence facing each other. Buber seemed to draw a certain strength from the brightness of the morning light that began to flow into the room. It was one of those moments when a man speaks from the depths of his being:

Yes, . . . it is the most heavy-laden of all human words. None has become so soiled, so mutilated. Just for this reason I may not abandon it. Generations of men have laid the burden of their anxious lives upon this word and weighed it to the ground; it lies in the dust and bears their whole burden. The races of men with their religious factions have torn the word to pieces; they have killed for it and died for it, and it bears their finger marks and their blood. Where might I find a word like it to describe the highest! . . . I do indeed mean Him whom the hell-tormented and heaven-storming generations of men mean. Certainly, they draw caricatures and write "God" underneath; they murder one another and say "in God's name." But when all madness and delusion fall to dust, when they stand over against Him in the loneliest darkness and no longer say "He, He" but rather sigh "Thou," shout "Thou," all of them the one word, and when they then add "God," is it not the real God whom they all implore, the One Living God, the God of the children of man? Is it not He who *hears* them? And just for this reason is not the word "God," the word of appeal, the word which has become a *name*, consecrated in all human tongues for all times? We must esteem those who interdict it because they rebel against the injustice and wrong which are so readily referred to "God" for authorization. But we may not give it up.[14]

With this the old man stood up, placed his hand on Buber's shoulder, and said: "Let us be friends." And Buber concludes: "The conversation was completed. For where two or three are truly together, they are together in the name of God."[15]

This second talk manifests more clearly the approach to God which marked so much of Buber's life. He could speak of God so freely because he was so open to Him in prayer; God can be addressed but never possessed. Buber was a man who lived in the presence of the divine, for whom God was constantly Thou, One whom man stands over against, One to whom man turns with the fullness of his being. The God who is the object of conversation and thought, "He, He," is too often the God of the philosophers, a God whom man grasps and possesses by reason. The God of Abraham, of Isaac, of Jacob is the God whom man addresses in prayer, who is known in the meeting, One to whom man can only say Thou.

This distinction may seem commonplace, but it is too often forgotten or abused; it is a distinction which is crucial in the thought of Martin Buber. It is to Buber's credit that he maintained in his writings and in his life the clarity of this distinction to which he refers time and again. It is little wonder that those who knew him were struck by "the prophetic force of his personality and the tremendous strength and sincerity of his religious conviction."[16] And it is this element of Buber's life and religious thought that he has so clearly portrayed for us in his "Report on Two Talks."

REAL LIVING IS MEETING

The third of these personal reminiscences was written in 1947 and is called simply "Books and Men."[17] Here we have a simple and beautiful insight into the humanity of Martin Buber, into his strong love for man. He speaks of a choice between books and men. He admits that in his early years he most certainly would have chosen books, but in his later years he realized this would be less and less the case. It is not that his experiences with men have been so much better than his experiences with books; "on the contrary, purely delightful books even now come my way more often than purely delightful men."[18] Both have gifts to share, but in the end it is a question of love. "I revere books ... too much to be able to love them. But in the most venerable of living men I always find more to love than to revere."[19]

Buber concludes the short essay with this pointed analogy:

> Here is an infallible test. Imagine yourself in a situation where you are alone, wholly alone on earth, and you are offered one of the two, books or men. I often hear men prizing their solitude but that is only because there are still men somewhere on earth even though in the far distance. I knew nothing of books when I came forth from the womb of my mother, and I shall die without books, with another human hand in my own. I do, indeed, close my door at times and surrender myself to a book, but only because I can open the door again and see a human being looking at me.[20]

This brief memoir speaks for itself. It brings home so clearly one of Buber's fundamental tenets: "All real living is meeting." Buber realized that for himself he could achieve authentic existence only in loving encounter with God and with his fellowman. He was a man rooted in this world, in the concrete responsibility of each lived moment. He was a man fully alive who savored the precious value and limitless possibilities which were open to man in every hour of life. And he combined this fullness of life with an extraordinary sensitivity for others.

One instance of the latter appears in his open letter to Mahatma Gandhi, who had been critical of Zionist aspirations for Palestine. Buber strongly opposed Gandhi's views throughout the letter, yet at the end of it he wrote:

> I have been very slow in writing this letter to you, Mahatma. I made repeated pauses—sometimes days elapsing between short paragraphs—in order to test my knowledge and my way of thinking. Day and night I took myself to task, searching whether I had not in any one point overstepped the measure of self-preservation allotted and even prescribed by God to a human

community, and whether I had not fallen into the grievous error of collective egoism. Friends and my own conscience have helped to keep me straight whenever danger threatened.[21]

OPENNESS AND CONCERN FOR OTHERS

Thus even when standing in opposition to another's views, Buber exhibits that openness and concern for others which was so characteristic of his life. Along with Gandhi, he has been hailed as one of the truly universal men of our era. One commentator says of him:

> The appreciation of being—the joy of life lived in the presence of God and in relation with fellow man—was the secret of Buber's amazing sense of presence and the feeling of grandeur he transmitted to all who came into contact with him. He is one of the very few universal men of our time. Like Gandhi and Schweitzer he transcended the bounds of space and locality.[22]

And the same writer adds later: "This was the essence of Martin Buber's life and work. To make known in the concrete moment the presence of the Divine. This is what made him a great Jew. This is what made him a great human being."[23]

The universality of this man can be attributed to his determination to live on the "narrow ridge," to choose the narrow way between opposing forces and views. This view is summed up in one of the Hasidic sayings to which he would refer: "The way in this world is like the edge of a blade. On this side is the underworld, and on that side is the underworld, and the way of life lies between."[24] His success in living on this narrow ridge can be indicated by the positions he held on some of the great problems of his age.

Buber was a lifelong Zionist and devoted much of his energies for the independence of his people in their own country—yet he preached friendship and love for the Arabs of Palestine, and at times was highly critical of affairs in Israel after it had gained independence. In the above-mentioned letter to Gandhi he pointed out that the love and faith of both Arab and Jew made a union in the common service of the land a definite possibility. "Where there is faith and love, a solution may be found even to what appears to be tragic opposition." And he goes on to say:

> The Jewish farmers have begun to teach their brothers the Arab farmers to cultivate the land more intensively; we desire to teach them further; together with them we want to cultivate the land

—to "serve" it. . . . The more fertile this soil becomes, the more space there will be for us and for them. We have no desire to dispossess them; we want to live with them. We do not want to dominate them, we want to serve with them.[25]

And in an address given in 1958 he stressed that the only peace between Arab and Jew can be that of genuine cooperation. "Today, under such manifoldly aggravated circumstances, the command of the spirit is still to prepare the way for the cooperation of peoples."[26]

In criticizing Israel, Buber charged that its leaders were cultivating a political secularism that was keeping men from hearing the voice of the living God. And he added:

> And now Ben-Gurion tells us that Zionist thought is dead but that the Messianic idea is alive and will live until the coming of the Messiah. And I answer him with the question: "In how many hearts of this generation in our country does the Messianic idea live in a form other than the narrow nationalistic form which is restricted to the Ingathering of the Exiles?" A Messianic idea without the yearning for the redemption of mankind and without the desire to take part in its realization is no longer identical with the Messianic visions of the prophets of Israel, nor can that prophetic mission be identified with a messianic ideal emptied of belief in the coming of the kingdom of God.[27]

We begin to understand the narrow ridge, the edge of the blade, on which Buber chose to live his life.

REVERENCE FOR JESUS

Although he was perhaps the greatest Jewish thinker of this century, and one of Judaism's foremost exponents, he revered Jesus as much as a Jew might, and perhaps more than most Christians. In the foreword to his book *Two Types of Faith*, Buber wrote:

> From my youth onwards I have found in Jesus my great brother. That Christianity has regarded and does regard him as God and Saviour has always appeared to me a fact of the highest importance which, for his sake and my own, I must endeavour to understand. A small part of the results of this desire to understand is recorded here. My own fraternally open relationship to him has grown ever stronger and clearer, and to-day I see him more strongly and clearly than ever before.

I am more than ever certain that a great place belongs to him in Israel's history of faith and that this place cannot be described by any of the usual categories. . . . There is a something in Israel's history of faith which is only to be understood from Israel, just as there is a something in the Christian history of faith which is only to be understood from Christianity. The latter I have touched only with the unbiased respect of one who hears the Word.[28]

As a leader of German Jewry until he had to leave as a refugee for Palestine in 1938, Buber fought Nazism with patriarchal dignity and considered himself to be one who could never get over what had happened; yet he begged Israel not to execute Adolf Eichmann, and earlier, in 1953, he accepted the Peace Prize of the German Book Trade—for which he was criticized in some Jewish circles. In his acceptance of this award he called for trust and openness among men, a characteristic which is becoming increasingly rare among men of our time. "This lack of trust in Being, this incapacity for unreserved intercourse with the other, points to an innermost sickness of the sense of existence." And he concluded: "The name Satan means in Hebrew the hinderer. That is the correct designation for the anti-human in individuals and in the human race. Let us not allow this Satanic element in men to hinder us from realizing man! Let us release speech from its ban! Let us dare, despite all, to trust!"[29]

A LIVING TESTIMONY

What becomes evident from this brief portrait of Buber, and receives support from those who knew him, is that Buber's influence as a person is almost as great as his influence as a thinker. According to the German educator Karl Wilker, Buber's greatest characteristic was his "consciousness of responsibility."

The more I have come to know him, not only through his works but also face to face, the more strongly I have felt that his whole personality tolerates no untruthfulness and no unclarity. There is something there that forces one to trace out the last ground of things. . . . He who is thus must have experienced life's deepest essence. . . . He must have lived and suffered . . . and he must have shared with us all our life and suffering. He must have stood his ground face to face with despair. . . . Martin Buber belongs to the most powerful renewal not only of a people but of mankind.[30]

Buber was one of the few men of our time whose life was a living testimony to all he had written; what he taught, he also lived; within his being there was an identity of truth and life. Paul Tillich has written that

> in almost all encounters with Martin Buber something happened which trespassed for me in importance the dialogue itself. It was the experience of a man whose whole being was impregnated by the experience of the divine presence. He was, as one could say, "God-possessed." God could never become an "object" in Martin Buber's presence. The certainty of God always preceded the certainty of himself and his world.[31]

This, then, gives us a brief glimpse of the man whose thought we will study in the following pages. In Martin Buber, the man and his writings are one; his work is a beautiful projection of his own person. With this picture of the man from his own reminiscences and from the comments of a few of his admirers and acquaintances in the intellectual world, we are in a better position now to understand his thought.

THE JUDAIC WRITINGS

The First Source of His Criticism of Religion

BIBLICAL THOUGHT

"The supposition for a decision between faith and unbelief is lacking in the world of Israel, the place for it is as it were missing," writes Martin Buber. "There is here no decision of faith or unbelief."[1] To the man of ancient Israel "the idea of the non-existence of God lies outside the realm of that which was conceivable by him."[2] Faith for the Jew is not a question of belief that God exists. "That has never been doubted by Jacob's soul. In proclaiming its faith, its *emunah*, the soul only proclaimed that it put its trust in the everlasting God, *that he would be present* to the soul, as had been the experience of the patriarchs, and that it was entrusting itself to him who was present."[3]

Any serious study of Martin Buber must recognize the fundamental importance of his faith as a Jew to his philosophical, sociological, and religious thought. And this is particularly true of this particular study of his critique of organized religion. Unless we understand his criticism as one rooted in his Jewish faith, and unless we understand something of his philosophy of dialogue which in itself strongly reflects his interpretation of Judaism, we will not be able to grasp the full dimension of the criticism he directs against the structure of religion and at the same time his deep reverence for the religious spirit of man. We begin then with his concept of faith.[4]

THE MEANING OF FAITH

For Buber, his faith as a Jew meant the total consecration of his life. "The relationship of faith is a relationship of my entire being," either in the sense of trusting someone or of acknowledging something to be true, without in either case being able to give a sufficient reason for this relationship. "The relationship of trust depends upon a state of contact, a contact of my entire being with the one in whom I trust"; this basically describes the faith of Israel. "The relationship of acknowledging depends upon an act of acceptance of my entire being of that which I acknowledge to be true"; and this basically describes the faith of the Christian.[5] The man of biblical faith is one who believes not in the existence of God but in the fidelity of God and in the presence of God so that he may trust himself to God completely. One has faith in the biblical sense when he "understands the fact of the divine existence as the fact of the actual Presence of God, and on his part realizes the relationship to God which is so indicated to him . . . , that is, whether he trusts in the God who exists 'as a matter of course' as truly his God." The Israelite of true faith is distinguished by "the exclusiveness of his relationship to his God and by his reference of all things to Him."[6]

Trust rather than belief

Thus the full realization of one's faith "does not take place in a decision made at one definite moment . . . but in the man's whole life, that is in the actual totality of his relationships, not only towards God, but also to his appointed sphere in the world and to himself." For Israel, and for Martin Buber, everything is dependent upon making faith effective as actual trust in God. "One can 'believe that God is' and live at His back; the man who trusts Him lives in His face."[7] Both the preaching of Israel's prophets and the word of Jesus demand, not a faith 'in God,' but rather the realization of this faith in the totality of one's life. The meaning of one's faith in God depends on the extent to which that faith enters the reality of personal life.[8] One cannot therefore divide life into two domains: one in which God's rule is paramount and another which is governed by man through politics, economics, and the like. The man who hears the voice of his Lord and then dares to set a limit to the area of life beyond which its rule must not extend is not simply one who is moving away from God; he is one who is standing up directly against God. The man of faith cannot prescribe to God how far His power may extend; such a prescription is a denial of faith.[9]

Biblical faith demands that teaching be lived; the God who gives meaning to life is wronged by a teaching which simply delights in itself. For Buber, the God of Israel makes one demand: "willingness to do as much as we possibly can at every single instant." Whereas Hellenic man believed that all virtue lies in knowledge, biblical man insists that knowledge is never enough; rather, the deepest part of man must be seized by the teachings. The Talmud criticizes the man who studies with some other intent than to act. Judaism is rich in sayings that praise the simple man who acts over the scholar who fails to express his knowledge in deeds. "He whose deeds exceed his wisdom, his wisdom shall endure; but he whose wisdom exceeds his deeds, his wisdom shall not endure." Again, the man whose wisdom exceeds his deeds is likened to a tree with many boughs but few roots, while the man whose deeds exceed his wisdom is likened to a tree with few boughs and many roots: the one is easily uprooted, the other cannot be budged. Buber comments on these teachings: "What counts is not the extent of spiritual possessions, not the thoroughness of knowledge, nor the keenness of thought, but to know what one knows and to believe what one believes so directly that it can be translated into the life one lives."[10]

Expressed in everyday living

The biblical man of faith is called upon to use the capacity of each day to the full; it is in the content of the everyday that man freely chooses or rejects God. Each man stands in the naked situation that was Adam's; to each the decision is given. The man of faith takes seriously his appointment and commitment to the earth. He is called upon to cooperate in the redemption of the world. Does this mean that God cannot redeem the world without the help of man? "It means," replies Buber, "that God does not will to be able to do it." Does God, then, need man for His work? "He wills to have need of man." Man's role in the world is to be a real partner in a real dialogue with God. The life of faith necessarily includes everything that a man does; it embraces "the whole concreteness of life *without reduction, grasped dialogically.*"[11] In the biblical view history consists of a dialogue between God and man. God speaks to man through the life which He gives him, and man responds to God by the life he lives. The response of man comprises the whole of his life, in each area and each circumstance of life. Biblical faith protests against a "religion" which is satisfied with a partial response to God; the God of the Bible lays claim to the whole of man's life and demands the hallowing of the everyday.[12]

THE ESCAPE FROM RESPONSIBILITY

It is this awesome responsibility of continual dialogue, of openness to the word, to which the man of biblical faith is called. Each day he is called upon to renew his faith by the life he lives, by a continual response to the word addressed to him, by a continual effort to hallow the everyday. Faith is so demanding because life is so demanding. It is not surprising that the biblical man of faith seeks to escape from these demands, to avoid the responsibility made by the demands of this continuing dialogue; for this purpose he sought refuge in what Buber calls "gnosis and magic." Biblical man sought by various means to control the Lord who confronted him with His demands for "responsible awareness," for the response of dialogue. Man was, and is, being constantly addressed; it is an address that calls for a total response; but if man can in some way "control" Him whose word he hears, if God could in some way be at man's disposal, then the roles would be reversed. God would then be at man's beck and call; it would be the Lord who should respond to man. And so Israel sought security in gnosis and magic; and nothing was so corruptive of Israel's relation with Yahweh, as today nothing so corrupts the dialogue between man and God, as this attempt to employ gnosis and magic in order to "control" God.

> The two spiritual powers of gnosis and magic, masquerading under the cloak of religion, threaten more than any other powers the insight into the religious reality, into man's dialogical situation. They do not attack religion from the outside; they penetrate into religion, and once inside it, pretend to be its essence. . . .
>
> The tribes of Jacob could only become Israel by disentangling themselves from both gnosis and magic. He who imagines that he knows and holds the mystery fast can no longer face it as his "Thou"; he who thinks that he can conjure it and utilize it, is unfit for the venture of true mutuality.[13]

Passion for success

Again and again in his biblical writings Buber points out the various subterfuges employed by the Israelites to escape from their responsibilities, a weakness which has by no means been limited to Israel, and which was condemned throughout the Bible from the time of Moses on through the prophets. It consists basically in the tendency to treat God as an object, as a source of power, as a means of bringing about success:

> Always and everywhere in the history of religion the fact that God is identified with success is the greatest obstacle to a steadfast religious life. In the Biblical narrative of the Exodus and the wanderings in the desert this identification becomes particularly acute. Moses has to engage in a never-interrupted, never-despairing struggle against the "stiff-neckedness" of Israel; that is, against this permanent passion for success.[14]

In all the various murmurings of the people against Moses during the desert wanderings this same religious problem lies in the background: the passion for success and security; "the people wish for a tangible security, they wish to 'have' the God, they wish to have Him at their disposal through a sacral system; and it is this security which Moses cannot and must not grant them."[15]

Images as a source of control

The people under Moses want an image of Yahweh so that He will in some way be visible to their senses and subject to their control. The imaging of Yahweh is in part a denial of His absolute power. The limitation to a definite form, the localization of Yahweh, is at the same time a limitation and localization of his power.

> The prohibition of "images" and "figures" was absolutely necessary for the establishment of His rule, for the investiture of His absoluteness before all current "other gods."
> No later hour in history required this with such force; every later period which combatted images could do nothing more than renew the ancient demand. . . . Moses certainly saw himself as facing . . . that natural and powerful tendency which can be found in all religions, from the most crude to the most sublime, to reduce the Divinity to a form available for and identifiable by the senses.[16]

Obviously, this is not a fight against art, but rather against the efforts of fantasy and imagination to replace faith. And it is a conflict found at the origins, the "plastic hours," of every "founded" religion, of every religion born of the meeting between the human person and the divine mystery. For Israel, it was Moses more than anyone else who established the principle of the "imageless cult."[17]

The Decalogue itself opens with a strong prohibition of idol worship, of image worship, of magic worship. And the reason these have been prohibited, says Buber, is to promote "the exclusive recognition of the exclusive rule of the divine lord, the exclusive leadership of the divine leader; and to this end it is necessary to recognize Him as He is, and not in the shape with which people would like to endow Him."[18]

Later the ark of the covenant becomes a "holy object" that is at once a paradox and a concession; a paradox, because the "invisible deity becomes perceptible as One who comes and goes"; a concession because God grants "that His 'face' will go with the people"; but it is the visibleness, not of an "image" or a "shape," but of a "place." Yet when the ark was captured and afterwards could have been returned to the people, it was not: this is a turning point for Israel's faith.

> We sense that which the narrator dared not say. . . . YHVH Himself allowed His ark to be captured: now He has brought it out of the hands of the Philistines, but still does not wish to restore it to the people of Israel, for He does not wish them to use Him instead of serving Him. The leader-God wishes only that they should harken to His voice.[19]

The pattern is clear: the people are to have a firm trust in God as absolute Lord; they are to be turned to Him in the fullness of their being; they are to express their faith in the living out of their daily life; they are to resist the urge for idol worship, which in all its various forms is an attempt to control Yahweh, avoid responsibility, and seek in religion their personal and collective security.

Abuse of cult and worship

But time and again the people of Israel succumbed to this temptation. An even more subtle, and therefore more dangerous, form of this temptation was the tendency to use worship as a means of putting Yahweh at the disposal of the people. From the beginning of the revelation to Israel it was indicated to them that Yahweh was indeed the Lord of the world and not a God removed to the high heavens, that man cannot establish on this earth his own regime, man's regime, and satisfy the Lord God simply by cult. The God of the universe is the God of history "Who walks with the creature of His hands, man, Who walks with His elect, Israel, along the hard way of history." He demands of man that "he should serve Him lovingly in all the breadth of historic life" and that his worship should be a "living worship," a worship of Yahweh as "He Who is present," by means of the whole presence of the worshiper, instead of the empty cultic worship of Yahweh *"as an idol."*[20] Yet man seeks constantly to use and possess, to worship by empty cult rather than to dialogue and to worship by all that one is and does.

Israel's sacrificial cult may well have had its origin in the need for a "living communion with God" through some type of sacramental or symbolic act such as the communal meal. However, the symbol soon became a substitute.

> The sacrificial cult was so elaborated and codified that in every phase of his life, at every moment of his destiny, man had at his disposal a prescribed sacrifice for establishing a communion with God; but this communion no longer consisted of anything but the sacrifice. It was now no longer necessary, when gripped by suffering or terrified by one's sins, to commit oneself to God in struggle and surrender, in a storm of decision, until the creature's cry was stilled before the secret voice. One offered a sacrifice, one acted according to regulations, and God was appeased. To be sure, this sacrificial cult with its claim to truth opposed the promiscuous idol-worship among the people. . . . But whether worship-service serves idols or serves God depends not on the name by which one calls one's God but on the way in which one serves Him. This is the great insight manifested by the later prophets.[21]

Reliance on cult and rite is rooted in a lack of faith which divides man's life into two realms: "the realm of myth and cult, heaven and the temple, subject to religion, and the civic and economic realm, the reality of everyday public life." Yahweh is not to be shut up in a "house of cedar"; men's hearts must be purified of the notion that "it is possible to satisfy Him merely with worship and cult."[22] Worship must not be used as a means of utilizing God in order to avoid the responsibilities of daily life. Moses had sought to uproot this type of "sacral assurance" and to replace it with the awareness of the "consecration of men and things, of times and places, to the One who vouchsafes

His presence amid His chosen people." Later, the prophets
wanted to demolish a sacrificial cult empty of personal involvement and devoid of intention.[23] But time and again the people
opted for the security of their sacral assurance.

God does not seek religion

One of Buber's most forceful criticisms of this escape by the
people is found in his comment on Jeremiah's attack against the
Temple (Jer. 7:1 ff.). Jeremiah realized that much of Josiah's
reforms were nothing in God's eyes because they did not re-
form the life of the people. The people calmed the anguish of
their hearts with the thought of the indestructible Temple;
Jeremiah sees himself as sent to the Temple gate to combat this
illusion.

> His words here mean simply this, that God does not attach
> decisive importance to "religion." Other gods are dependent on
> a house, an altar, sacrificial worship, because without these things
> they have no existence, their whole nature consisting only of
> what the creatures give them; whereas . . . [YHVH] is not depen-
> dent upon any of these things, since He is. He desires no religion,
> He desires a human people, men living together, the makers of
> decision vindicating their right to those thirsting for justice, the
> strong having pity on the weak . . . , men associating with men.
> He rejects this people here, which "enter these gates to throw
> themselves down before YHVH." . . . He rejects them, because
> by the iniquity they commit one with another they frustrate the
> divine order of the people and profane God's name.

Jeremiah tries to make it quite clear that "God seeks something other than religion. Out of a human community He wills
to make His kingdom; community there must be in order that
His kingdom shall come; therefore here where He blames a
people for not having become a community, man's claim upon
man takes precedence of God's claim." It is not cult itself which
is the object of Jeremiah's wrath, but rather the deterioration
of cult. More than any of his predecessors, he believed that "for
the sake of hallowing the whole life, the partition between
sacred and profane should be removed."[24]

Any form of worship, therefore, that tends to remove God's
presence from the midst of His people to the heavens above is
degrading to true faith and leads to that point where men
worship in order to utilize God rather than to face their respon-

sibilities before the living God. Working from within, the magical element supplants the true meaning of worship and cult; it becomes no longer "a venture of true mutuality" but a means whereby the people "conjure" and "utilize" the divine mystery. What the prophets of Israel demand is a living faith, constantly renewed, constantly open, a faith in God's presence in the midst of His people and in the word He addresses to His people.

THE LAW

If the danger of magic is most clearly expressed in the use of images and cult, the danger of gnosis is best exemplified in dogma and in the codification of the law. Almost from its beginnings the religion of Israel suffered from the tendency to structure, to codify, to objectify its faith; at a later stage it would proceed from formula to formula, leading to a regular confession in creeds, a process which "belongs no longer in essence to living religion itself, but to its intellectually constituted outposts, to the theology and the philosophy of religion."[25]

Meaning of Torah

Buber draws a clear distinction between Torah and law: "In the Hebrew Bible Torah does not mean law, but direction, instruction, information. . . . It includes laws, and laws are indeed its most vigorous objectivizations, but the Torah is essentially not law." What makes the Torah essentially different from law is the presence of the voice of the living God speaking to the people through the Torah. A trace of the actual speaking voice always adheres to the commanding word. To identify Torah with law is to destroy its dynamic and vital character.[26] At the same time Buber admits that from the very beginning there was a tendency in Israel toward objectivizing the Torah. Its results are clearly seen in Jeremiah's accusation (8:8–9) that the popular saying, "We are wise, the Torah of Yahweh is with us," means in actuality a scorning of the divine word. By the beginning of the Christian Era, the Torah became even more closely blended with the concept of law. The narrow outlook that the Torah has been given to Israel as its own possession tends effectively to supplant "the vital contact with the ever-living revelation and instruction, a contact which springs from

the depths of the primitive faith." The Torah must remain a
"*dynamic* concept." Once it becomes objectified in law, it loses
its essence; it is no longer Torah.[27]

Torah preserves the living voice

It is precisely this contact with the "ever-living revelation"
that prevents Torah from becoming empty law and formality;
only the undying effort to hear the word that is being addressed
can prevent this torpidity and "liberate again and again the
living idea"; only the actuality of faith can preserve the voice
of the spirit that speaks to Israel through the Torah. To fulfill the
Torah means "to extend the hearing of the Word to the whole
dimension of human existence"; this is what was meant by
fulfillment of the Torah both in biblical Judaism and in the
Sermon on the Mount. And to extend the word to the whole of
human existence demanded a constant struggle against that
hardening of the spirit "which knew of no other fulfillment than
the carrying out of rules, and so made the Torah in fact into a
'law' which a person merely had to adhere to as such, rather
than to comprehend its truth with every effort of the soul and
then to realize it." This indeed is for Buber the constant danger
of every form of faith which seeks to realize a revealed divine
will: that the fulfillment "can persist apart from the intended
surrender to the divine will" simply by the performance of
certain prescribed duties. This process of making the gesture
independent of the surrender has its origins in the earliest days
of Israel's existence; the struggle against it runs throughout the
history of the Israelite-Jewish faith. It begins in the accusation
of the prophets, mentioned above, against a worship robbed of
its decisive meaning because there is no self-surrender to the
Lord; it gains new impetus in the zeal of the Pharisees against
the 'tinged ones,' that is, those whose inwardness is a mere
pretence; and it continues to the very threshold of our own era
through Hasidism, "in which every action gains validity only by
a specific devotion of the whole man turning immediately to
God."[28]

Direction to the human heart

When the Torah is fulfilled, when it is brought into life, the
result is a direction given to the human heart. The heart of man

is "by nature without direction, its impulses whirl it around in all directions." No direction which man gathers from his world stands firm. "Only in Emunah is persistence: there is no true direction except to God." And the human heart can receive this direction "only from a life lived in the will of God." The Torah assigns man such a life; it assigns him actions agreeable to God; in doing these actions, man learns to direct his heart to God. Thus the decisive element is not the bulk of actions prescribed by the Torah but in "the direction of the heart in them and through them." Far from encouraging a rote performance of duties, Torah insists that these actions have value only when they are performed with, or lead to, the direction of one's heart to God. It is the failure of man to direct his heart to God which is the essence of sin; he who commits sin refuses to direct his heart to God. "Therefore the project of sin and the reflecting upon it and not its execution is the real guilt." The play of the imagination upon the sin is considered "even more serious than the sin itself, because it is this which alienates the soul from God."[29]

Danger of outward conformity

Thus once again in Buber's analysis of biblical faith we come to the ever-present danger of outward conformity without inward surrender. Once precepts or laws are codified, there will always be the tendency to a performance of the prescribed actions with a heart that remains closed, devastated, without direction. One imagines that he is fulfilling the divine will because he is fulfilling certain precepts, whereas he lacks the one essential element for which the divine legislation exists: a heart open to God, a heart genuinely directed to God, a heart that listens to the divine voice. So also when Buber treats of the Decalogue, he emphasizes that the soul of the Decalogue is found in the word "Thou." The word "Thou" demands a *listener.* To grasp the meaning of the Decalogue, one must feel that he himself is being addressed. The Decalogue is not a set of precepts to be codified into a fixed pattern of life; it is not a list of rules of behavior or articles of faith; man is being addressed by God through the Decalogue; he must be able to hear the living Voice, to experience himself being addressed. "Thanks to its 'thou,' the Decalogue means the preservation of the Divine Voice."[30] Conformity to law and precept unaccompanied by a living faith, an inner direction of the heart to God, puts one in the position of believing "he holds the mystery fast," he no longer hears the eternal Thou addressing him in the law; such a man has succumbed to what Buber has called the power of gnosis "masquerading under the cloak of religion."

Need of law and structure

This must not be taken as a condemnation of the very notion of law itself. God rules His people through men "who have been gripped and filled by His Spirit" and who, in turn, carry out His will not merely by decision made for the moment, but also "through lasting justice and law." If the authority of these men is disputed and given to the people as a whole, then the actual dominion is taken away from God. Without law there is no "clear-cut and transmissible line of demarcation between that which is pleasing to God and that which is displeasing to Him"; without law "there can be no historical continuity of divine rule upon earth." However, the problem arises from the fact that "in the world of the law what has been inspired always becomes empty of the spirit," yet in this state "it continues to make its claim of full inspiration"; in other words, when the "living element" of the law dies off, as it always does, the empty shell that is left "continues to rule over living men." Hence, says Buber, "the law must again and again immerse itself in the consuming and purifying power of the spirit, in order to renew itself and anew refine the genuine substance out of the dross of what has become false. This lies in the continuation of the line of that Mosaic principle of ever-recurrent renewal."[31]

Thus there is need of law, there is need of structure, but in structure and law lie two of the great dangers to the religious spirit of man; without the spirit of renewal and without the spirit of a deep faith, structure and law become the embodiment of all that is harmful and obstructive in a religious community. Buber summed up very well this problem of biblical faith when he wrote: "Centralization and codification, undertaken in the interests of religion, are a danger to the core of religion, *unless there is the strongest life of faith*, embodied in the whole existence of the community, and not relaxing its renewing activity."[32]

DIVINE PRESENCE

Where does this renewing activity which thwarts the temptations to gnosis and magic in the religion of Israel come from? Ultimately, for Buber, it comes from the faith in the presence of God in the midst of His people; this in turn is rooted above all in the revelation of God to Moses in Exodus 3:14. The importance of this revelation for Buber can be judged by his numerous comments on that key passage.[33] The revelation made once to Moses is basically a revelation that God is revealing Himself always in the present, in the here and now.

"I am with you"

Moses made the request to know God's name. "But if they ask me what his name is, what answer shall I give them?" According to primitive beliefs, once a people seized the secret of the name, they could call upon the god to save them in their hour of need. The answer to Moses is not a theological statement, it is not an answer which reveals what God is, it is not "I am who am," as some have alleged. Rather, God's answer is in terms of His relationship with the people; it is at once a revelation and a concealment. "YHVH, that is to say He will be there, He will be present, this is the Deity's name." *Ehyeh asher ehyeh:* "I will be there as I will be there"; that is, in whatever appearance I choose, I will be there. "Thus YHVH does not say that He exists absolutely or eternally, but—without pledging Himself to any particular way of revelation ('as I will be there')—that He wants to remain with His people, to go with them, to lead them."[34]

Thus Yahweh is saying to His people through Moses: "You need not conjure Me for I am here, I am with you"; and further: "You cannot conjure Me, for I am with you time and again in the form in which I choose to be with you time and again; I Myself do not anticipate any of My manifestations; you cannot learn to meet Me; you meet Me when *you* meet Me."[35] Yahweh is to be ever-present to His people, but always in the form peculiar to the moment. Man cannot foretell "in the garment of what existence and what situation God will manifest himself. It is for man to recognize him in each of his garments."[36] This point cannot be overemphasized for the man of biblical faith: Yahweh "is always present but in every given hour in the appearance that pleases Him, that is to say He does not allow

Himself to be limited to any form of revelation and He does not limit Himself to any of them."[37] Yahweh is the One who is present here, "not merely some time and some where, but in every now and in every here." And again and again when it is said in the Exodus narrative, "Then will the Egyptians recognize that I am YHVH," it means that "the Egyptians shall come to know that I (unlike their gods) am the really Present One in the midst of the human world, the standing and acting One; you will know that I am He who is present with you, going with you and directing your cause."[38]

Source of religious spirit

It is this recognition of Yahweh's presence "in every now and in every here," under the guise in which He chooses to be present, which is the strongest bulwark against those elements which tend to undermine the religion of Israel. It is this recognition of Yahweh's presence which is the source of Israel's religious spirit. There can be no imaging of Yahweh, because an image means "fixing to one manifestation, its aim is to prevent God from hiding Himself, He may not be allowed any longer to be present as the One Who is there as He is there . . . , no longer appear as He will."[39] There can be no cult of a God hidden in the heavens above, as though apart from this world of the everyday; worship entails the recognition of Him who is present to the worshiper calling forth his internal surrender. There can be no true fulfillment of law and precept which does not recognize the voice of Him who speaks through the law, and the law itself must be continually renewed in order to be a suitable vehicle of the living Voice of the Present One. There can be no dogmatic formulation which in any way "holds fast" the divine mystery, because Yahweh does not reveal what He is but only that He is present to His people as He is present.

The God of Israel, then, is the God of history, the God who acts. The biblical revelation of God consists in man's encounter with God, God's presence to His people, God's presence through the saving acts in the history of Israel. God reveals Himself by His presence, and man himself must respond by being present to God in the fullness of his being; this is the only response open to the man of faith: to enter fully and completely into this personal relationship with the God present to him. Rightly understood, faith in Yahweh as the Present One, revealing Himself here and now, is the strongest protection against those elements which have been so destructive of the religion of Israel and of almost every religious undertaking of man: gnosis, magic, codification of the law, and dogma.

There remain two other aspects of Buber's writings on biblical faith that are important for this study: the biblical concept of man and the biblical teaching on community.

MEANING OF MAN

Although much of the preceding could be considered as part of the biblical image of man, it is primarily in his commentaries on the psalms, particularly Psalm 73, that Buber expresses his insights into the biblical meaning of human existence, of life, of death. His proposition can be stated in very simple terms: only the man of prayer, the pure of heart, the good man, really shares in existence; the wicked man has denied his existence.

Wickedness is nonexistence

Who are the wicked? They are men "who are far from God"; they are the ones "who have no share in existence." The evil man does not last "because he has no existence in himself. ... To be without God means not to be." And again he writes: "Those who walk about in wickedness . . . have been revealed in their nothingness by the working of salvation; rather, their nothingness has become their reality, the only thing they have is their nothingness."[40]

Of the wicked it is said that they are on a way of life that simply "peters out," it comes to nothing. "The men who go this way learn somewhere or other, at some point in their journey, that what they all the time had taken to be a way is no way, that this alleged way leads nowhere. And now they can see neither before nor after, their life now is wayless."[41]

Death and judgment become for the wicked simply an affirmation of what their life has been. The wicked do not stand in judgment, for in the judgment "existence is at stake." But the wicked have already negated their existence and so they end in nothing; their way is their judgment; in the end they have a "direct experience of their non-being."

> The bad do not truly exist, and their "end" brings about only this change, that they now inescapably experience their non-existence, the suspicion of which they had again and again succeeded

in dispelling. Their life was "set in slippery places"; it was so
arranged as to slide into the knowledge of their own nothingness;
and when this finally happens, "in a moment," the great terror
falls upon them and they are consumed with terror.[42]

The pure of heart

On the other hand, the biblical man of prayer, the man who
is pure of heart, is the man who experiences the goodness of
Yahweh. And to experience Yahweh's goodness is to experience
that all that happens to man, all that happens to Israel, is good.
If things go ill with Israel, one may conclude that God is not
good; but such a conclusion can be drawn only by one who is
not pure of heart. To experience the goodness of God, which is
the experience of the pure of heart, does not mean that God
rewards man for his goodness; rather, it is an experience that
what God does is goodness. No matter what may be the judgment of other men, the pure of heart experience in all circumstances the goodness of God. "Goodness does not come to them
as a reward for purity of heart but, in virtue of that purity, they
experience God's act as goodness."

The essential dividing line is between those who are pure of
heart and those who are impure of heart. As Israel purifies its
heart, it experiences that God is good to it. The state of one's
heart determines "whether a man lives in the truth in which
God's goodness is experienced, or in the semblance of truth,
where the fact that it 'goes ill' with him is confused with the
illusion that God is not good to him." Even the erring and
struggling man who "imagines that he is driven far from God,"
who is tempted "by doubt and despair into treason," eventually
in his struggles comes to the realization that he is continually
with God.[43]

> As he has become pure of heart, he knows that he remains con-
> stantly with God, Who has taken him by the right hand and leads
> him. . . . He does not turn his eyes away from the sufferings of
> the earth, persistent as they are, he does not turn to the delights
> of heaven, it is not heaven with which he is concerned, but *God*,
> Who is no more in heaven than on earth, but is near him. . . . If
> his flesh and with it his heart will fail, . . . He Who lives in this
> perishable heart as the imperishable "rock" . . . remains forever,
> and this is enough. Lasting is of God: he lasts who is near to God.
> Those who keep away from God dwindle. . . . Verily God is good

to Israel, to the pure of heart, who are allowed to be near to Him.[44]

Yahweh guides the pure of heart with His counsel, but this counsel does not consist in answers to life's problems; it does not exonerate man from the duty of personally deciding, in each new situation, what he must do.

> The guiding counsel of God seems to me to be simply the divine Presence communicating itself direct to the pure in heart. He who is aware of this Presence acts in the changing situations of his life differently from him who does not perceive this Presence. The Presence acts as counsel: God counsels by making known that He is present. He has led his son out of darkness into the light, and now he can walk in the light. He is not relieved of taking and directing his own steps.[45]

The meaning of death

This revealing insight of the pure of heart changes the whole meaning of life's experience and radically alters the perspective of death. Death now becomes the event "in which God—the continually Present One, the One who grasps the man's hand, the Good One—'takes' a man"; it becomes a "direct experience of the Being of God." The pure of heart knows that after death "being with Him" will no longer mean, as it does in this life, "being separated from Him."

Death is the end of everything that we know as human. But the pure of heart knows God as his true part and true fate, his "rock," and he knows that God is eternal. It is into God's eternity that the pure of heart moves in death, and God's eternity is something absolutely different from time.[46] The man who is pure of heart is convinced that God does not remove His presence even in death; he is convinced that God, who is actively present to him in life, will remain actively present to him in death. The concept of God simply becomes more real and more powerful than the concept of death. This belief concerns not the immortality of the soul, but the eternity of God. It is not a question of what dying appears to be in man's eyes. The man who lives in communion with God knows that God is eternal and that He is his "portion."[47]

Since God is his "portion," the good man *is*, he shares in existence, he has life; the evil man is lost in his own abyss, without direction, without life, without existence. There is no genuine existence for biblical man unless he is in some way turned toward God, struggling to become pure of heart so that he may live his life as man; he seeks to respond to a revelation that deals not so much with the mystery of God as with the life of man. Revelation imposes upon man the obligation to respond. "There is no revelation without commandment. Even when he who addresses us talks to us about himself, he is really talking about us. What he says of himself does not refer to his own being, but gives the reasons and the elucidation of his demands on us."[48] Biblical revelation deals with what is right and wrong in human life. The man of biblical faith is called upon to respond. He is called upon to concern himself with this life of man and with this earth of man. He is called upon, within this human world, to have a special concern for the weak and the afflicted, for the wretched and the needy, for the poor and the powerless.[49] He is called upon to distinguish between right and wrong, between justice and injustice. He is called upon above all to form a community of man, a community of justice, a community of God's people.

ELECTION TO COMMUNITY

For Martin Buber, the primary obligation imposed upon Israel by Yahweh was, and is, the obligation to become a true people. When Yahweh formed a covenant with Abraham, it was for the sake of a new people, a people not yet existing. It was a covenant which was dialogic: it promised the formation of a people, and it imposed as response the obligation of a people. Yahweh addressed this people in the name of Abraham, promising and demanding that it become a blessing, a blessing for the whole world of nations.[50]

A true people

It is the aim of the Mosaic covenant to unite the tribes into a people, and then to bind the people to their God. They are to become truly a people, a people of Yahweh. He wants to rule over them, not as a crowd but as a community.[51] Moses brings to the tribes the offer of Yahweh to establish a covenant which would unite both God and people into a living community. Israel is to come under Yahweh's personal ownership; Yahweh is to be the hallowing leader and Israel the people hallowed by Him, a nation made holy through Yahweh.[52]

Yahweh makes His demand that the people should be entirely His people, a holy people. This means a people whose entire life is hallowed by justice and loyalty, a people that exists for God and also for the world. Israel is to be dedicated to Yahweh as *goy*, that is, with its corporate national existence. Israel as a nation must dedicate itself to Yahweh as its Lord. It must dedicate its substance and its functions, its laws and its institutions, its internal and external relations. Only then will Israel be a holy people.[53]

Only as His people can Israel come into being and remain in being. There simply is no Israel and there can be none except as the people of Yahweh.[54] Israel is to become a true nation-community; it is to proclaim by what it is that the ideal service of God is the establishment of a truly human community. God wants man to become man in the truest sense of the word. He seeks this not simply in isolated instances, as among other nations, but in the life of an entire people. Israel was chosen to become a true people in order to provide a pattern of life for the future of mankind. To become a true people means to become God's people.

> Biblical man is man facing and recognizing such election and such a demand. He accepts it or rejects it. He fulfills it as best he can or he rebels against it. He violates it and then repents. He fends it off, and surrenders. But there is one thing he does not do: He does not pretend that it does not exist or that its claim is limited.[55]

God's people

A true people means God's people, but time and again Israel glories in its election; it substitutes election for social responsibility, for justice, for mercy. To establish itself as God's people, Israel must place its whole common life under God's order and rule. The idea of election points not to superiority, but to responsibility and to destiny. It is rooted in Israel's response to a task, a task which originally molded the people into a nation and which was formulated again and again by the prophets: "If you boast of being chosen instead of living up to it, if you turn election into a static object instead of obeying it as a command, you will forfeit it."[56]

The people must constantly be reminded that election is for service, not for self-aggrandizement. Israel's doctrine of election is entirely different from the theories of election of other nations in that her election is completely a demand. Biblical election does not express a people's wishful dreams; it is not an unconditional promise of greatness. Rather, it imposes a stern demand on the people; their future hinges on whether this demand is met. Yahweh is not a God created by the people in their own image. He confronts them, He opposes them, He demands, He judges. He calls for truth and righteousness, not just in certain isolated spheres of life, but in the whole life of man and in the whole life of the people. He wants both the individual and the people to be wholeheartedly with Him.[57]

Yahweh awaits this response from His people, He awaits the human fulfillment. Buber points out how the prophet Isaiah stresses this role of the people: if Israel will walk now in the ways of Yahweh, He will not hide His face any longer from them, but will make His light shine for them. It is for Israel to begin this "going" so that the nations may follow and so that there may arise among them all the great peace of God for which Israel will stand as a "blessing in the midst of the earth."[58]

The servant of Yahweh

Israel is to prepare for God the proper instrument for His work among mankind. But what Israel was called upon to do as a nation it failed to do. For this reason the servant of Yahweh is called, in order to fulfill this task for the world of nations— the bearing of afflictions and the establishment of the order of the kingdom. The servant suffers and acts in the name of Israel; he suffers and acts as Israel. Rightly, both servant and Israel are spoken of in one breath, in one utterance, for he is Israel as servant. "When the nations look at him, they look at the truth of Israel, the truth chosen from the very beginning."[59] And the truth for Israel is that it must become more faithfully God's servant, and Israel becomes God's servant by becoming a true people, for a true people means God's people. There is no Israel, there can be no Israel, except as God's people. Only in fulfilling this biblical demand will Israel become genuinely a blessing, a light, to the nations of mankind.

*   *   *

With this picture of biblical faith, of the revelation and the demands made to Israel, of its service to the nations of the world, we turn now to the insights of Buber's studies in Hasidism, insights which may be very fruitful to man confronting the problems of faith and religion and church.

HASIDIC WRITINGS

Whatever can be said of the influence of Buber's Jewish faith on his religious, philosophical and sociological thought, the same must also be said of his studies in Hasidism. For Buber came to Judaism only through Hasidism, a movement of renewal within Judaism which was founded by Rabbi Israel of Mesbiez, the "Baal Shem Tov," during the first half of the eighteenth century in Poland.

EARLY ACQUAINTANCE WITH HASIDISM

Buber became acquainted with Hasidism during his childhood summers, when with his father he visited a town in Galicia in which there was a Hasidic community. Buber recalls:

> The palace of the rebbe, in its showy splendor, repelled me. The prayer house of the Hasidim with its enraptured worshippers seemed strange to me. But when I saw the rebbe striding through the rows of the waiting, I felt, "leader," and when I saw the hasidim dance with the Torah, I felt, "community." At that time there rose in me a presentiment of the fact that common reverence and common joy of soul are the foundations of genuine community.[1]

But it was only in his early adulthood that Buber undertook a serious study of Hasidism. It came after a period of several years during which his spirit was caught in a whirl of confusion, when he lived "in versatile fullness of the spirit, but without Judaism, without humanity, and without the presence of the divine." Then through his interest in Zionism Buber became newly vowed to Judaism, although, as he admits, "I professed Judaism before I really knew it." It was in his efforts to know Judaism, in his search for the "eye-to-eye knowing of the people," that Buber came to Hasidism. His real conversion took place while reading a passage from the testament of Israel Baal

Shem: "He takes unto himself the quality of fervor. He arises from sleep with fervor, for he is hallowed and become another man and is worthy to create and is become like the Holy One, blessed be He, when He created His world."

> It was then that . . . I experienced the Hasidic soul. The primally Jewish opened to me, flowering to newly conscious expression in the darkness of exile: man's being created in the image of God I grasped as deed, as becoming, as task. And this primally Jewish reality was a primal human reality, the content of human religiousness. Judaism as religiousness, as "piety," as *Hasidut*, opened to me. . . . I recognized the idea of the perfected man. At the same time I became aware of the summons to proclaim it to the world.

At this point, at the age of twenty-six, Buber retired from his other activities to devote his efforts to gathering quietly the scattered Hasidic literature. In this work he immersed himself and discovered "mysterious land after mysterious land."[2]

Influence on Buber

At a much later date Buber would write of his great affection for Hasidism:

> I am morally certain that, had I lived in that period when one contended concerning the living Word of God and not concerning its caricatures, I, too, like so many others, would have escaped from my paternal home and become a Hasid. In the epoch into which I was born such things were forbidden according to both generation and situation. . . . My heart is at one with those among Israel who today, equally distant from blind traditionalism and blind contradictoriness, strive with a striving meant to precede a renewal of the forms of both faith and life. This striving is a continuation of the Hasidic striving; it takes place in a historic hour in which a slowly receding light has yielded to darkness. Assuredly not my entire spiritual substance belongs to the world of the Hasidim. . . . But my foundation is in that realm and my impulses are akin to it. "The Torah warns us," . . . Rabbi Mendel of Kozk said, "not to make an idol even of the command of God." What can I add to these words![3]

While Buber made it quite clear toward the end of his life that his interpretation of Hasidic teaching should not be confused with his own thought or be taken as a presentation of his own religious philosophy, he nevertheless acknowledges his in-

debtedness to Hasidic ideas, to which his own thinking is closely
bound.

> Hasidism has exercised a great personal influence on me; much
> in it has deeply affected my own thinking, and I have felt myself
> called ever again to point to its value for the life of man. . . .
> Hasidic theology always comes into contact with my own at those
> points where the relation between God and the world is con-
> cerned, as it manifests itself to us in our own experience of the
> relation between him and us.[4]

Proclaiming the message

Hasidism contains a message which Buber considered "vitally
important" for all men, and more important in this era than
ever before. "For now is the hour when we are in danger of
forgetting for what purpose we are on earth, and I know of no
other teaching that reminds us of this so forcibly."[5]

Hasidism may be called a mysticism, but it is a mysticism
rooted in the world. The world is not an illusion from which
man must turn in order to find God; rather, it is the reality
between God and man in which "reciprocity manifests itself."
The world bears the message of creation to man, and it bears
man's response, his service of creation; through this "meeting
of divine and human need" the world is destined to be redeemed. It is given to man "at each time and at each place to
receive the divine." Each action of man which expresses total
dedication, which involves man's whole being, each such action
is the "way to the heart of the world." Hasidism demands of
man that quality which is so basic to Buber's thought, to his
"human religiousness"; Hasidism demands of man "presentness."[6] And this "presentness," this "ever-anew" of each moment, is the key to Buber's "holy insecurity," one of the great
bulwarks of Hasidism's protest against gnosis and magic in religion. Hasidic man lives in the holy insecurity of the ever-anew
of each present moment.

SUMMARY OF HASIDISM

For Buber the core of Hasidic teachings is "the concept of a
life of fervor, of exalted joy." Every great religious movement
seeks to instill in its followers a life of joy and fervor which is
based on man's relation to the eternal, and which therefore

cannot be stifled by any individual experiences. But since most of man's experiences with the world do not rouse him to such fervor, religious concepts often refer him to another world, a "world of perfection in which his soul may also grow perfect." Life on earth then becomes "either an antechamber, or mere illusion"; the prospect of a higher life creates that fervor which is lacking in the face of the disappointments which man experiences. But for Judaism, and in particular for the Hasidic renewal of Judaism, there has always been, in addition to its faith in a life hereafter, a strong tendency to "provide an earthly residence for perfection." The great messianic ideal of Judaism looked forward to this "coming perfection on earth," but it could not endow life with that "constant, undaunted and exalted joy in the Now and Here, which can spring only from fulfillment in the present, not from hope in a future fulfillment."

> The hasidic movement did not weaken the hopes in a Messiah, but it kindled . . . its . . . followers to joy in the world as it is, in life as it is, in every hour of life in this world, as that hour is. Without dulling the prick of conscience . . . , hasidism shows men the way to God who dwells with them "in the midst of their uncleannesses." . . . Without lessening the strong obligation imposed by the Torah, the movement suffused all the traditional commandments with joy-bringing significance, and even set aside the walls separating the sacred and the profane, by teaching that every profane act can be rendered sacred by the manner in which it is performed.[7]

Again the emphasis on the present must be noted; fulfillment in the present is open to man. Man is fully human, fully alive, when he is fully present. This is what Buber meant when he wrote that the teachings of Hasidism could be summed up in a single sentence: "God can be beheld in each thing and reached through each pure deed."

> The least thing in the world is worthy that through it God should reveal himself to the man who truly seeks Him; for no thing can exist without a divine spark, and each person can uncover and redeem this spark at each time and through each action, even the most ordinary, if only he performs it in purity, wholly directed to God and concentrated in Him. Therefore, it will not do to serve God only in isolated hours and with set words and gestures. *One must serve God with one's whole life, with the whole of the everyday, with the whole of reality.* The salvation of man

does not lie in holding himself far removed from the worldly, but
in consecrating it to holy, to divine meaning: his work and his
food, his rest and his wandering, the structure of the family and
the structure of society. It lies in his preserving the great love of
God for all creatures, yes, for all things.[8]

Not concerned with knowledge

Buber classifies Hasidism among those genuine religious
movements that "do not want to offer man the solution of the
world mystery, but to equip him to live from the strength of the
mystery; they do not wish to instruct him about the nature of
God, but to show him the path on which he can meet God."
Hasidism is not concerned with a knowledge, valid always and
everywhere, of what is and of what ought to be, but rather it
is devoted to the "here and now of the human person, the
eternally new shoot of the eternal truth." And so the real contribution of Hasidism cannot be codified.

> It [Hasidism] is not the material of a lasting knowledge of obliga-
> tion, only light for the seeing eye, strength for the working hand,
> appearing ever anew. . . . Of highest importance to it is not what
> has been from of old but what again and again happens; and,
> again, not what befalls a man but what he does; and not the
> extraordinary of what he does, but the ordinary; and more still
> than what he does, how he does it.

Hasidism emphasized the ancient Judaic idea that man is responsible for God's fate in the world, a responsibility that emphasizes the "mysterious, inscrutable value of human action,
the influence of the acting man on the destiny of the universe,
even on its guiding forces."[9]

Rise and fall of Hasidism

Buber saw the Hasidic teachings as eagerly welcomed by a
people accustomed to religious rigidity and the dominance of
the law; for them it was a joyful liberation. But in a sense Hasidism contained the seeds of its own downfall. It demanded from
the people a spiritual intensity and awareness that they did not
possess. It offered the people fulfillment, but at a price they
could not pay. Its spiritual ideals were so high that only a few
would ever be capable of them; yet it spoke to the many. This
situation led to the institution of leaders called zaddikim, who

acted as mediators "through whom prayers are borne above and blessing brought below." While the zaddik made the Hasidic community richer in security of God, he helped deprive it of the one thing that really counted: "one's own seeking."

Furthermore, the quality of the zaddik radically changed. At first, only the really worthy became zaddikim, "but because the zaddik received from his community an ample livelihood in order to be able to devote to it the whole of his service, soon lesser men crowded to the benefice, and because they could offer nothing else, acquired a claim through all kinds of wonder-working."[10] Naturally such a situation could not long endure; it contained the elements of its own destruction, primarily because the believer who is seriously concerned about his "own seeking" is all too rare, yet the appeal of Hasidism was always to the many. So whatever remains of Hasidism can only be a hollow shell of the original religious renewal. And this type of decline from within is obviously not something limited to Hasidism. As Buber himself observed, original Hasidism "has almost as little in common with the Hasidism of today as early Christianity has with the Church."[11]

Perhaps the real problem is inertia in one form or another: man's inability to cope with the responsibility of "presentness." Buber points to the core of the problem in a remark concerning Hasidism, but one which he also applies to every genuine religious movement: "No teaching finds it so difficult to preserve its strength as one which places the meaning of life in the working reality of the here and now and does not tolerate man's fleeing before the taxing infinity of the moment into a system of Is and Ought."[12] Because inertia won out, Hasidism declined.

Opposition to gnosis and magic

In what he called his "summons" to proclaim Hasidism to the world, Buber has preserved the rich religious qualities of Hasidic teaching. In the pattern presented to us we can discover Hasidism's strong, but often silent, protest against the great enemies of all religion: magic and gnosis. The meeting of man with God takes place only in "the lived concrete," and the lived concrete exists only insofar as each moment retains its character of presentness and uniqueness. Man has devised many types of "once for all," but all share the same characteristic: they make unnecessary the real response to the unique situation that confronts man in each hour. The God who can be put into a system or enclosed in an idea is not the God who can be met in the lived concrete. Any type of once-for-all dogma becomes what Buber has called "the most exalted form of invulnerability against revelation," for it is an opening to gnosis on one hand and to magic on the other. A God that can be fixed in dogmatic pronouncements, whose mystery is encased in a theology, is also a God who can be possessed and used.

Magic exists whenever one worships God without really being turned to Him, without presentness, whenever one celebrates "without being turned to the Thou and . . . really meaning its Presence." In magic God becomes a bundle of powers, present at man's command and present in the form in which man commands them. Gnosis attempts to raise the veil which divides the revealed from the hidden; it seeks to lead forth the divine mystery. Gnosis and magic are the twin threats to man's life of dialogue, to his turning to God. Gnosis seeks an answer to the contradiction of existence in order to be free from it; Hasidism seeks to endure the contradiction and attempts to redeem it.

In its own sphere Hasidism is agnostic; it is "not concerned with objective knowledge that can be formulated and schematized, but with vital knowledge, with the Biblical 'knowing' in the reciprocity of the essential relation to God." Gnosis never stops short, it never prostrates itself. But it is precisely in stopping short, it is in holy insecurity, that Hasidic piety has its true life, in the "defenseless outstretched hand of the insecure."

> It would be contrary to the faith and humor of our existence (Hasidism is both faithful and humorous) to suppose that there is a level of being into which we only need to lift ourselves in order to get "behind" the problematic. The absurd is given to me that I may endure and sustain it with my life; this, the enduring and sustaining of the absurd, is the meaning which I can experience.

Against magic, Hasidism emphasizes the fullness of the living act; when a man acts with the whole of his being turned toward the living God there is no room for magic. There is no fixed procedure and no fixed effect known in advance. What approaches us cannot be known beforehand: "God and the moment cannot be known beforehand; and the moment is God's moment; therefore, we can indeed, prepare ourselves ever again for the deed, but we cannot prepare the deed itself."[13]

Let us look now more closely at the meaning of Hasidism as it appears in the writings of Buber in order to understand more clearly its effect on his thought in general, and in particular on his critique of organized religion.

UNIQUENESS OF THE INDIVIDUAL

Hasidism places great emphasis on the "inextinguishable uniqueness" of the individual. Uniqueness is the "essential good of man that is given to him to unfold."[14] Buber comments on the saying of Rabbi Pinhas[15] that "in everyone is something precious that is in no other":

> The uniqueness and irreplaceability of each human soul is a basic teaching of Hasidism. God intends in His creation an infinity of unique individuals, and within it he intends each single one without exception as having a quality, a special capacity, a value that no other possesses; each has in His eyes an importance peculiar to him in which none other can compete with him, and He is devoted to each with an especial love because of this precious value hidden in him.[16]

There is an obvious rapport between this teaching on uniqueness and the emphasis placed on "one's own striving." It is by personal striving, personal turning, that each man fulfills the uniqueness that is his. By the turning of his whole being, a man who had formerly set himself as his goal now finds a way to God, that is, he finds "a way to the fulfillment of the particular task for which he, this particular man, has been destined by God."[17]

Listening to the Voice

So much depends on man's listening to "the Voice"; without this listening and turning he will never find his way as man. Whatever success he achieves, whatever power he attains, whatever deeds he accomplishes, man's life will be wayless "so long as he does not face the Voice"; to listen is to begin to find the way.[18] And this way, this task, is always a way in the world;

it demands that a man do what he must do at this moment with his "whole strength" and with "holy intent."

> The world in which you live, just as it is and not otherwise, affords you that association with God, which will redeem you and whatever divine aspect of the world you have been entrusted with. And your own character, the very qualities which make you what you are, constitutes your special approach to God, your special potential use for Him.[19]

In a reply to a request to indicate the general way man is called to serve God, the "Seer of Lublin"[20] replied: "It is impossible to tell men the way they should take. For one way to serve God is through learning, another through prayer, another through fasting, and still another through eating. Everyone should carefully observe what way his heart draws him to, and then choose this way with all his strength."[21] For Buber, this means that we are to revere and learn from the genuine service of those before us, but we are not to imitate it. The great and holy deeds done by others are examples which point to what greatness and holiness is, but they are not models which we are to copy. "However small our achievements may be in comparison with those of our forefathers, they have their real value in that we bring them about *in our own way and by our own efforts.*"[22] Thus Buber confirms the teaching of the Hasidic rabbi of Kotzk:[23] "Everything in the world can be imitated except truth. For truth that is imitated is no longer truth."[24] And Rabbi Bunham[25] had no desire to change places with Abraham: "Rather than have this happen, I think I shall try to become a little more myself." Rabbi Susya[26] expressed this same idea even more strongly: "In the world to come I shall not be asked: 'Why were you not Moses?' I shall be asked: 'Why were you not Susya?'"[27]

Something precious in each man

Buber goes on to elaborate this doctrine of uniqueness as it is found in Hasidism:

> Every person born into this world represents something new, something that never existed before, something original and unique. "It is the duty of every person in Israel to know and consider that he is unique in the world in his particular character and that there never has been anyone like him in the world, for

if there had been someone like him, there would have been no need for him to be in the world. Every single man is a new thing in the world and is called upon to fulfill his particularity in this world. For verily: that this is not done is the reason why the coming of the Messiah is delayed." Every man's foremost task is the actualization of his unique, unprecedented and never-recurring potentialities, and not the repetition of something that another, be it even the greatest, has already achieved.

This doctrine is based on the fact that men "are essentially unlike one another"; it does not aim at making them alike. If a man should study the achievements of another man for the sake of equaling them, he would miss precisely "what he and he alone is called upon to do." God does not say: "This way leads to Me and that does not," but rather: "Whatever you do may be a way to Me, provided you do it in such a manner that it leads you to Me."[28]

Buber reminds us of the words of Rabbi Baruch:[29] "Each man is called to bring something in the world to completion. Each one is needed by the world." Perhaps the best summary of this Hasidic teaching is found in the words of the Baal Shem: "Everyone has in him something precious that is in no one else."[30] It was one of the consistent tasks of Hasidism to develop this "something precious" that is unique for each man by bringing him to decision in the present moment, by helping him to flee the props and securities of gnosis and magic and to depend upon "one's own seeking."

ROOTEDNESS IN THE WORLD

Man is called upon to develop his own unique qualities, he is called to self-fulfillment, not for his own sake, but for the world. Hasidic man begins with himself, but he does not end with himself; he starts with himself, but he does not aim at himself; he is not to be occupied with himself but with the world. This is the basis upon which Hasidism divides men into two classes: "the proud who, if sometimes in the sublimest form, think of themselves, and the humble, who in all matters think of the world."[31]

In most systems of belief the believer considers that he can achieve a perfect relationship to God by renouncing the world of the senses and overcoming his own natural being. Not so the

hasid. Certainly, "cleaving" unto God is to him the highest aim
of the human person, but to achieve it he is not required to
abandon the external and internal reality of earthly being, but to
affirm it in its true, God-oriented essence and thus so to transform it that he can offer it up to God.

Hasidism is no pantheism. It teaches the absolute transcendence of God, but as combined with his conditioned immanence. . . .

The task of man, of every man, according to hasidic teaching,
is to affirm for God's sake the world and himself and by this very
means to transform both.[32]

Hasidism turns man toward the world, for it is here that man
enters into relation with God. Man's bond with God "authenti-
cates and fulfills itself in the human world." The human world
is "the world of authentication." The world needs man for its
redemption, for its hallowing. Man's concern is in this world in
order "to let the hidden life of God shine forth." Everything
seeks to become sacrament; "the creature, the things seek us
out on our paths; what comes to meet us on our way needs us
for its way. . . . Everything wants to come to us, everything
wants to come to God through us."[33]

Here and now

The fulfillment of existence, the fulfillment of man's role in
the world, can only be found in one place, "the place on which
one stands." Hasidism emphasizes that the rich treasure of
fulfilled existence is had here and now, in *this* place, at *this*
moment, if we will only recognize it. This is the sense of the
Hasidic tale:

> God says to man as he said to Moses: "Put off thy shoes from
> off thy feet"—put off the habitual which encloses your foot and
> you will recognize that the place on which you happen to be
> standing at this moment is holy ground. For there is no rung of
> being on which we cannot find the holiness of God everywhere
> and at all times.[34]

Only rarely do we realize our failure to taste the fulfillment
of existence; only rarely do we realize that our life does not
participate in true, fulfilled existence, that it passes true existence by. We nevertheless feel the deficiency at each moment,
and in some measure "strive to find—somewhere—what we are
seeking."

Somewhere . . . except where we stand, where we have been set
—but it is there and nowhere else that the treasure can be found.
The environment which I feel to be the natural one, the situation
which has been assigned to me as my fate, the things that happen
to me day after day, the things that claim me day after day—
these contain my essential task and such fulfillment of existence
as is open to me. . . . For it is here, where we stand, that we should
try to make shine the light of the hidden divine life.

If we had power over the ends of the earth, it would not give
us that fulfillment of existence which a quiet devoted relationship to nearby life can give us. If we knew the secrets of the
upper worlds, they would not allow us so much actual participation in true existence as we can achieve by performing, with holy
intent, a task belonging to our daily duties. Our treasure is hidden beneath the hearth of our own home.[35]

Hasidism teaches that every encounter in the course of our
life has a deeper, hidden spiritual significance, if only we live in
the present moment and develop a genuine relationship to the
persons and things in whose life we ought to take part. The
people we live with and meet, the soil we till, the materials we
shape, the tools we use all contain a "mysterious spiritual substance which depends on us for helping it toward . . . its perfection." If we neglect this, if we think only in terms of momentary
purpose and use without developing a genuine relationship,
then we bar ourselves from true, fulfilled existence. To this,
Buber adds a personal remark: "It is my conviction that this
doctrine is essentially true. The highest culture of the soul remains basically arid and barren unless, day by day, the waters
of life pour forth into the soul from those little encounters to
which we give their due."[36]

True life in the world

Hasidism gives the fullest expression to the Jewish doctrine
that life in this world is no less true or real than life in a world
to come. One of the sayings of Rabbi Hanokh[37] reflects this
teaching: "The other nations too believe that there are two
worlds. They too say: 'In the other world.' The difference is this:
They think that the two are separate and severed, but Israel
professes that the two worlds are essentially one and shall in fact
become one." The two worlds are essentially one but have
moved apart. Man was created for the purpose of bringing
about their unity, and he does this by "holy living in relationship

to the world in which he has been set, at the place on which he stands."[38]

God puts Himself in man's hands. "God wants to come to His world, but He wants to come to it through man. This is the mystery of our existence, the superhuman chance of mankind." This is why Hasidism teaches that man is responsible for God, for he is responsible for God's presence in the world. We read in another Hasidic tale:

> "Where is the dwelling of God?"
> This was the question with which the rabbi of Kotzk surprised a number of learned men who happened to be visiting him.
> They laughed at him: "What a thing to ask! Is not the whole world full of his glory!"
> Then he answered his own question: "God dwells wherever man lets him in."

And Buber adds his own commentary: "This is the ultimate purpose: to let God in. But we can let Him in only where we really stand, where we live, where we live a true life. If we maintain a holy intercourse with the little world entrusted to us . . . then we are establishing, in this our place, a dwelling for the Divine Presence."[39]

Thus Hasidism calls upon man to "live a true life" in the world and thus to let God into the world. The exemplary religious man is no longer the one versed in theological knowledge or the one secluded in ascetic contemplation, but rather "the pure and unified man who walks with God in the midst of the world, who participates in the life of the people and raises it to God."[40] Hasidism seeks to elaborate the traditional belief that "God wants to win *through man* the world created by Him." He wants to make this truly His world, His kingdom, *"but through human deed."* And divine revelation has for its purpose the formation of men who will work on this redemption of creation.[41]

Danger of "religion"

It is clear that for Hasidic man there can be no relation with God apart from relation with the world. It is in the world that man's bond with God is fulfilled; it is only in the world that man can find an authentic relation with God, "a direct relation to God that includes no direct relation to the world is, if not deception, self-deception; if you turn away from the world in order to turn to God, you have not turned toward the reality of God but only toward your concept of God; the isolated religious is also in reality the not religious."[42]

The fundamental danger of man's relationship with God, that is, of the religious element in man, is that it will become isolated from the world; and the isolated religious is actually the irreligious. And this danger often becomes reality under the guise of "religion." The real communion of man with God takes place in the world; "religion" seeks to divert this communion of man with God from the world to itself. "Religion" is the great temptation of man:

> God speaks to man in the things and beings that He sends him in life; man answers through his action in relation to just these things and beings. All specific service of God has its meaning only in the ever-renewed preparation and hallowing for this communion with God in the world. But there is a danger, in fact, the utmost danger and temptation of man, that something becomes detached from the human side of this communion and makes itself independent, rounds itself off, seemingly perfects itself to reciprocity, yet puts itself in the place of real communion. The primal danger of man is "religion."[43]

One area in which this independence asserts itself is the "cultic-sacramental," the forms by which man "hallows the world for God." Once these forms succumb to the temptation of "religion," they no longer imply the "consecration of the lived everyday," but rather its amputation. Life in the world is divorced from the service of God; it is a mere semblance; the cultic "gestures of intercourse fall on the empty air."

Another area in which this independence may appear is in the state of the soul, the devotion, the intention, the absorption, the ecstasy.

> What was destined and directed to flow into confirmation in the fullness of life is cut off from that fullness. The soul wants to have to do with God alone, as if God wished that one exercise one's love for Him toward Him alone and not toward His world. Now the soul imagines that the world has disappeared from between it and God, but with the world, God Himself has disappeared; only it alone, the soul, is there. What it calls God is only an image within it, what it conducts as dialogue is a monologue with divided roles; the real partner of communion is no longer there.[44]

Man is to find communion with God in the world. Hasidism does not identify the world and God; rather, God transcends the world yet dwells in it, and because of this indwelling the world becomes, in general religious terms, a sacrament. Man has been given charge of this "sacramental possiblity" of beings and things—this constitutes his existence in the world, this constitutes his task. This concrete world, the world of this moment of personal existence, is ready to be a sacrament. It is in this world that "God addresses me and in which He wants to receive an answer from me."[45]

Hence isolation from the world implies isolation from God, and this is the great danger of religion. Buber sums up this problem:

> He who divides his life between God and the world, through giving the world "what is its" to save for God "what is His," denies God the service He demands, the giving of direction to all power, the hallowing of the everyday in the world and the soul.
>
> In the Hasidic message the separation between "life in God" and "life in the world," the primal evil of all "religion," is overcome in genuine, concrete unity. . . . Hasidism preserves undiminished God's distance from and superiority to the world in which He nonetheless dwells. In this distance Hasidism sets the undivided wholeness of human life in its full meaning: that it should receive the world from God and act on the world for the sake of God. Bound to the world, receiving and acting, man stands directly before God—not "man" rather, but this particular man, you, I.[46]

Buber then adds this personal remark, indicating the importance of this aspect of Hasidic teaching in his own life: "This very teaching of man's being bound with the world in the sight of God . . . was the one element through which Hasidism so overpoweringly entered my life. I early had a premonition, indeed, no matter how I resisted it, that I was inescapably destined to love the world."[47]

HALLOWING ALL THINGS

Man is called to the world in order to hallow it, to redeem it. The world needs man for its hallowing, it is waiting to be hallowed by man; and in hallowed contact with the world, with the things and people he meets on his way, man finds his way to

God. A man may turn away from the world from time to time, but only in order to return to it more fully. Hasidism teaches that "rejoicing in the world, if we hallow it with our whole being, leads to rejoicing in God."[48]

No division of sacred and profane

Basic to this effort to hallow all things is Hasidism's attempt to overcome the fundamental separation between the sacred and the profane. This separation has formed a part of the foundation of every religion. "Everywhere the sacred is removed and set apart from the fullness of things"; it forms a type of self-contained holiness outside of which the profane "must pitch its tent." As a result, religion becomes a sort of untouchable province, and it is limited to this province with almost no power in the rest of life. Judaism, and in particular Hasidism, rejects this split; the profane is only a designation for that which is not yet hallowed. The profane is regarded "only as a preliminary stage of the holy; it is the not-yet-hallowed. But human life is destined to be hallowed in all its . . . created structures." Basically, for Hasidism, the holy "is nothing other than what is open to transcendence, as the profane is nothing other than what at first is closed off from it, and hallowing is the event of opening out."[49]

No renunciation of a desired object is necessary. Man can and should live genuinely with everything, but he should live with it in consecration, he should hallow all that he does.

> One eats in consecration, one savors one's taste of food in consecration, and the table becomes an altar. One works in consecration. . . . One walks over the fields in consecration. . . . One drinks to one's companions in consecration, each to the other. . . . One dances in consecration, and a splendor radiates over the community. A man is united with his wife in consecration, and the Shekina rests over them.[50]

What is important here is not the object in question, but man's relationship to the object. Man consecrates an object by a genuine relation which is open to the transcendent; the object is hallowed or redeemed by opening it to the transcendent.

For Hasidism, the world is ugly and wretched insofar as it resists the entrance of the holy into lived life. Our age knows how to speak about things and beings in an illuminating fashion, but it is alienated from the great insight that it is our relation to these things and beings that forms the marrow of our existence. Hasidism constantly emphasizes the "living power of meeting" by calling for a "holy intercourse with all existing beings"; it thus opposes the "progressive evasion of man before the meeting with God in the world."[51]

The call to responsibility

Buber records an interesting Hasidic tale which points out man's constant evasion of his real responsibility in the world. A zaddik is asked why God said to Adam: "Where art thou?" and he replies that "in every era, God calls to every man: 'Where are you in your world? So many years and days of those allotted to you have passed, and how far have you gotten in your world?' God says something like this: 'You have lived forty-six years. How far along are you?' " The rabbi's answer means: "You yourself are Adam, you are the man whom God asks: 'Where art thou?' "

Adam hides himself to avoid rendering account, to escape responsibility for his way of living. "Every man hides for this purpose, for every man is Adam and finds himself in Adam's situation. To escape responsibility for his life, he turns existence into a system of hideouts. . . . A new situation thus arises, which becomes more and more questionable with every day, with every new hideout. This situation can be precisely defined as follows: Man cannot escape the eye of God, but in trying to hide from Him, he is hiding from himself."[52]

This call to responsibility is the call to enter the path of true intercourse with beings and things; only on this path can man actively participate in the redemption or hallowing of the world. It is a call to fulfill the Hasidic command "to do all that one does with one's whole being" and "to hallow the intercourse with all beings and things in the life of the everyday."[53] Creation awaits the liberation and fulfillment of the man who gives himself completely. The man who hallows existence is no magician or wonder-worker; he "really and simply gives himself; he exercises no power but a service, *the* service. He gives himself in service." For the man who hallows, for the man who redeems,

> no kind of acquired rules . . . no inherited methods of working avail, nothing "known," nothing "learned"; he has to withstand

ever again the unforeseen, the unforeseeable moment, ever
again to extend liberation, fulfillment to a thing or being that he
meets in the moment flowing toward him. And he can undertake
no selection, no separation. . . . The not-holy, in fact, does not
exist; there exists only the not yet hallowed, that which has not
yet been liberated to its holiness, that which he shall hallow.[54]

The event of hallowing begins in the depths of man where
choosing and deciding take place. The true hallowing of man is
the hallowing of the human in him. "Man cannot approach the
divine by reaching beyond the human; he can approach Him
through becoming human. To become human is what he, this
individual man, has been created for. This, so it seems to me,
is the eternal core of Hasidic life and of Hasidic teaching."[55]
This understanding of the hallowing of man is at the basis of
Buber's comment: "The real existence of a human person can
itself be symbol, itself be sacrament."[56]

Hallowing begins here and now

The event of hallowing always begins here and now. Each
action can be a hallowing one; it depends on the presentness
with which man acts. This is brought out in the simple Hasidic
tale in which one of the disciples of Rabbi Moshe[57] is asked:
" 'What was most important to your teacher?' The disciple
thought and then replied: 'Whatever he happened to be doing
at the moment.' "[58] This is the way that man will hallow all
things: by considering each action here and now as the most
important, by entering into it fully and genuinely. "There are
no actions which, in themselves, are useless," said Rabbi Pinhas,[59] "but one can make them useless by doing them use-
lessly."[60]

This emphasis on each individual action is what Buber calls
elsewhere "the renewal of the deed-idea." For Hasidism, the
deed reveals the true meaning of life. What counts here is not
what one does, but *how* one does it. There is nothing of itself
that is evil; every deed is hallowed if it is oriented toward God
and toward salvation. The very being of the doer determines
the character of his deed. Thus the action or deed becomes the
life center of all religiosity. By his actions man brings about the
world's redemption; the fate of the world is placed in his
hands.[61]

Once again we come back to the Hasidic theme that man is
responsible for the redemption of the world. God wills to need

man for the work of completing His creation; God waits for man. Each man, each action, each moment may be a source of redemption. But there can be no reliance on any type of magical approach to redemption that would divert man from his responsibility to seek a genuine relation with all things and beings:

> There is no definite, exhibitable, teachable, magic action in established formulae and gestures, attitudes and tensions of the soul, that is effective for redemption; only the hallowing of all actions without distinction, only the bearing to God of ordinary life as it comes to pass and as it happens, only the consecration of the natural relationship with the world possesses redemptive power. Only out of the redemption of the everyday does the All-Day of redemption grow.

Man's work toward redemption consists in "turning the whole of his life in the world to God and then allowing it to open and unfold in all its moments until the last." For Hasidism, man lives in an unredeemed world, but out of each human life that is bound to the world "a seed of redemption falls into the world, and the harvest is God's."[62]

LOVE OF ALL THINGS

Man's task to hallow all things by entering into a genuine relationship with them is actually the task to love all things. Man finds communion with God through his relation with the world, that is, by his love of the world, and especially by his love for his fellowmen.

> You cannot really love God if you do not love men, and you cannot really love men if you do not love God.
> This is the stage that Hasidism reached, even if the new life established by it remained fragmentary and fleeting. One shall, says Kierkegaard, have to do essentially only with God. One cannot, says Hasidism, have to do essentially with God if one does not have to do essentially with men.[63]

To love more

Some of the richest of Buber's collection of Hasidic tales deal with this subject. Buber records the example given by Rabbi Pinhas and his disciples:

> When you see that someone hates you and does you harm, rally your spirit and love him more than before. That is the only way

you can make him turn. For the whole of Israel is a vehicle for holiness. If love and unity prevail among them, then the Divine Presence and all holiness is about them. But if—God forbid!— there should be a schism, a rift appears, and through the opening holiness falls down into the "shells." And so, if your neighbor grows remote from you in spirit, you must approach him more closely than before—to fill out the rift.[64]

One of the disciples of Rabbi Rafael[65] tells this story about his master:

> When he was going on his summer trip, he called me and asked me to share his carriage with him. I said: "I am afraid that I should crowd you." Then he said to me in the manner he always used to express special affection: "Let us love each other more and we shall have a feeling of spaciousness." And after we had prayed, he said to me: "God is a great-hearted friend."[66]

Elsewhere Buber adds the wise comment to this story: "The feeling of being too crowded in the human world has its origins in insufficient love." Whenever "at one place there is too little love, at the other one must love so much the more" in order to bring about agreement and to restore wholeness.[67]

The emphasis here is always "to love more." The same Rabbi Rafael used to warn his disciples against being moderate in their dealings with others: "Excess in love is necessary in order to make up for the lack in the world."[68] And when a father complained to the Baal Shem, "My son is estranged from God— what shall I do?" he replied: "Love him more." Buber comments: "This is one of the primary hasidic words: to love more. Its roots sink deep and stretch out far. He who has understood this can learn to understand Judaism anew." And then he adds further advice from Rabbi Rafael:

> If a man sees that his companion hates him, he shall love him the more. For the community of the living is the carriage of God's majesty, and where there is a rent in the carriage, one must fill it, and where there is so little love that the joining comes apart, one must love more on one's own side to overcome the lack.[69]

True love of God

This love of others is higher than any other service that one can give to God. Without it there is simply no love of God. Buber quotes a Hasidic master: "If someone says to you that he has love for God but has no love for the living, he speaks falsely and pretends that which is impossible."[70] And this is simply a rewording of the Hasidic saying: "To love God truly, one must first love man. And if anyone tells you that he loves God and does not love his fellow man, you will know that he is lying."[71]

In the eyes of Hasidism, true human love is a religious attitude in the most proper sense of the term, so much so that "in the development of the person the religious itself can most easily be built just on this love."

> It should be noticed that, despite the saying in which mere goodness is condemned, still nowhere, as far as I can see, is it said that no one can feel love for men without love for God: the former is always regarded as the foundation. . . . While elsewhere in the Scriptures one is commanded to love God and then the stranger because God loves him, here the converse way is indicated. Certainly both together are the truth: for each of the two loves in its truth demands the other for its completion and helps the other along; but it is significant that in Hasidism it is the way from the world to God that is ever again indicated as decisive for personal development.[72]

How does one come to this love of man? Again the Hasidic tales provide an insight:

> Question: It is written in Proverbs: "As in water face answereth to face, so the heart of man to man." Why does the verse read "in water" and not "in a mirror"?
> Answer: Man can see his reflection in water only when he bends close to it, and the heart of man too must lean down to the heart of his fellow; then it will see itself within his heart.[73]

And Buber elsewhere adds the comment: "So the heart of man comes to man, and not this one to this other alone, but all to all."[74]

The test of love

The true test of this love is in the love of one's enemies and of those burdened with sufferings. Buber frequently refers to the advice of Rabbi Mikhal[75] to his sons: "Pray for your enemies that all may be well with them. And should you think this is not serving God, rest assured that more than all prayers, that is, indeed, the service of God."[76]

And Buber records the moving prayer of Rabbi Shmelke[77] after someone had tried to destroy his reputation before all the community on the eve of the Day of Atonement. He spent the night in prayer with his congregation, and

> when, in the forty-first psalm, he came to the verse: "By this I know that Thou delightest in me: mine enemy will not triumph over me," he repeated it over and over, and translated it, but not in the usual way but freely and boldly: "By this I know that you delight in me: my enemy will suffer no ill because of me." And he added: "Even though there are persons who are hostile to me and try to make me an object of ridicule, forgive them, Lord of the world, and let them not suffer because of me." And he said this in a voice so full of power that all those who were praying burst into tears, and each repeated his words from the bottom of his heart.[78]

And there is the simple advice of Rabbi Moshe Leib[79]: "To know the needs of men and to bear the burden of their sorrow —that is the true love of men." On another occasion, when a disciple expressed his astonishment at the capacity of Rabbi Moshe to share the sufferings of others, he replied: "What do you mean 'share'? It is my own sorrow; how can I help but suffer it?"[80]

Finally, there can be no genuine love of God that is not rooted in fear. Buber records the Hasidic saying, "Fear without love is something imperfect; love without fear is nothing at all." Only through great fear can man attain to great love. "He who has not this fear does not love the great and terrible God himself, but only a small convenient idol."[81]

Love, then, is the one response that God expects from man; for Hasidism, God is the great lover who has set man into the world in order to be able to love him. But there is no perfect love without reciprocity, and so God longs for man to love Him.

> Everything follows from this, all teaching, all "morality," for ... nothing is wanted and nothing is demanded from above but love of God. Everything follows from this; for man cannot love God in truth without loving the world in which He has set His strength and over which His Shekina rests. People who love each other in holy love bring each other toward the love with which God loves His world.[82]

COMMUNITY AND LEADERSHIP

In his earliest acquaintance with Hasidism, Buber writes that he recognized the "living double kernel of humanity: genuine

community and genuine *leadership.*" The Hasidic community
was a genuine human community because it possessed "common reverence and common joy." And the Hasidic zaddik was
a genuine leader because he was the "perfected man," the
"true helper."[83]

In its emphasis on community lies the uniqueness and essence of Hasidism. "What constitutes the uniqueness and greatness of Hasidism is not a teaching, but a mode of life, a mode
of life that shapes a community and that is consonant with
community by its very nature."[84] For Hasidism, "nothing can
be concretely realized in the world if the individual does not
find his realization in the community."[85] And there is no real
prayer except within the community, for "in every true prayer,
it is the community that is praying."[86]

Furthermore, the whole personal attitude of faith that constitutes the essence of Hasidic life works to form a community, but
never a community apart from the world. And in each community the zaddik plays a decisive role. This does not mean forming a brotherhood removed from public life and guided by an
esoteric teaching. Rather, it means forming a community of
men who remain in families and in public life, and whose leaders live, not in seclusion, but in the world. The formation of
communities and of disciples who form communities was at the
heart of the Hasidic movement. Each of the zaddikim was surrounded by a community, and each community was empow-
ered to live its brotherly life because a leader was there who
brought them all closer together by bringing them closer to
what they believed.[87]

Community and redemption

The formation of community for Hasidism was intimately
bound up with its understanding of the role of Israel in the
redemption of the world. There can be no real response to
God's revelation except through a people. In Buber's historical
novel, *For the Sake of Heaven,* Rabbi Israel, the maggid,[88] says:

> No one can wholly serve God except a people. For the service
> of God means just this, and all individual justice can supply but
> the single stones toward a structure. A people alone can build
> justice. This is the meaning of Isaiah when he said: Intertwine not

your destiny with the injustice of the mighty but build up justice
with your own lives. Then will the love of the peoples rush
toward you and you will become a blessing in the midst of the
earth.[89]

Israel was born from the common experience of exile and
redemption, a historical work which it declared to be the work
of God and a sign of the covenant between God and Israel. For
the prophets, the redemption of humanity and its transformation into the kingdom of God is intimately connected with the
redemption of Israel and its transformation into a center of this
kingdom. Hasidism strongly emphasized this prophetic idea of
redemption; its teaching of redemption was so oriented to the
nation that it was prevented from becoming the property of the
whole of humanity; it could never consider the redemption of
Israel as "merely a tiny part of the great redemption"; it could
never separate "the redemption of the soul from the redemption of the nation."

Hasidism strongly contrasts with Christianity on this point. In
Christianity there is no longer a "relation between the nation
as a nation and God"; the kingdom of God is established within
individual souls; people become Christian only as individuals,
while the nations as nations remain "idol worshippers" and "as
long as nations exist, the world will not become Christian." For
Hasidism, the kingdom of God remains what it always was in
the eyes of Judaism, namely,

> the establishment of the kingship of God over the "human na-
> tion" as a nation of nations, a nation consisting of nations; and this
> kingdom will not come about until one nation, which has been
> destined for this purpose, shall begin to establish in its own way
> of living the will of God for the redemption of the world. Cer-
> tainly this does not mean the weakening of the national exis-
> tence, and of course not its abolition, but . . . its decisive concen-
> tration. Therefore Hasidism announced with great enthusiasm
> that Israel, the heart of humanity, and Eretz Israel [the Land of
> Israel], are required by each other, and without their unity re-
> demption will not come.[90]

Role of the zaddik

For Buber, the zaddik, or leader, of the Hasidic community,
is the perfected man, the true helper. He is a true helper because he elevates the needs of the people before he satisfies

them. "There is nothing corporeal that cannot be transfigured, nothing material that cannot be raised to the spirit." And the zaddik does this for all; he is a genuine helper of souls in need: "He is the helper in spirit, the teacher of world meaning. . . . The world needs him, the perfected man; it awaits him, it awaits him ever again."[91]

To fulfill his role of leadership within the community, the zaddik must not only be "ahead upon the way," he must also "keep the flock that he leads together." But togetherness is not just the common following of the foremost. "A bellwether is no leader. Togetherness means that each is intimate with the other and each feels loving-kindness for the other."[92]

For Buber, the zaddik is "the true human being"; he is one who is more "concentratedly devoted than other men to the task of salvation that is for all men and all ages." Constant renewal is his characteristic life principle. Yet zaddikim are not separated into a special class of men. There is nothing of the magical in his role, no special effect produced by special gestures and words; the zaddik deals with the ordinary life of man. There are no magical actions, there are no "secret formulae," but rather "the dedication of everything." Hallowing of the worldly is the central motive of the zaddik. "His meal is a sacrifice, his table an altar. All his movements lead to salvation."[93] The zaddikim are men who are "open to the world, pious toward the world, in love with the world." They possess no special approach to God limited to the knowing and initiated few: "Here stands the brotherhood of the sons of the Father, the mystery is valid for all or none, to none or all the heart of eternity is open. What is reserved for a knowing segment of mankind, what is withheld from the simple, cannot be the living truth."[94]

Thus around each zaddik a community was formed, a community of brothers rooted in the world, and more genuinely a community because theirs was the genuine leader, the true helper, the perfected man who helped create a real sense of brotherhood in his followers. Genuine community and genuine leadership: these are the twin characteristics which for Buber make Hasidism a living source of real humanity.

THE HASIDIC MESSAGE

In this brief treatment of Buber's Hasidic writings, many interesting aspects of Hasidism have necessarily been omitted, such as its beautiful attitude toward suffering, its emphasis on the need for decision, and especially its emphasis on the real joy of living. Perhaps one remark of Buber's will serve to point out the richness here: he speaks of prayer as the purest and most perfect way that man finds God; prayer should take place, not in pain and repentance, but in great joy. And he adds: *"Joy alone is true service of God."*[95] The profound truth of this statement is often missed in our lives today.

Ultimately the Hasidic message is rooted in its understanding of love. The true meaning of love of neighbor is that through this love and in it man meets God. God is never far away from man, for in loving his neighbor, man finds God. The man who loves unites both God and the world. This teaching of Hasidism represents, for Buber, the consummation of Judaism.

The Hasidic message to each one of us is simply that we ourselves must begin. Existence will continue to remain meaningless until we penetrate it with active love and find its meaning for ourselves. The world awaits us; it awaits hallowing; it awaits the disclosure and realization of its meaning. But we must begin. For the sake of this beginning God created the world. "Meet the world with the fullness of your being and you shall meet Him. That He Himself accepts from your hands what you have to give to the world is His mercy. If you wish to learn to believe, love!"[96]

The effect of Hasidic Judaism on Buber's thought should be quite evident, especially on his philosophy of dialogue. He himself, toward the close of his life, admitted that the biblical and Hasidic expressions of Judaism constitute "the strongest witness for the primacy of the dialogical that is known to me." At the same time, he admits:

> I have not been able to accept either the Bible or Hasidism as a whole; in one and in the other I had to and I have to distinguish between that which had become evident to me out of my experience as truth and that which had not become evident to me in this manner. Many of my readers . . . will protest against such a "subjectivism." Those with whom I am in dialogue and whose experience confirms mine know otherwise.[97]

Perhaps it is best to add nothing further. The influence of Hasidism will witness for itself. There remains then a final important aspect of Buber's Judaic writings: his thoughts on Judaism in this era and on Israel as a nation. To oversimplify, we might say that the biblical and Hasidic expressions of Judaism represent an ideal; Judaism today represents the reality. We will now look at Buber's reflections on this reality.

ADDRESSES ON JUDAISM

The writings and addresses of Martin Buber on the meaning of Judaism in the first half of this century are among the richest sources for the subject of this study. We discover here a criticism of his religion, of his people, and of Israel that is rooted in a passionate thirst to achieve that purity of Judaism which he came to understand in his biblical and Hasidic studies, and which was revealed to him in his own experience of faith. It is with no small justification that we can apply to Buber in these efforts words which he himself applied to the biblical prophets in their persistant efforts to right the abuses current in the Israel of their era:

> Compromise with the status quo is inconceivable to them; but escape from it into the realm of a contemplative life is equally inconceivable. Through torment and humiliation, their impassioned words storm against the rich, the powerful, the princes. They have neither a home in the world nor a shelter in the desert; inexorably, the hand of the Lord has set them their hopeless task.

Prophets know in the depth of their being that the ultimate is at stake; they do not hesitate to condemn any achievement of civilization which ultimately impedes genuine human living, or which threatens to destroy the relationship between man and man. In the final analysis, the realm of God for the prophet is nothing more than the "realm of man as it is to be."[1]

This admirably sums up Buber's attitude toward Judaism: the realm of God is the realm of man as it is meant to be; Judaism directs man's efforts toward making the realm of man what it ought to be. And in a similar way, the same can be said of Christianity and of every great religion. Buber was adamant in his criticism of whatever he thought was an obstacle in Judaism toward the achievement of God's realm on earth: the community of man as it ought to be. And in one form or another the obstacles that have been present in Judaism have also made their appearance in the other great religions of man. It is in this light that we should read Buber's critique of Judaism—it is a critique that is not limited necessarily to his own Judaic beliefs, and it is made with great love and reverence for that which is most dear to him.

During the tumultuous days of his early youth when he was without religion, without the presence of God, Buber's first step toward a return to Judaism was through Zionism. It gave him the one thing that he needed so desperately at that time: rootedness in community once again. Buber wrote that no one needs this saving connection with a people so much as the youth seized by spiritual seeking; and among such youths, none needs it so much as the Jew. Nothing, neither intellectual gifts nor material success, can compensate the detached man who lacks the "holy insignia of humanity—rootedness, binding, wholeness." This ultimately was the meaning of Buber's return to Judaism.[2]

In one of his earliest addresses on Judaism after his five-year immersion in Hasidic studies, Buber spoke of the relationship of Judaism to all mankind, recalling the uniqueness of his people, for it involves values that are "archhuman and universally human." Judaism lives not only in its history and in the life of its people, but in every man who calls himself a Jew. Its task is momentous and universal. Every man who decides for the pure and against the impure, for freedom and against bondage, for creativity and against conformity, every man who drives the moneylenders out of his temple, every such man, for Buber, participates in "the great process of Judaism."[3]

Several years later, in another address on Judaism, he spelled out this process; the true task of Judaism, and of every great religion, is and remains "man's response to the Divine . . ., the unity of the spiritual and the worldly . . . , the sanctification of the relationship to all things."[4] We will begin Buber's study on present-day Judaism by examining its approach to these three great tasks.

MAN'S RESPONSE TO THE DIVINE

Among men who are believers there are those who hold that God spoke once to man, but now remains silent; there are others who can never reconcile the idea of God's addressing man and of His being addressed by man. But the basic teaching of Judaism, the teaching that fills the Hebrew Bible, is that "our life is a dialogue between the above and the below." And for Buber, "a faithful and unbiased reader of Scripture must endorse the view he has learned from it: what happened once happens now and always." The Bible has given "vivid, decisive expression to an ever recurrent happening," and this decisive happening is that "transcendence speaks to our hearts at the essential moments of personal life." Judaism teaches that we can respond to this address: we respond by "our actions and our attitudes, our reactions and our abstentions"; this is man's responsibility in the proper sense of the word; this is the fundamental interpretation of our existence. And whenever we truly listen and respond to this address, whether it be in the form of its glorified remembrance in the Bible or its occurrence here and now, "our self-understanding is renewed and deepened."[5]

The God who addresses

This, for Buber, is the great contribution of Judaism to the religions of man: not that it teaches anything about God, but that it recognizes that God speaks to man and that man can speak to God.

> The great deed of Israel is not that it taught the one real God, who is the origin and goal of all being, but that it pointed out that this God can be addressed by man in reality, that man can say Thou to Him, that he can stand face to face with Him, that he can have intercourse with Him. Wherever there is man, to be sure, there is also prayer, and so it has always been. But only Israel has understood, or rather actually lives, life as being addressed and answering, addressing and receiving answer. . . . God in all concreteness as speaker, the creation as speech: God's call into nothing and the answer of things through their coming into existence, the speech of creation enduring in the life of all creation, the life of each creature as dialogue, the world as word —to proclaim this Israel existed. It taught, it showed that the real God is the God who can be addressed because He is the God who addresses.[6]

And Judaism teaches further that no man is exempt from the address of God. God speaks to each man, and each is summoned to answer with his doing and not doing. This dialogue between God and man, between God and the world, is the historical hour, the present hour, and each hour which is granted to us is "real in faith".[7] One can almost say that for Judaism the fundamental reality is speech: the speech or address of God to man. The very act of God's creation is speech; each lived moment carries on this dialogue. The whole life of man is looked on as a giving and a receiving; all the great and small events of life occur in this framework of dialogue. Man responds, or fails to respond, by what he does, or fails to do. The whole of world history in its deepest sense is an expression of the dialogue between man and God, a dialogue in which man as true partner speaks his own word from the depth of his being.[8]

The biblical leaders of Israel are the ones who foreshadow this dialogical man, the man who commits his entire being to God's dialogue with the world and who stands firm throughout the dialogue. Biblical man, as well as the true Jew of this era, is one who is absorbed in this dialogue, and who, no matter what the obstacles, enters again and again into it; his response may be imperfect but it is not refused; he is determined to persevere in the dialogical world. For the true Jew, all that happens is experienced as dialogue, what befalls him is taken as a sign, what he tries to do and what miscarries is taken as "an attempt and a failure to answer, as a stammering attempt to respond as well as one can."[9]

The whole process is one of "being-led." Insofar as these men allow themselves to be led, insofar as they freely take upon themselves "that which has been laid upon them from outside of themselves," they are true leaders of Judaism. It is an attitude which demands that "one hold oneself free and open." Man cannot produce genuine dialogue, but he can be at its disposal. And it is a process that involves risk, "the risk of giving oneself, of inner transformation"; it is the risk of moving out of and beyond one's present state. This is what the prophets of Israel understood by "the turning," namely, that the person one is intended to be penetrates that which one has appeared to be up till the present moment.[10]

Risk of dialogue

This process of "being-led," the risk of entering into the dialogue between God and man, does not assure one of vindication or comfort or justification. In the biblical dialogue between God and Job, Job not only laments, he also charges God with having acted against justice. And he receives an answer in this dialogue, but God's answer does not even touch upon Job's charge. "Nothing is explained, nothing adjusted; wrong has not become right, nor cruelty kindness. Nothing has happened but that man again hears God's address." So it is, Buber explains, for the Israel of this era, for all those "who have not got over what happened and will not get over it," for an Israel that has suffered far more than Job ever suffered. How is Israel to react? It must remain open to dialogue. It must struggle for its redemption and not simply accept its earthly condition. It must await His voice, whether He speaks out of the storm or in the stillness that follows. Though his coming is like no earlier appearance, Israel will recognize again its cruel and merciful Lord.[11]

This is in essential agreement with what Buber wrote earlier at the dawn of the terror that was to engulf European Jewry. Man has not the capacity to judge current history. If history is a dialogue between God and man, we can understand its meaning only when we consider ourselves as the ones addressed. "This, in one way or another, is history's challenge to me; this is its claim on me; and this is its meaning as far as I am concerned." It is the meaning that *I* perceive and experience and hear in reality; it is not a meaning which can be formulated independently of my personal life and experience. It is only in my life *as person* that I am able to grasp the meaning of history, for it is a dialogical meaning. We can only search for the Voice and listen to it, not in order to soothe our suffering, nor to give reasons for it, but simply in order to remain open in dialogue. Buber confirms this point with the beautiful Hasidic tale of the rabbi who does not dare ask God "why everything happens as it does, why we are driven from one exile to another, why our enemies are allowed to torture us."

> I do not beg you to reveal to me the secrets of your way—for I could not endure them. But I implore you to reveal to me with great clearness and profundity what this, which is happening at the moment, means to me, what demands it makes upon me, and what you, Lord of the world, wish to tell me through it. Ah, I do not long to know why I suffer, but only if it is for your sake that I am to suffer.[12]

The man who is led, the man who gives himself completely to the dialogue between God and man, is the man who must suffer.

Religious truth is dynamic

If man remains true to his attempt to seek constantly a response to the divine, he cannot take refuge in dogma, in any kind of once-for-all understanding of divine revelation. The dialogical view of history, which is the biblical view, seeks to preserve the mystery of the dialogical encounter between God and man from all tendencies toward rigid dogmatism. One cannot deny the existence of dogma in Judaism, but dogma remains always of secondary importance to that which is primary: the encounter between God and man. Dogma arises only after man turns aside from the lived moment, and the dogmatist too easily mistakes this detachment from the concrete situation as superior to the lived moment itself. Religious truths are dynamic; they can be understood only in the dynamic of their changing forms. Whatever is enunciated in the third person about the divine, on the distant side of the confrontation between I and Thou, has lost its dynamism; it takes place outside the dialogue and is only a movement into the conceptual area which, while indispensable, proves itself again and again to be unessential.[13]

Religious truths are not merely abstract concepts; they must have "existential relevance." Words can only point the way, but religious truth is adequately manifested only by its actualization *(Bewährung)* in the life of the individual or of the community. Religious teachings lose their character when they are taken out of the context of the life of the individual or community and transformed into a nonpersonal, autonomous maxim, into a dogma. But when they are viewed as part of a life of dialogue which can never be adequately conceptualized, then they are beyond the sphere of any ideology, they are "truth *sui generis,*" dependent upon no other truth. Words do not embody this truth, but rather life as it has been and will be lived. Since religious truth is dynamic and not static, since it pertains to the life of dialogue, to the historical moment, it is never fulfilled at any one moment in time. Every moment of the past, no matter how precious its revelation, represents one phase of this truth, as in fact does each religiously creative period. Religious truth is "not a maxim but a way, not a thesis but a process."

Buber thus rejects any understanding of Jewish teaching as a finished product. Rather, it is constantly in flux, an ever-incomplete and creative response to the address of God. Judaism beckons man to participate actively and creatively in this dialogic process.[14]

Buber regards history as a dynamic process in which God is operative, addressing man at each moment. God is not a wound-up machine that keeps on running until it wears down. He is always the *living* God. Even the word which God speaks at a certain hour must not be idolized or hung up like a placard. "God has truth, but he does not have a system. He expresses his truth through his will, but his will is not a program." At any given hour, God wills this or that for mankind, but He has also endowed mankind with a will of its own, and with sufficient power to carry out its will. But at each hour we must not rely simply on our knowledge; we must go our way and listen all over again. We must listen to this God who addresses each one of us personally, and who says to each of us, not "I am God," but rather "I am your God."[15]

Man's imperfect response

In this Jewish view of history as a dialogue between God and man, man's response is always imperfect. The idea of the messianic leader means that at last the perfect response shall be given. "From out of mankind itself the word shall come, the word that is spoken with the whole being of man, the word that answers God's word." This messianic belief centers on a leader who will set right the dialogue and bring to an end the disappointment of God. Thus Buber sees in the apocryphal saying of God to Jesus, "In all the prophets have I awaited thee, that thou wouldst come and I rest in thee, for thou art my rest," a concept that is truly Jewish.[16]

Opposed to this ideal is the pagan, the man who fails to recognize God in His manifestations. A man is pagan to the extent that he does not recognize God in His revelation, and hence makes no response to the God who addresses him. God is ever-present to man, but always in the form peculiar to the moment, so that man cannot foretell in what garment, in what situation, in what circumstances, God will manifest Himself. It is for man to recognize God in each of His garments. Paganism in man is the failure to recognize the Presence which confronts him, whereas the Jewish in man is the striving for the "ever renewed discernment of God."[17]

God as Father

The response of Judaic man to God is one which admits that God is wholly Other, that He is beyond the grasp of man; yet it is also a response which insists that God faces man, that He is immediately present in relationship with man. To know both of these aspects as inseparable constitutes "the living core" of every believing Jew. The emphasis, however, is always on the God who is present, who addresses; and because of this, even in pre-Christian times Jews called their God "Father." It is not as though such Jews did not realize that God is also utterly distant; but rather they knew at the same time that no matter how far away God is, He is never unrelated to them, and that even the man who may be farthest away from God cannot cut himself off from immediate mutual relationship.[18]

This dialogical relationship with God demands a strong assertion of man's "I" confronting the "Thou" of God. Buber criticizes Simone Weil, who, he claims, turned away from a Judaism she did not know and opted for the destruction of one's "I" and hence for the destruction of dialogue. Buber insists that Judaism's idea of dialogue between God and man rests firmly on a double foundation: the "I" of man and the "I" of his eternal partner. Judaism clearly rejects the "I" of selfishness and pride, but it welcomes and affirms the "I" of genuine relation and love between I and Thou. Love does not negate the "I," saying, "Thou art loved," but rather affirms it, saying, "I love thee." Buber also criticizes Weil's concept of the "We" in her saying that "one should not be I and even less should one be We." Judaism clearly rejects a "We" rooted in the conceit of group or party or nation, but it affirms a "We" rooted in genuine relations and genuinely related to other groups, a "We" that may say in all truth: "*Our* Father."[19]

It is a basic Jewish belief that when God created man, He set the mark of His image upon man's brow and embedded it in man's nature; however faint God's mark may become, it can never be entirely wiped out. There is a Hasidic legend concerning the Baal Shem who had ordered a demon to depart from his disciples, and the demon asked: "Sons of the living God, permit me to remain a little while to look at the mark of the image of God on your faces." And Buber adds the simple comment: "God's real commandment to men is to realize this image."[20] And the realization of this image of the Father is the goal to which man is constantly called, hour by hour, in his dialogue with God in the world.

UNITY OF SPIRITUAL AND WORLDLY

In the religion of Israel there is no division between those who have faith and those who do not, because there is simply no decision here of belief or unbelief. Rather the division takes place between those who effectively realize their faith and those who do not. Faith for the Jew is trust in the Lord; by its very nature this faith implies the maintenance of trust in the fullness of life no matter what the adversity that one experiences.[21] Judaic faith is to be *realized;* it has no true meaning apart from this realization. Thus a life lived in faith for Buber means "concreteness itself, the whole concreteness of life *without reduction,* grasped dialogically, included in the dialogue."[22]

Division between religion and life

Since religion implies the "whole concreteness of life," there can be no division between the spiritual and the worldly. Yet this is often the case of man today: the life of the spirit does not permeate the everyday aspects of life. The world appeals to religion to bring about this union, but what goes by the name religion today is for the most part far removed from life, a "structure erected over and above life," possessing a special atmosphere all its own. Religion is no longer that which embraces the whole of life; it has lost its own unity and hence its ability to lead man to inner unity. If religion is to exert an influence on man today it must return to reality. And religion is most real when it makes the spirit incarnate, when it sanctifies the here and now, when it shoulders the burden of everyday life instead of rejecting it as something inferior.[23]

If man could really grasp the Bible, he would understand it as expressing an outlook that comprises all of life. But contemporary man is scarcely able to do this. If he takes any interest at all in Scripture, it is a purely abstract or "religious" interest,

often from the point of view of the history of religion or civilization. Man today "no longer confronts his life with the Word; he
locks life away in one of the many unholy compartments, and
then he feels relieved." He no longer takes his stance before the
biblical word, and thus he "paralyzes the power which, of all
powers, is best able to save him."[24] And so he remains divided
between the spiritual and the worldly. The Jew who professes
this division of life and faith has forfeited his justification for
living.

And what is true of the individual is also true of the nation.
If Israel were just one nation among the many it would have
perished long ago. Israel exists because it dares to be serious
about the undivided unity of God and His absolute sovereignty.
If Israel turns from God, God will turn from Israel. And Israel
does this whenever it professes God in synagogue and personal
life while denying Him in communal and social life. What is
wrong for the individual cannot be right for the nation. If it
were, then the God of Sinai would no longer be the Lord of
peoples but only of individuals. The Jew believes that God's
commands are to be observed in the whole of one's life and that
the meaning of life depends on one's fidelity to these commands. In Jewish eyes, God does not build His own house; He
wants man to build it, with the strength of his hands and the
dedication of his heart; ultimately, God's "house" means simply
that man begins "to live God's word on earth!"[25]

God's word is lived by *bemishpat* (justice). If a Jew does not
believe this, says Buber, then he should stop talking about Judaism, its spirit and its teachings. For Judaism is the teaching that
there is only one Power and that whatever is done in the service
of that Power, in the spirit of justice, will survive, even though
it may have to struggle temporarily and seem in great peril.[26]

Buber again and again pleaded for this union of faith and life.
"It remained for our time to separate the Jewish people and the
Jewish religious community." As a result, Israel has become "a
nation like unto other nations, and a religion like unto other
religions." The nation is on the rise; the religion is in a sharp
decline, confined to a narrow sphere of rituals and sermons. But
Israel as a nation cannot exist without its religious spirit. Its
salvation lies in becoming Israel again, in becoming the unique
whole of a people and a religious community—a renewed people and a renewed religion. "If we want to be nothing but
normal, we shall soon cease to be at all."[27]

A *return to the spirit*

Judaism must strive for nothing less than the concrete transformation of life as a whole. Inner transformation must be expressed in an outward form, in the transformation of the life of
the individual as well as that of the community. What a great
many Zionists overlook, says Buber, is that the power generated
by a return to the soil is not sufficient of itself to accomplish a
complete and genuine transformation. Above all, there must be
in Judaism a return to the spirit, to the spirit "which made us
such as we are."

> This spirit has not vanished. The way to it is still open; it is still
> possible for us to encounter it. The Book still lies before us, and
> the voice speaks forth from it as on the first day. But we must not
> dictate what it should and what it should not tell us. If we require
> it to confine itself to instructing us about our great literary pro-
> ductions, our glorious history, and our national pride, we shall
> only succeed in silencing it. For that is not what it has to tell us.
> What it does have to tell us, and what no other voice in the world
> can teach us with such simple power, is that there is truth and
> there are lies, and that human life cannot persist or have mean-
> ing save in the decision in behalf of truth and against lies; that
> there is right and wrong, and that the salvation of man depends
> on choosing what is right and rejecting what is wrong; and that
> it spells the destruction of our existence to divide our life up into
> areas where the discrimination between truth and lies, right and
> wrong holds, and others where it does not hold.[28]

What matters is that in every hour of decision we be aware
of our responsibility, especially the responsibility of never setting aside a certain sphere in which God's command would not
hold. This, for Buber, is our "arch-sin" today, circumscribing
God, confining Him to a narrow sector of life called "religion."
Biblical man is a sinner like ourselves, but he never dared commit this sin, the insolence of drawing boundaries around God's
commands, of recognizing His sovereignty to a certain point
and beyond this recognizing only the sovereignty of "science or
society or the state."[29]

In Scripture the divine Voice addresses man not as an isolated
individual but rather as an individual member of the people:
thus there can be no duality of a private versus a public morality. What is reprehensible in the relations between persons
cannot be commendable in the relations between peoples. Yet

this is precisely the division that is so often found in modern life: man's existence is divided into a private and a public sphere, governed by very different laws. Lying degrades the private individual, but it is regarded as a political asset when practiced skillfully and successfully. This dualism in morality is intolerable from the viewpoint of biblical faith.[30]

Faith manifested in life

The prophets of Israel warned against this division of faith and life; they fought against all those who evaded the consequences of divine truth in our everyday life by formalizing and ritualizing this truth; they fought against all those who taught and practiced such evasion, thereby degrading the divine name; they fought for the wholeness and unity of society, which can be whole and united only if consecrated to God. Yet this division manifests itself again and again in Judaism; Buber recognized its dangers throughout his life. In one of his earliest addresses he pointed out the lack of that religious fervor among Jews that would drive them from the scattered emptiness of modern society into an authentic life, a life which would bear witness to God, transforming Him from an abstraction into a reality. There is an adherence to Judaism out of pride, out of loyalty, or simply out of inertia. But there is no fulfillment, and there is no community, no community dominated by "Jewish religiosity in its immediacy, by an elemental God-consciousness."[31]

In an address given in 1951 Buber pointed out that a home, and the freedom to realize the principle of its being, had been granted Israel anew, but "Israel and the principle of its being have come apart." People try to conceal the rift by applying religious terms—like God of Israel and Messiah—to purely political processes, but the reality once meant by such terms is no longer present, namely, the fulfillment of divine truth and justice on earth. No matter where he searched in the Jewish community, Buber saw the same weakness: nowhere in it could one sense a powerful striving to heal the rift and to hallow the communal life. And so he asks:

> Are we still truly Jews? Jews in our lives? Is Judaism still alive?
> . . . Where does the world stand? Is the ax laid to the roots of the

trees . . . ? Can the roots be saved? How can they be saved? Who
can save them? In whose charge are they?
 Let us recognize ourselves: we are the keepers of the roots.
How can we become what we are?[32]

For Buber, the answer will not be found in dogma, whose
purpose is to formulate into concepts beliefs that lie beyond
conceptual thinking; it will not be found in ritual cult, whose
purpose is to express the relationship to the unconditional by
means of ordered and regular exercises. There is only one
thing that really matters: the personal existence of the individual. This gives actuality to religion and attests to its living
force. This personal existence means the effective living of
one's religious faith, and for Judaism faith can be realized only
when Jews become a true people, a people of God. And what
does it mean to become a people of God?

A common belief in God and service to His name do not constitute a people of God. Becoming a people of God means rather
that the attributes of God revealed to it, justice and love, are to
be made effective in its own life, in the lives of its members
with one another: justice realized in the indirect mutual relationships of these individuals; love in their direct mutual relationships rooted in their personal existence.[33]

Or, as Buber expressed it at an earlier time, what really matters is life itself, religious life itself, that is, "the total life of an
individual or of a people in their actual relationship to God and
the world." Jews must understand that to "realize God" means
to "prepare the world for God, as a place for His reality—to help
the world become God-real *(gottwirklich)*; it means, in other
and sacred words, to make reality one. This is our service in the
Kingdom's becoming." In a sense, this is the one thing "for
whose sake we are on earth, the one thing that God will not
achieve without us." All men are in some way aware of this our
human task; but the Jew has heard and preserved this summons
as a people. All men, at some time, are aware of an encounter
with God; but the Jew is enduringly aware of it. All men, somewhere, "in the loneliness of their pain or of their thought, come
close to God"; but the Jew, bound up with the world, "dares to
relate himself to God in the immediacy of the I and Thou—as
a Jew." This, concludes Buber, is Judaism's "primal reality."

This people must continue to prepare itself for His word to come.[34]

Redeeming the world

Again and again for the Jew it is a question of making faith effective in his life. The Jewish people are constituted by their faith; their existence depends on their living this faith in their *whole* life; the faith of Judaism claims one's *whole* life. It is a claim to realize God's image; it is a claim to realize God's kingdom; it is a claim to redeem the world by completing God's creation. The "irreducible element" in this faith is that man "shall have his share in the work of the completion of creation. *God needs man because he wills to need him.* God has chosen him for this comradeship." For Buber, this belief means that "we cannot talk with God if we abandon the world to itself. We can only talk with God when we put our arms, as well as we can, around the world, that is, when we carry God's truth and justice to all."

God gives to each historical hour its sign; it is of the utmost importance that man recognize this sign and answer it rightly with the whole of his being; there is no dogma or ritual or law that will aid him.

> There is no firmly established law, formulated once for all, but only the word of God and our current situation which we have to learn by listening. We do not have codified principles that we can consult. But we must understand the situation and the moment.
>
> We must begin with the realization of God here where we are placed. There is no realization unless we live from faith. Living from faith, I may not will the realization of holy ends by unholy means. If I do not use holy means, then no holy way can exist. ... The real faith must take in everything. That is often fearfully difficult and many times a dangerous undertaking. . . . On this road one often has fearful experiences, but they cannot be spared one. Each in his responsibility in his life must approach realization by bowing before God and being sure that before this King all power of the world is unreal.[35]

SANCTIFYING THE RELATIONSHIP TO ALL THINGS

Judaism calls man to hallow all things here and now in the world. Biblical revelation is concerned not with the mystery of

God but with the life of man. It calls man to live his life in the face of the mystery of God, and when man does this, he is truly man. The Bible does not deal with the essence of God, but with His manifestation to man; it deals with the human world.[36] It is a revelation made to man today. If a man is really serious, he can "open up to this book and let its rays strike him where they will." He must face the book with a new attitude, "as something new." He is called to yield to it, to hold himself open, to withhold nothing of his being, and in this way to experience its revelation. But this is often too difficult for modern man since it demands that he recognize an origin and a goal, namely, creation and redemption. It demands that he recognize a meaning to his life, a meaning that he does not create for himself, a meaning he is to live, not to formulate. Man no longer recognizes an origin or a goal, because he no longer wishes to recognize the consequence: that revelation is a *present experience.* Man resists Scripture because he cannot endure revelation; he cannot endure this present moment with its fullness of possibility, responding to, and being responsible for, each moment. Man turns aside from Scripture because he fears responsibility. Modern man thinks he risks a great deal, but he assiduously avoids the one great risk, that of responsibility.[37] If man is to be man, he must *listen;* each life event is the bearer of revelation, and each man who experiences an event in its fullness can experience also its revelation. He can hear the voice which speaks forth from the event, speaking to his life and to his sense of duty. Only in this way, in Buber's mind, can modern man discover the approach to biblical reality.[38]

Revelation implies responsibility

Revelation involves responsibility, for there is no revelation without commandment. Even when in addressing us God talks about Himself, He is really talking about us. What He says of Himself does not refer to His being but supplies the reasons for His demands on us. Our own life is the sphere in which we point Him out, our life as it is lived in the face of God.[39] This demand is ultimately the demand to sanctify all things: "not their glorification or conquest, but their sanctification, and consequently their transformation."

The world is not so much a reality to be overcome as a reality to be hallowed. The meaning of man and of the world is fulfilled through hallowing. This does not entail transforming the world into something wholly spiritual; it does not imply the spirit, as the source of holiness, floating above an unholy world, clutching all holiness to itself. But rather it implies making the world itself holy.[40]

It is always man who is responsible for this hallowing, and he accomplishes it by living each day to the full, by entering into each day with all the active fullness of the whole person. Buber recognizes no overpowering original sin which could prevent man from deciding as freely as did Adam: "As freely as Adam let God's hand go, the late-comer can clasp it." Man is dependent on grace; but he does not do God's will when he takes it upon himself to begin with grace instead of beginning with himself; man must not remain passive before God. God made no tools for Himself and He needs none; instead, He created a partner in the dialogue of history, a partner capable of response who is to complete creation by working for the redemption of the world.[41] ·

Emphasis on the deed

The great emphasis of Judaism, therefore, is on the deed. Doing is far more essential than experiencing. Not faith but the deed is central to Judaism. The books of the Bible speak much less of faith than they do of deeds. This does not mean an empty glorification of works or rituals devoid of any interior significance; but it does mean that every deed is capable of being orientated toward the divine. In one of his earliest addresses on Judaism, Buber insisted that Jews must restore the greatness to the struggle for the deed idea if they want Judaism to be great once again. If Jews are once more to experience all the pride and all the magnificence of Judaism, "they must demand that the striving of the people's spirit for the deed be renewed." Indeed, every great renewal of Judaism, beginning with the prophetic, proclaimed the holiness of the deed. But time and again the deeds became prescribed acts, and the acts lost their meaning; ritual law replaced the religiosity of the deed, demanding continued observance of that which had become meaningless. Ritual law became more rigid and alienated from life. Christianity was one of the great attempts to break away from the ritual law and to restore the emphasis on the deed as the source of man's bond with God. To earliest Christianity the deed was central. Original Christianity in Buber's eyes was a renewal of Judaism. It was much more closely related to Judaism than to what is known today as Christianity. What was creative in early Christianity was its Jewish element. The Christian revolution of ideas originated in a Jewish land; it was proclaimed by Jews and addressed to Jews; and what was proclaimed was the "religiosity of the deed," the genuine renewal of Judaism.

Early Christianity taught what the prophets taught: "the unconditionality of the deed." But it too, in Buber's estimation, soon succumbed to the inflexibility of the ritual law.

> Whatever in Christianity is creative is not Christianity but Judaism; and this we need not reapproach; we need only to recognize it within ourselves and to take possession of it, for we carry it within us, never to be lost. But whatever in Christianity is not Judaism is uncreative, a mixture of a thousand rites and dogmas; with this—and we say it both as Jews and as human beings—we do not want to establish a rapprochement.

Christianity failed because it was unable to overcome the "increasing ossification of the law."[42]

Religion stifles the deed

Religiosity, that which is genuinely religious, is man's desire to establish a living communion with the unconditional; it is "man's will to realize the unconditioned through his deed, and to establish it in his world." It is by his actions, undertaken in faith before the mystery of God, that man realizes God's image and assumes his responsibility for the redemption of the world. "Genuine religiosity is *doing*. It wants to sculpt the unconditioned out of the matter of this world. The countenance of God reposes, invisible, in an earthen block; it must be wrought, carved, out of it. To be engaged in this work means to be religious—nothing else." The community of man, which is our share in preparing for the reign of God, is as yet "only a projected opus that is waiting for us, a chaos we must put in order." But we can accomplish this only if each of us, in his own place, will perform "the just, the unifying, the in-forming deed." For ultimately, in Buber's view, "God does not want to be believed in, to be debated and defended by us, but simply *to be realized through us.*"[43]

The history of Judaism has witnessed the imprisonment of genuine religiosity, the stifling of the deed.

> Ever since the destruction of the Temple, tradition has been at the center of Judaism's religious life. A fence was thrown around the law in order to keep at a distance everything alien or dangerous; but very often it kept at a distance living religiosity as well. To be sure, to manifest itself in a community of men, to establish and maintain a community, indeed, to exist as a religion, religiosity needs forms; for a continuous religious community, perpetuated from generation to generation, is possible only where a common way of life is maintained. But when, instead of uniting them for freedom in God, religion keeps men tied to an immutable law and damns their demand for freedom; when, instead of viewing its forms as an obligation upon whose foundation genuine freedom can build, it views them as an obligation to exclude all freedom; when, instead of keeping its elemental sweep inviolate, it transforms the law into a heap of petty formulas and allows man's decision for right or wrong action to degenerate into hairsplitting casuistry—then religion no longer shapes but enslaves religiosity.[44]

The prophetic, early Christian, and Hasidic renewals all tried to restore religiosity, to free it from the burden of law and tradition. All three shared in common the desire to restore freedom of decision as the key element in all religiosity. Only through his deeds rooted in freedom can man realize God. But it is precisely this freedom that is endangered by religion through its ossification of cult, Scripture, and tradition. It is no longer decisive action that leads to God, but rather adherance to rules and regulations. The prophetic, early Christian and Hasidic renewals of Judaism emphasized decision as the heart of Jewish religiosity. But these forces never won favor with official Judaism, burdened with its dearth of vitality, and were subsequently suppressed. Yet they are the forces that eternally fight Judaism's battle against bondage. They are the unique source of that religiosity without which no renewal of Judaism can succeed.[45]

Disposition toward realization.

This emphasis on the deed, this renewal of true Jewish religiosity, is closely allied with what Buber calls the most precious heritage of traditional Judaism: "its disposition toward realization." This means that the true human life is conceived to be a life lived before the presence of God. It is not the man who turns his back on the world who will remain steadfast and live in God's presence, but rather the man who breathes, walks, and bathes himself and all other things in the sunlight of the world. "He who turns his back on the world comprehends God solely as an idea, and not as a reality; he is aware of Him in some experiences in life *(Erlebnis)*, but he is unaware of Him in life itself."

Yet even when a man turns toward the world he does not necessarily live in God's presence. God is realized only *between* beings; His radiance glows dimly in every human being, but does not shine in its fullness within them—only between them. The divine attains its earthly fullness only between men, that is, when individuals open and disclose themselves to one another and where immediacy is established between one human being and another. When this happens, the eternal "rises in the Between," and true community, the realization of the divine between man and man, is established. For Buber, this teaching forms the basis of Judaism's vocation, "not the intellectual grasping of the spiritual, nor the artistically creative expression of it, but its realization."[46]

For Buber, Judaism can never be content with truth as idea; its goal must always be "truth as deed." It is not concerned with a God who lives in the beyond, but with the God whose realization on earth is fulfilled not within man, but between man and man. Divine realization may have its beginning in the life of the individual, but it is consummated only "in the life of true community." Being the firstborn, Judaism knows that realization is incumbent upon it, the realization of community. So long as the kingdom of God does not come, Judaism will not recognize any man as the true Messiah, yet it will always look for redemption to come from man, for it is man's task to establish God's reign on earth. Judaism must give itself to this realization. To accomplish the truth as deed is to fill the world with God.[47]

Jesus: man of realization

Buber cites one example in particular of a Jew who strove to bring about this ideal of deed or realization: "I cannot today trace history step by step. But I must mention a man, a Jew to the core, in whom the Jewish desire for realization was concentrated and in whom it came to a breakthrough. His is the original Jewish spirit of true community when he teaches that two who become one on this earth can gain everything from God."

What Jesus called the kingdom of God was no vague heavenly bliss, or a church, or an ecclesiastical association. Rather, he meant true community, the perfect life of man with man. God's earthly kingdom implied a community in which all who thirst for justice will be satisfied. It will come about only through the mysterious union of divine grace and human will. Whatever else may separate Jesus from traditional Jewish teachings, he sought not to abolish society, but to perfect it, as did the prophets before him. He sought not to flee the world, but to build within it a true spiritual community. This understanding, that God wants to be realized through the purification and perfection of the world, is, for Buber, Jesus' "most deep-seated Judaism."[48]

Jesus strove to create a new structure that would reflect a genuine communal life born out of man's renewal. He wanted to build "the temple of true community out of Judaism," a community whose mere presence would cause the walls of despotism to crumble. But unfortuantely this is not how later generations were to understand him. While Western history is filled with "massive interpretations of his teachings," the true Jewish consciousness of Jesus has been lost. Christianity no longer seeks true community in hallowed worldliness, in the totality of man's life with man, but rather in the church, in the community of grace and spirit apart from the community of the world. For Buber, when the peoples of the West took over the teaching of Jesus, they lost its Jewish essence. The drive for realization did not become part of the spiritual foundation of Christianity.[49] To put it more simply, genuine realization was thwarted by religion.

Importance of decision

Closely allied with this thrust toward realization and the deed is Judaism's emphasis on the importance of decision in the realization of the divine. Of all the religions of man, Judaism alone endows man's decisions with such centrality and such meaningfulness. When the will to decision awakens in man, the cover of routine life bursts open and primal forces break through, storming the heavens. In the man who decides, creation begins anew, and the substance of the world is renewed. When a man chooses with all his being, the mystery of creation is consummated, and the "spirit of God hovers over the waters." The man who decides with all his being decides for God, for he thus becomes whole; and all wholeness is of God.[50] The act of decision implies that man's whole power is included in the direction for which he has decided, and man can only decide for one direction: the direction of God.[51]

For Buber, Judaism has always placed the essence of religiosity in man's act of decision as the realization of divine freedom and of unconditionality on earth. To decide means to be alive; it is the supreme moment in the life of man. Every man is called to strive toward this divine freedom and unconditionality through the shattering force of personal decision.

No one and no thing can facilitate this act; outside help only weakens the force of decision. This is why Buber sees Christianity as repugnant for Judaism, for it changed the truly Jewish teaching of Jesus—that every man by living unconditionally could become a son of God—into the doctrine that only belief in the only-begotten son could bring eternal life to man. The act of genuine decision is for Buber *the* religious act in Judaism because it brings about God's realization through man.[52]

Sin as indecision

God remains a being unknown and beyond this world only for the "indolent, the decisionless, the lethargic, the man enmeshed in his own designs." For the man who chooses and decides, God is the closest and most familiar being, realized ever anew by man through his decision. Whether God is immanent or transcendent in respect to the world does not depend on God; it depends upon man, that is, it depends upon man's decision and on the sanctity of his intention. Every deed, even the most profane, is holy when performed in holiness, in unconditionality.[53]

On the other hand, inertia and indecisiveness are "the root of all evil." A man who is divided, who cannot bring himself to the point of decision, is in a state of "sin"; for sin implies decisionlessness, "a divided, unfree existence"; it is basically "nothing more than inertia." The divided man experiences within himself the fate of a world which has fallen from freedom into slavery, from unity into duality. Paul, a "Jew who in this respect is representative," expressed this insight with simple clarity when he wrote: "For I do not the good which I will, but the evil which I hate that I do." Sin means, then, to live not in freedom but in bondage, not in deciding to act but in being acted upon.[54]

Sin, lack of decision or inertia, renders impossible the Judaic ideal of realization of the divine, for there can be no realization without man's free, decisive action. If a man knows this, and knows it not just conceptually or by feeling but "through genuine awareness of a life of decision," then no matter how far he may seem to have strayed from tradition, he has in reality committed himself "to the great course of Judaism.[55]

THE NEED FOR OPENNESS

Another great obstacle to the realization of Judaism's ideals is a mentality which is narrow and fixed and unopen. Buber was greatly concerned about the generations of Jews to come. Can the Judaic ideal for the realization of faith be conveyed to a generation that has separated the world of faith from all that makes life worth living? Can the sacredness of the deed be taught to a generation that possesses an almost inflexible self-assurance? Buber was convinced that men today can be made receptive, that their ears and hearts can be opened to the voice of the mystery that speaks in each happening. They can listen to the voice and hear its message addressed to their hour and their work; they can learn to trust the voice and through this trust come to faith, to a faith rooted in the very life they live.[56]

Men of all ages, including the young, suffer from prejudices which tend to cut them off from the full experience of life. They do not want experiences which contradict or question their emotional concepts; they only want to experience that which will confirm them in their "position." This type of prejudice, which locks a man out of the world and keeps him from admitting anything new, prevents him also from fulfilling his role in redeeming and hallowing the world. Thus for Buber an open mind was a quality of the utmost importance; he calls it "the most precious human possession." Remaining open to the world, seeing and experiencing what it has to offer, is not incompatible with taking a stand and defending it passionately. Openness implies that wherever a man stands, he stands free and unbiased. Even though his outlook constantly changes, it remains ever true to itself and to reality. Ultimately, to be open means to listen: "I have pointed out that it is of the utmost importance not to lose one's openness. But to be open means not to shut out the voice—call it what you will. It does not matter what you call it. All that matters is that you hear it."[57]

Openness of youth

Youth is the time of "total openness"; it is youth which gives itself to "life's boundlessness." Buber asks if youth should be concerned with religion, but behind this question is another of much greater importance: Is total openness compatible with religion? In its openness, youth has not sworn allegiance to any one truth for whose sake it would have to close its eyes to all other viewpoints; it has not yet chosen to abide by any one norm that would silence all its other yearnings. And so it is argued that if youth accepts religion, it closes all but one of the thousand windows that look out onto the world, all but one of the thousand roads that lead into the world. But there is a basic misunderstanding of religion here.

If religion were essentially a source of norms and guidelines or a sum of dogmas and rules, this fear would be justified. But religion is neither of these things. Dogmas and rules spring from man's efforts to make comprehensible his experience of the unconditional; they are in a certain sense symbols of transcendent reality. Ultimately, Buber hopes that no symbol will be any longer needed; life itself, man's relation to man, will become the symbol "until God is truly present when one man clasps the hand of another."[58]

We should not be concerned, then, with imposing religion upon youth; we should not try to force it into a system of things which must be known and practiced. Rather we should attempt to awaken within youth its own latent religion, namely, its own willingness to confront in its fullness the impact of the unconditional. We must not preach to youth that God reveals Himself in one, and only one, way, but rather that everything may become a vehicle of revelation. We must not proclaim to youth that God can be served only by certain types of privileged actions, and no other; but rather that every deed is hallowed if done with the right intention. We must not ask youth to bind itself exclusively to something which emanated at an hour long past, but rather affirm that each man has his hour when the word becomes audible to him. We do not wish to teach youth a fixed knowledge of God's nature, but rather a sense of awe in the face of mystery. We do not want to regulate the lives of young people by "divine" laws and rules, but rather make them aware that life is itself more divine than laws and rules. If we do this we do not limit youth's openness, but rather promote and affirm it; we do not curtain any of its windows, but rather provide an all-encompassing view; we do not block any road, but rather show that all roads, walked in truth and sincerity, "lead to the threshold of the Divine."[59]

Dogma opposed to openness

In contrast to this spirit are those who seek realization in idol worship and dogma, no matter what form it takes. Buber scored particularly those in Judaism today who make an idol of the nation and of the law. He severely criticized those who would readily approve any idol worship in Israel, "if only the idols bear Jewish names!" Such Jews have succumbed to the ruling dogma of this century, "the unholy dogma of the sovereignty of nations"; it is the dogma which teaches that every nation is its own master and judge, obligated only to itself, answerable only to itself. Buber's response to these dogmatists is clear and concise: "No people on earth is sovereign; only the spirit is." So long as the nations turn their back on the spirit and avoid its command, they will only succeed in devouring one another. Buber appealed to his fellow Jews to keep faith with the spirit and to avoid the pitfalls of dogma and idolatry. Such a course will not be easy, but then it is not meant to be easy. Jews must again and again strive to subordinate themselves to the spirit; only in this way will they carry within themselves the seed of true life. "On the day we become like all the nations, we shall indeed deserve to be no more than that."[60]

Buber was even stronger in his condemnation of the dogmatists of the law, those who believed that to be truly Jewish and to realize Judaism one must return to a "pious submission to God and His law." For such dogmatists, the spirit of true community can be found only in the fount of Jewish tradition; its law is in the word God spoke to His people. The law offers the only solid and secure means to Jewish realization. To Buber's mind such a dogmatism was an escape from confrontation with the living God.

> Oh, you who are safe and secure, you who take refuge behind the bulwark of the law in order to avoid looking into God's abyss! Yes, you have solid, well-trodden ground under your feet, whereas we hang suspended over the infinite deep, looking about us. Oh, you heirs and heirs of heirs who have but to exchange the ancient golden coins into crisp new bills, while we, lonely beggars, sit at the street corner and wait for the coming of the One who will help us. Yet we would not want to exchange our giddy insecurity and our untrammeled poverty for your confidence and your riches.

To the dogmatist God created but once, He revealed Himself but once—and never again. To the openhearted "lonely beggar," God renews the work of creation each day, desiring to enter through man into a new reality; He speaks again from the burning bush of the now and from the innermost being of man.

It is not a question of Judaism's rejecting the law; the true Jew honors the law, but he resists those who would use it to keep man from entering into dialogue with the living God. Ever anew man must try to apply the eternal command to his concrete life. Again Buber inveighs against the dogmatizers who seek to escape this responsibility:

> For you, the road is mapped out in books, and you know your way; but we must feel around it with our hands in the beclouded chaos of the present. We are, however, guided not by arbitrariness but by the most profound need, for we are guided by the voice. It bids us work for what is most profoundly Jewish . . . . realization, reconstruction of God's community, and a new beginning. . . . We want to obey this voice. We want to walk on the way . . . to lived truth.

It is not simply by the law that the Jew becomes one with his people, but by his beginning anew, by his sharing in the work of realizing and reconstructing God's community. The genuine Jew will hear the word spoken in the life between man and man; the Sinai to which he is being called is true community. In this, then, lies the realization of Judaism: the establishment of a genuine community by which Israel will be a light unto the nations.[61]

Openness toward Christianity

One other aspect of Buber's stress on openness should be noted: the need for openness between Christian and Jew. It has already been pointed out that he regarded original Christianity as a return to the deed idea of Judaism; early Christianity was in reality a renewal of Judaism. But even granted the differences that have divided Judaism and Christianity in these two millennia, each can learn from the other. Jew and Christian have in common "a book and an expectation." For the Christian, the Book is a forecourt; for the Jew, it is the sanctuary. But Jew and Christian can dwell and listen together to the Voice that speaks here; together they can work to redeem "the imprisoned living word."

The Christian expectation is directed toward a second coming, the Judaic toward a coming not yet anticipated by a prior one. But Jew and Christian can wait together for the one who is to come and they may even prepare the way before him together. In Christian eyes the Jew is the "incomprehensibly obdurate man" who refuses to see what has taken place; in Jewish eyes the Christian is the "incomprehensibly daring man" who affirms in a world obviously unredeemed that redemption has already taken place. For Buber, this is an abyss which no human power can abridge. But Jew and Christian can keep common watch for a unity that will come from God, a unity which replaces all the creedal truths of this earth with the ontological truth of heaven which is singular. Each should hold fast to his own understanding of faith as his deepest relationship to truth. Each should reverently respect the true faith of the other, acknowledging how each stands in relation to the truth. And each should care more for the reality of God than for his particular image of God. When this happens, Christian and Jew are united in realizing that their Father's house far surpasses any of our human models.[62]

At the close of his *Two Types of Faith*, a study in which he pointed out the divergences and similarities of Christianity and Judaism, Buber wrote:

> The faith of Judaism and the faith of Christendom are by nature different in kind, each in conformity with its human basis, and

they will indeed remain different, until mankind is gathered in from the exiles of the "religions" into the Kingship of God. But an Israel striving after the renewal of its faith through the rebirth of the person and a Christianity striving for the renewal of its faith through the rebirth of nations would have something as yet unsaid to say to each other and a help to give one another— hardly to be conceived at the present time.[63]

By his writings and by his life Buber has indeed demonstrated that the right kind of openness is of the utmost importance and the most precious of human possessions.

NATION AND COMMUNITY

It is clear that Judaism rejects a dualism of a "religious" life that is opposed to a "secular" life. Man's commitment to God is to be manifested in daily living, rather than in solemn cult or in an asceticism that rejects the world. And the real manifestation of this commitment is in the establishment of the truly human community. This, in Buber's mind, is Judaism's ultimate task: to create the true community on earth. Judaism's longing for God is its longing to prepare Him a place in the true community; its expectation of the Messiah is the expectation of true community; its awareness of Israel is the awareness that from it the true community will emerge. The very ideal of Judaism, holiness, implies true community with God and true community with man, both in one.[64] Buber is insistent on this idea: "Not truth as idea nor truth as shape or form but truth as deed is Judaism's task; its goal is . . . the establishment of true community."[65]

Vocation to community

Israel must survive, not for its own sake, not simply to extend its span of life, but in order to fulfill its vocation, the realization of a truly great Jewish human community. From the very beginning the people have taken upon themselves this task, which is at once national and supranational. Thus every attempt to regard the nation as an end in itself is more fatal for Israel than for any other nation. For Israel is not the result of mere biological and historical development, but rather it springs ultimately from a decision made long ago, a decision for the true God and against the baal. It was a decision for a God of justice and against a god of selfish egoism; a decision in favor of a God who leads His people into the land to prepare it for its messianic role and against a god who whispers to all comers to Canaan: "Take possession and enjoy." The uniqueness of Israel lies in this original decision and in its attempts to realize this decision.[66]

Israel assumes that it is not like unto the nations because it possesses a specific spirit. But if that spirit is no more than the personification of the nation, an attempt to justify a collective egoism, then Israel is indeed like the other nations. The biblical prophets knew that if Israel intended to exist only as a political structure, it could not exist at all. Israel can endure only "if it insists *on its vocation of uniqueness,* if it translates into reality the divine words spoken during the making of the Covenant." The prophets knew that there was no security for Israel save in God; by this they meant not something unearthly or "religious" in the common sense of the term, but rather the realization of that true communal life to which Israel was summoned by its covenant with God, and which it must sustain in history in its own unique way. This call represented "the *first real attempt at 'community'* to enter world history"; it sought to encourage the nations to change their inner structure and to better their relations with one another. Israel was called to bring peace and justice to the nations.[67]

Fidelity to the spirit

If Israel is to be faithful to its spirit, it must proclaim the simple truth that man has been created for a purpose, that there is a purpose to creation and to the human race, one that we have not made up ourselves. Israel knows this purpose because it has "revealed its face to us and we have gazed upon it." It cannot be clearly defined, but basically it is the realization that unity, not division, is the purpose of creation. Israel must strive for the great upbuilding of this unity and peace among nations. The nations of the world are meant to become a single body, even though at present they are more like a heap of limbs each thinking it constitutes the entire body. It is man who is charged with bringing about this unification of the human world. And there is one nation which long ago received this charge into the very depths of its soul. As a nation it accepted this charge, and as a nation it must strive for its fulfillment in itself and by all the nations of man, by the human race as a whole.[68]

To fulfill the truth it has received, Israel must become again a spiritual force; this implies an espousal of spirit and people; it means *lived* religion, the religion of communal living, the religion of God's revelation in the community. In this crucial age in which we live, no other force but lived religion can withstand the stress and impact of our times. Only when Judaism is lived will it reach its goal of community, "the realization of the Divine in the shared life of men."[69]

The achievement of this goal is threatened by a variety of obstacles: the rigidity of traditionalists and the irresponsibility of revolutionists; miserly egotism and hysterical self-effacement; the intransiency of the purists and the disoriented compromise of realpolitik: all the established forces that do not want to be disturbed in the exercise of their power. These are the forces that rage in a bewildering whirlwind around "the lonely and dedicated individual who boldly assumes the task of building a true community."[70] This is the task of every human being, and in particular of every Jew: to realize the divine in the shared life of men.

Not the individual alone

For Judaism it is never the individual alone, but rather the community as such that is involved in this task, because Israel has received its decisive religious experience *"as a people."* In the hour of its experience of faith the group became a people, and only as a people can it hear what it is destined to hear. The charge given to Israel is not laid upon isolated individuals but upon the nation. Only an entire nation, involving every kind of people, can demonstrate that unity and peace, that righteousness and justice to man, which could serve as an example and a beginning. A true humanity, a nation of nations, must begin with a single true nation. Israel has been charged to become this true nation. In fulfilling this charge, Israel will point the way to a true community of nations. Only true nations, each upholding righteousness and justice, are capable of entering upon genuine mutual relations. It is the task of Israel to lead the way toward this realization.[71]

Although justice and righteousness may be reflected somewhat in the life of an individual, they become wholly visible only in the structured life of a people. These structures enable justice to be realized in an abundant diversity of functions and

in regard to the whole spectrum of social, political, and historical situations. Buber borrows the body metaphor from Christian
mysticism to emphasize this point: "We too may say only the
people can—as it were—represent God, so to speak, cor-
poreally, representing in its own life what God had in mind in
creating man 'in his image.'" This *tzelem*, or image of God, is
an outline which can be completed only by a people; it can be
fully revealed only corporately, through a people varied in
character and personality, yet living harmoniously with one
another, "a human circle around a divine center." Only a people as a people, in their relations to one another, can inaugurate
the realization of a community of mankind and thus point to
God himself. The life and thought of the individual can shake
the throne, but nothing save the life of the people "can erect
the throne for the true king."[72]

Judaism's mission to establish a just way of life simply cannot
be achieved by individuals in their private existence, but only
by a nation in the establishment of a full society. Yet Israel has
never fulfilled this task, and its failure mirrors the wider failure
of faith in the life of mankind. Buber sensed this failure shortly
after he took up residence in Palestine after leaving Germany.
He saw in Judaism's lack of faith the concentrated expression of
mankind's inability to believe in God, although in Judaism the
failure was more dangerous and more fateful than anywhere
else. No solution is to be found in the lives of isolated individuals. A true solution can come only from the life of a community
responding faithfully to the will of God, often without being
aware of doing so or even believing that God exists. Believing
people must support and share this common life and be ready
for the moment when they are called upon to respond to the
inquiry of mankind. This is the innermost meaning of Jewish life
in Israel: to be that true community from which a solution may
come for this crisis of faith, not only to Judaism, but to the whole
of humanity.[73]

Israel's failure

For Buber, as for the biblical prophets before him, Israel has
betrayed its mission. Israel must seriously ask itself if it still seeks
to fulfill God's truth, if it still seeks to establish a human people
whose king He is, if it still seeks to become a true nation whose

members live in peace, and which exerts its influence in behalf of peace and which lives in peace with other nations as well. Israel must realize God's truth "by living a life of truth, both inwardly and outwardly." Only when Israel can point to itself as an example of an evolving pattern of a true people, only then will it be able to impart to a despairing mankind "the doctrine of a nation composed of many nations, which is the doctrine of the Kingdom of God."[74]

Israel is doomed unless it genuinely seeks to fulfill its mission. Buber is relentless on this point. Israel cannot be like unto the nations. "It is not my office to discuss what may happen to other nations because of their denial of the spirit. But I know that we, who believe that there can be no teaching apart from doing, will be destroyed when our doing becomes independent of the teachings."

Judaism must not delude itself: all that is merely social, merely national, merely religious lacks the fiery spirit of the teachings; it cannot ward off decay. "The teachings cannot be severed from the deed, but neither can the deeds be severed from the teachings!" For Buber, this is not a contradiction of his emphasis on the importance of action; rather, it is a recognition that "the teachings are central and that they are the gate through which we must pass to enter life." Men can live the true life in simplicity without the teachings, provided they are linked with God; but they can do this "only because the teachings which represent just such a link to God have, although they are unaware of it, become the very foundation of their existence." In order to do the right thing in the right way, the deed must be rooted in our bond with God. The function of the teachings is to make us aware of our bond with God. The teachings are the way; their full content will be found in no book, in no code, in no formulation. Nothing exists that can comprehend the teachings in their entirety; hence the need of community, for the teachings must be handed on from generation to generation within the community: "Generations must continue to meet, and the teachings assume the form of a human link, awakening and activating our common bond with our Father."[75]

Israel must not be like unto the other nations; it cannot regard its task solely as that of preserving and asserting itself. Just as an individual who wishes simply to preserve and assert himself leads an unjustified and meaningless existence, "so a nation with no other aim deserves to pass away." Buber was a Zionist from his early youth; he sought vigorously for an Israel that would be rooted again in the soil and that would govern itself. "But these are mere *prerequisites!*"[76] Only when they are recognized as such can they play their proper role in the development of the true Israel, a people that strives to become a genuine community where justice and righteousness thrive, a nation that will become a light unto all other nations because it will have realized the divine in the shared life of men.

BUBER'S CHALLENGE

Martin Buber, in his biblical and Hasidic writings, in his addresses on Judaism, by the very life he lived has issued a challenge to Judaism. It is a challenge to recognize its greatness and its uniqueness, its failings and its prejudices, its responsibilities and its potential. Through Judaism this same challenge is flung forth to every great religion, and especially to that religion which had its origins in Judaism and which for Buber was an attempt to restore Judaism to its original purity. For we can understand here also a challenge to Christianity to recognize its greatness and its uniqueness, its failings and its prejudices, and above all its responsibilities and its potential. In each case it is a challenge addressed both to the individual and to the community, whether it be a nation or a church. It is the challenge framed in Buber's own haunting question: How can we become what we are? It is the challenge, and ultimately the appeal, to work for the achievement of God's realm on earth: the community of man as it ought to be.

PART II

II

THE PERSONALISM OF BUBER

The Second Source of His Criticism of Religion

THE DIALOGUE BETWEEN MAN AND MAN

In this section on the personalism of Martin Buber insofar as it is relevant to his critique of religion, it should be noted that these two chapters are divided along somewhat arbitrary and artificial lines. This cannot be helped. The very attempt to conceptualize the life of dialogue is in itself artificial, yet altogether necessary. And so, even though there will be unavoidable repetitions, we will concentrate first on the dialogue between man and man, and in the following chapter we will consider primarily the dialogue between man and God.

Buber himself designated as central to his life's work the basic insight that "the I-Thou relation to God and the I-Thou relation to one's fellow man are at bottom related to each other"; this insight is at the heart of the "dialogical reality that has ever more disclosed itself to me." All of Buber's work on the Bible and on Hasidism ultimately served this insight.[1] We are thus dealing in these two chapters with a theme central to Buber's thought, a theme which is of the utmost importance for understanding his criticism of the structures of religion.

LIFE BETWEEN MAN AND MAN

Buber, writing in 1919, sees modern man as imprisoned in the shell of his own pride, imprisoned in the shells of "society, state, church, school, economy, public opinion," imprisoned by his own indirectness. He appeals to man: "Break through your shells, become direct; man, have contact with men!"

> Ancient rot and mould is between man and man. Forms born of meaning degenerate into convention, respect into mistrust, modesty in communicating into stingy taciturnity. Now and then men grope towards one another in anxious delirium—and miss one another, for the heap of rot is between them. Clear it away, you and you and you! Establish directness, formed out of meaning, respectful, modest directness between men![2]

Man must not withhold himself. He must become aware of the "two solitudes" that are interwoven in his life. One of them must be rooted out, namely, the solitude of "shutting oneself up, withdrawing into oneself, standing apart—the solitude of the men incapable of community." When this rooting out is achieved, man can establish and consolidate the solitude of the strong, the solitude that gives renewed strength. Man needs the opportunity from time to time to "call home his forces into a solitude," pondering his relations to things past and to those ahead, so that he may go forth "with new strength to the community of those who now exist." Otherwise there is a danger that man will never recognize the service he is able to render to others. In renewed service, man himself is renewed.

> You shall help. Each man you meet needs help, each needs *your* help. That is the thousandfold happening of each moment, that the need of help and the capacity to help make way for one another so that each not only does not know about the other but does not even know about himself. It is the nature of man to leave equally unnoticed the innermost need and the innermost gifts of his own soul, although at times, too, a deep hour reminds him of them. You shall awaken in the other the need of help, in yourself the capacity to help. Even when you yourself are in need—and you are—you can help others and, in so doing, help yourself.
>
> He who calls forth the helping word in himself, experiences the word. He who offers support strengthens the support in himself. He who bestows comfort deepens the comfort in himself.[3]

This appeal for man to go forth, to give of himself, to cease withholding himself is in accord with all that Buber writes on the meaning of man. We can understand the essence of man by beginning "neither with the individual nor with the collectivity, but only with the reality of the mutual relation between man and man."[4]

The essence of man

In an encounter with another person, in a conversation, an embrace, a lesson, what is essential does not take place in each of the participants, but rather between them, in a dimension "accessible only to them both." When two persons encounter one another, the complete "happening" is not simply the sum of what takes place within each individual; there is always something more, a remainder, and "this remainder is what is essential."

This fact can be found even in the tiniest and most transient events which scarcely enter the consciousness. In the deadly crush of an air-raid shelter the glances of two strangers suddenly meet for a second in astonishing and unrelated mutuality; when the All Clear sounds it is forgotten; and yet it did happen, in a realm which existed only for that moment. In the darkened opera-house there can be established between two of the audience, who do not know one another . . . a relation which is scarcely perceptible and yet is one of elemental dialogue, and which has long vanished when the lights blaze up again.

From the least events "which disappear in the moment of their appearances" to the pathos of "pure indissoluble tragedy," the dialogical situation can be adequately grasped only in an ontological way, as that which has its being between two persons and transcends both. "On the far side of the subjective, on this side of the objective, on the narrow ridge, where *I* and *Thou* meet, there is the realm of the 'between.' "[5]

That which is specifically human, that which decisively sets man apart from all other beings cannot be expressed by the concept of "spirituality." What is human in man consists of the whole body person; it is this wholeness which is involved when he goes forth to his meeting with the world.[6] That which is specifically human extends beyond man's reason. Man is man "through and through"; man's hunger is not the same as an animal's hunger; human reason can be understood only when complemented by human nonreason. Man's essence is not found in isolated individuals, for his relations with others are a part of his essence.[7] And by "others" Buber means not only other men, as individuals or as a community, but also the world of things and of animals, and "the mystery which points beyond these, and also beyond himself"; all of this must be included in man's situation.

The question what man is cannot be answered by a consideration of existence or of self-being as such, but only by a consideration of the essential connexion of the human person and his relations with all being. . . . Only when we try to understand the human person in his whole situation, in the possibilities of his relation to all that is not himself, do we understand man.

For Buber, man is the being capable of entering into relation with the world of things, with other men, and with God.[8]

It is always the relation with other men that is of primary importance here. The essential human reality is something that takes place *"between* man and man, *between* I and Thou."

> The fundamental fact of human existence is man with man. What is peculiarly characteristic of the human world is above all that something takes place between one being and another the like of which can be found nowhere in nature. Language is only a sign and a means for it, all achievement of the spirit has been incited by it. Man is made man by it; but on its way it does not merely unfold, it also decays and withers away. It is rooted in one being turning to another as another, as this particular other being, in order to communicate with it in a sphere which is common to them but which reaches out beyond the special sphere of each. I call this sphere, which is established with the existence of man as man but which is conceptually still uncomprehended, the sphere of "between." Though being realized in very different degrees, it is a primal category of human reality.[9]

That which is proper to man can be directly known "only in a living relation." Only man, among all the creatures of earth, can say *Thou.* Any philosophical understanding of man must take as its starting point "man with man." Only man with man provides a full and complete image. "Consider man with man, and you see human life, dynamic, twofold, the giver and the receiver . . . always both together, completing one another in mutual contribution, together showing forth man." We may come nearer to answering the question of what man is, Buber adds, when we come to see him as "the eternal meeting of the One with the Other."[10]

Need for confirmation

Man and man alone is able to enter into relation with those like himself. This "fundamental fact" of human existence, man with man, rests on a twofold basis: "the wish of every man to be confirmed as what he is, even as what he can become, by men; and the innate capacity in man to confirm his fellow men in this way." Real humanity exists only where this capacity is actualized, and the real weakness of the human race is rooted in the fact that this capacity so often remains fallow, untouched. Man is rarely with man! Men need to confirm one another by means of genuine meetings: "Human life and humanity come into being in genuine meetings." Here man learns not only his own finitude and need of completion, but his relation to truth is heightened by the other's different relation to the very same truth, a difference in accord with his own individuality and destined to develop differently. Man helps to convey truth to man, and in doing so he is confirmed.[11]

Man is the sole living creature whose reality is "incessantly enveloped by possibilities"; hence he alone among living creatures needs confirmation. "Again and again the Yes must be spoken to him"; without this man is in danger of being overwhelmed by the dread of abandonment, the foretaste of death.[12]

Man's need and responsibility for confirmation have been expressed by Buber in a particularly moving passage:

> Man wishes to be confirmed in his being by man, and wishes to have a presence in the being of the other. The human person needs confirmation because man as man needs it. An animal does not need to be confirmed, for it is what it is unquestionably. It is different with man: sent forth from the natural domain of species into the hazard of the solitary category, surrounded by the air of a chaos which came into being with him, secretly and bashfully he watches for a Yes which allows him to be and which can come to him only from one human person to another. It is from one man to another that the heavenly bread of self-being is passed.[13]

It is through the Yes spoken to him by another that man receives the confirmation he needs in order to face the uncertainty, the insecurity, which is so much a part of human life. The "heavenly bread of self-being" is that awareness of confirmation which every man needs from deep within his person in order to accept the great challenge and risk of living a truly human life.

Danger of "seeming"

Man's need for confirmation is also the source of a grave danger for humanity, the danger of false confirmation, or what

Buber calls "seeming," as opposed to "being." This duality of being versus seeming is the essential problem of interhuman relations; both elements are generally found mixed together, with one being dominant. By "being" in this context, Buber means that a person proceeds from what he really is; by "seeming" Buber means that a person proceeds as he wishes to appear to be in the eyes of others. For example, two persons look at one another. The first lives from his being and looks at the other spontaneously, without reserve, uninfluenced by the thought of the impression he should make on the other; it is a look dominated by being. The second is concerned about the image he should produce in the other, so he produces a look that is meant to have the air of spontaneity; it is a look dominated by appearance. Where seeming dominates, there can be no genuine interhuman life. Seeming destroys the authenticity of human existence in general.

> Whatever the meaning of the word 'truth' may be in other realms, in the interhuman realm it means that men communicate themselves to one another as what they are. It does not depend on one saying to the other everything that occurs to him, but only on his letting no seeming creep in between himself and the other. It does not depend on one letting himself go before another, but on his granting to the man to whom he communicates himself a share in his being. This is a question of the authenticity of the interhuman, and where this is not to be found, neither is the human element itself authentic.[14]

The tendency toward seeming is rooted in the need for confirmation, "in men's dependence upon one another." It is no small thing to be confirmed in one's being by another; seeming appears to offer itself as a help in this. "To yield to seeming is man's essential cowardice, to resist it is his essential courage." A man must struggle to come to his authentic self, to come to confidence in being, and it is a costly struggle. "One must at times pay dearly for life lived from the being; but it is never too dear." In every effort, even if unsuccessful, the will of man is stirred and strengthened to be confirmed in his being as what he really is and nothing else, and to confirm the other as he really is. True confirmation means that I confirm my partner as this existing being, as he is in himself. It requires a bold swinging toward the other as "the particular real person who confronts me . . . in his wholeness, unity and uniqueness." It is true that this basic attitude can remain unanswered, and the dialogue can die in seed. "But if mutuality stirs, then the interhuman blossoms into genuine dialogue."[15]

This relation of genuine dialogue is the only hope for man today. We live in an age in which seeming predominates, in which the look between man and man has become analytical, and a radical effort is being made to destroy the mystery between man and man. Man's need for confirmation is so rarely fulfilled. We must throw off all seeming and strive for a real trust in man and in existence. Every man must be given what he needs for a really human life. The hope for man lies in our overcoming the mutual mistrust which is everywhere so prevalent. Buber expressed this sentiment in a 1952 address:

> The hope for this hour depends upon the hopers themselves, upon ourselves. I mean by this: upon those among us who feel most deeply the sickness of the present-day man and who speak in his name the words without which no healing takes place: I will live.
>
> The hope for this hour depends upon the renewal of dialogical immediacy between man. But let us look beyond the pressing need, the anxiety and care of this hour. Let us see this need in connection with the great human way. Then we shall recognize that immediacy is injured not only between man and man, but also between the being called man and the source of his existence. At its core the conflict between mistrust and trust of man conceals the conflict between the mistrust and trust of eternity. If our mouths succeed in genuinely saying "thou," then, after long silence and stammering, we shall have addressed our eternal "Thou" anew. Reconciliation leads toward reconciliation.[16]

Man with man in genuine dialogue: for Buber, this is the focal point for understanding the meaning of man, it is the source of real humanity, it is the basis for the ever-renewed hope for man in the present hour.

GENUINE DIALOGUE

While something of the meaning of dialogue has already been given, and while much more will be said below in treating of the I-Thou relation, nevertheless it will be valuable at this point to clarify further the meaning of genuine dialogue. Its importance cannot be overemphasized. In genuine dialogue "man becomes revealed as man"; only through dialogue does man reach "that valid participation in being that is reserved for him"; it is genuine dialogue, the saying of Thou by the I, that "stands in the origin of all individual human becoming."[17]

Importance for mankind

When there is genuine dialogue between partners who have turned to one another in truth, who express themselves without reserve and are free of all semblance, "a memorable common fruitfulness which is to be found nowhere else" comes into being. Dialogue brings out an aspect of man which would otherwise remain dormant.[18] However, it is not only on the level of persons that dialogue is important. If real peace is ever to appear on earth, if the devastated life of man is to renew itself, then "peoples must engage in talk with one another through their truly human men." What is needed above all between nations today is a hearkening and replying to the human voice wherever it speaks forth unfalsified.

Speaking during the era of the cold war following World War II, Buber sensed that "the living word of human dialogue . . . now seems to have become lifeless." Political and ideological debates "no longer have anything in common with a human conversation." And this condition is universal: "Men are no longer willing or no longer able to speak directly to their fellows." They cannot speak to one another because they no longer trust one another; each one knows that the other does not trust him. If man today reflects on his relations with others, he will see that trust is almost nonexistent.

> Trust is increasingly lost to men of our time. And the crisis of speech is bound up with this loss of trust in the closest possible fashion, for I can only speak to someone in the true sense of the term if I expect him to accept my word as genuine. . . . This incapacity for unreserved intercourse with the other points to an innermost sickness of the sense of existence. One symptom of this sickness, and the most acute of all, is the one from which I have begun: that a genuine word cannot arise between the camps.[19]

The very depth of the political crisis leads Buber to hope. It is in times of crisis that man's power of turning manifests itself. Instead of allowing himself to be overwhelmed by despair, man "calls forth his primal powers and accomplishes with them the turning of his very existence." The very absence of authentic dialogue imposes on man an urgent demand; it calls for naked decision.

> I believe, despite all, that the peoples in this hour can enter into dialogue, into a genuine dialogue with one another. In a genuine dialogue each of the partners, even when he stands in opposition to the other, heeds, affirms, and confirms his opponent as an existing other. Only so can conflict certainly not be eliminated from the world, but be humanly arbitrated and led towards its overcoming.
>
> To the task of initiating this conversation those are inevitably called who carry on today . . . the battle against the anti-human . . . by speaking unreservedly with one another, not overlooking what divides them but determined to bear this division in common.[20]

It was Buber's analysis of mistrust in the world, his own profound hope in man, and his appeal for trust that attracted the attention of Dag Hammarskjøld, then secretary-general of the United Nations. When the two men met at the request of Hammarskjøld at the United Nations in New York, Buber perceived that "both of us were indeed concerned about the same thing: he who stood in the most exposed position of international responsibility, I who stand in the loneliness of a spiritual tower."

> We were both pained in the same way by the pseudo-speaking of representatives of states and groups of states who, permeated by a fundamental reciprocal mistrust, talked past one another out the windows. We both hoped, we both believed that still in sufficient time before the catastrophe, faithful representatives of the people, faithful to their mission, would enter into a genuine dialogue, a genuine dealing with one another out of which would emerge in all clarity the fact that the common interests of the people were stronger still than those which kept them in opposition to one another. A genuine dealing with one another in which it must occur that a working together . . . must be preferred to the common destruction. For there is no third possibility, only one of these two: common realization of the great common interests or the end of all that, on the one side and the other, one is accustomed to call civilization.

For both Buber and Hammarskjøld, genuine dialogue was of absolute importance for the very survival of man.[21]

Becoming aware

Dialogue does not require vocalization; "no sound is necessary, not even a gesture." Buber gives the picture of two men sitting beside one another in solitude. They do not speak to one another, they do not look at one another, they are not in one another's confidence, they are not thinking of one another. One man, as is his custom, is calm, openly disposed to everything that might come. For him, it is not enough to be ready; he is also present, he is "really *there.*" The attitude of the other reveals a man who holds himself in reserve; there is an "impenetrable inability to communicate himself." Then there occurs one of those rare moments which succeed in "bursting asunder the seven iron bands about our heart—imperceptibly the spell is lifted." No word is spoken, no gesture made; but communication streams forth unreservedly, and the silence bears it to his neighbor, who receives it unreservedly. "He will be able to tell no one, not even himself, what he has experienced. What does he now "know" of the other? No more knowing is needed. For where unreserve has ruled, even wordlessly, between men, the word of dialogue has happened sacramentally."[22]

Dialogue implies *becoming aware,* becoming aware that we are addressed and that the address demands an answer. It is not necessarily a man of whom I become aware; it can be an animal, a plant, a stone. Nothing is excluded from the things through which from time to time something is said to me. "Nothing can refuse to be the vessel for the Word. The limits for the possibility of dialogue are the limits of awareness." The signs of address are not something extraordinary, but just those things that happen again and again; nothing is added by the address; they are the events of personal everyday life, the great and the small. But man does not want to hear the address: "The waves of aether roar on always, but for most of the time we have turned off our receivers." We try to protect ourselves from the word addressed to us:

> Each of us is encased in an armour whose task is to ward off signs. Signs happen to us without respite, living means being addressed, we would need only to present ourselves and to perceive. But the risk is too dangerous for us, the soundless thunderings seem to threaten us with annihilation, and from generation to generation we perfect the defence apparatus. All our knowl-

edge assures us, "Be calm, everything happens as it must happen, but nothing is directed at you, you are not meant; it is just 'the world,' you can experience it as you like, but whatever you make of it in yourself proceeds from you alone, nothing is required of you, you are not addressed, all is quiet."

Each of us is encased in an armour which we soon, out of familiarity, no longer notice. There are only moments which penetrate it and stir the soul to sensibility.[23]

It is clear that for Buber one of the great weaknesses of man today is that he does not want to listen.

Need to listen

Man must listen. Each concrete hour allotted to man, with its content drawn "from the world and from destiny," is speech for the one who is attentive. Yet the whole apparatus of our civilization is geared to preserve man from this attentiveness, from its consequences, from its responsibility. For the attentive man would no longer be "master" of the situation that confronts him. None of the things that he has relied on in the past would be of help to him, "no knowledge and no technique, no system and no program; for now he would have to do with what cannot be classified." For the man who listens, each sound is a new creation, calling him to respond, to be true to the present moment. Only then does he experience a life that is something other than a sum of moments. "A newly-created concrete reality has been laid in our arms; we answer for it."[24]

Dialogue implies turning toward the other, regarding the other as the very one he is. If the other becomes merely a part of my experience, then dialogue becomes a fiction, this "mysterious intercourse between two human worlds" becomes only a game. Buber cites his personal experience during a summer spent on his grandparents' estate when he was eleven years old. He would often steal unnoticed into the stable to stroke the neck of his favorite horse. This was not a casual delight, but a deeply meaningful event. What he experienced in touch with the horse was "the Other, the immense otherness of the Other."

When I stroked the mighty mane . . . and felt the life beneath my hand, it was as though the element of vitality itself bordered on my skin, something that was not I, was certainly not akin to me, palpably the other, not just another, really the Other itself; and yet it let me approach, confided itself to me, placed itself elementally in the relation of *Thou* and *Thou* with me. . . . But once . . . it struck me about the stroking, what fun it gave me, and suddenly I became conscious of my hand. The game went on as before, but something had changed, it was no longer the same thing. And the next day, after giving him a rich feed, when I stroked my friend's head he did not raise his head . . . I considered myself judged.[25]

Whenever in dialogue I try to "bring attention to my *I*, I have irrevocably miscarried what I had to say; . . . the dialogue is a failure." Dialogue demands a turning fully toward the other as he is, in the unique way peculiar to him, aware that he is essentially different from myself; I accept him as the person he is; I am aware of the other when I step into relation with him, that is, when he becomes present to me.

I affirm the person I struggle with: I struggle with him as his partner, I confirm him as creature and as creation, I confirm him who is opposed to me as him who is over against me. It is true that it now depends on the other whether genuine dialogue, mutuality in speech arises between us. But if I thus give to the other who confronts me his legitimate standing as a man with whom I am ready to enter into dialogue, then I may trust him and suppose him to be also ready to deal with me as his partner.[26]

Making present

In genuine dialogue the turning takes place in all truth, it is a turning of the whole being; I make the other as present as it is possible at this moment, present in his wholeness and uniqueness, as the person he is. I receive him as my partner, which means I confirm and accept him as far as this is possible. Confirmation does not mean approval; but despite any disagreement, by accepting him as my partner in genuine dialogue, "I have affirmed him as a person."

Furthermore, if there is to be genuine dialogue, each participant must bring himself into it; he must be willing to say what he really thinks about the subject at hand. If genuine dialogue is to be had, it must be given its right "by keeping nothing back"; but to keep back nothing "is the exact opposite of unreserved speech." Everything depends on the legitimacy of what a man has to say. It is not necessary for all actually to speak, but each must be determined not to withdraw if the time comes for him to say what he has to say. No one can know in advance what he has to say: "Genuine dialogue cannot be arranged beforehand." For most it involves listening to the call of the spirit.[27]

Dialogue, then, is not merely the intercourse of words. It involves the response of my whole being to the otherness of the other, an otherness which is comprehended only when I open myself to him in the present concrete situation and respond to his need, even when he is not aware that he is addressing me.[28] This is the dialogue that is the source of real humanity. In our life and experience we are constantly being addressed. For the most part we do not bother to listen to the address, or we break into it with chatter. "But if the word comes to us and the answer proceeds from us," then there exists in the world, even though brokenly, the reality of human life.[29]

Objections to dialogue

Buber poses the question that his life of dialogue is too idealistic; it does not consider the actualities of life; it can only take place in a utopia. It is objected that dialogue concerns only intellectuals who have leisure. It may be quite interesting for those who are not bearing the normal burdens of life, but what of the office worker, the laborer, the factory worker, or the business magnate? Can he "communicate himself without reserve," or "feel himself addressed in what he experiences"? Such demands are simply out of reach for the ordinary person.

In his reply Buber points out that there is no such thing as demanding dialogue; dialogue is not something that can be commanded. "It is not that you *are* to answer but that you *are able.*"

> You are really able. The life of dialogue . . . begins no higher than where humanity begins. There are no gifted and ungifted here, only those who give themselves and those who withhold themselves. . . .
> You put before me the man taken up with duty and business. Yes, precisely him I mean, him in the factory, in the shop, in the office, in the mine, on the tractor, at the printing-press: man. . . . I have him in mind, the yoked, the wheel-treading, the conditioned. Dialogue is not an affair of . . . spiritual luxuriousness, it is a matter of creation, of the creature, and he is that, the man of whom I speak, he is a creature, trivial and irreplaceable.[30]

Dialogue is concerned with the dull, ordinary, pedestrian aspects of everyday life—and with the breakthrough: breaking through from the dull and routine, not into the heroic and exalted, but simply into "this tiny strictness and grace of every day." Only now there appears the effective reality, given to me "in trust and responsibility." We do not find meaning lying in things, nor do we put meaning into things; but between us and things meaning can happen.[31]

Dialogue always possible

The daily routine that engulfs man is never so formalized that dialogue would become impossible.

> No factory and no office is so abandoned by creation that a creative glance could not fly up from one working-place to another, from desk to desk, a sober and brotherly glance which guarantees the reality of creation which is happening—*quantum satis*. And nothing is so valuable a service of dialogue between God and man as such an unsentimental and unreserved exchange of glances between two men in an alien place.

At each moment man stands before concrete reality which reaches out to him and wishes to receive an answer from him. "Even now a real decision is made in him, whether he faces the speech of God articulated to him in things and events—or escapes. And a creative glance towards his fellow creature can at times suffice for response."[32]

It is a question of renouncing the bureaucratic and technological craze with its easy "mastery" of every situation, and instead bringing everything into the power of dialogue. "The task becomes more and more difficult, and more and more essential, the fulfillment more and more impeded and more and more rich in decision." All the regulated chaos of our age is awaiting the breakthrough, and whenever a man "perceives and responds," he is working to that end.

> He who really knows how far our generation has lost the way of true freedom, of free giving between I and Thou, must himself, by virtue of the demand implicit in every great knowledge of this kind, practice directness—even if he were the only man on earth who did it—and not depart from it until scoffers are struck with fear, and hear in his voice the voice of their own suppressed longing.[33]

If man wishes to be man, if he wishes to bring others to a realization of their humanity, then he must persevere in dialogue, in directness, in openness. This is man's greatness; this is man's awesome responsibility.

I AND THOU

Perhaps one of the highest tributes given to Buber's best-known work, *I and Thou*, came indirectly from the author himself. In August 1961, Dag Hammarskjøld wrote to Buber expressing his deep interest in Buber's philosophical works. Hammarskjøld wanted to translate into Swedish the most suitable of these writings. Buber replied that the work which was most representative of his thought was *I and Thou*. Recalling this occasion, Buber writes:

> He [Hammarskjøld] went to work immediately. In the letter in which he informed me of this, he described this book as the "key work," "decisive in its message." I received that letter an hour after I had heard the news of his death on the radio. As was later reported to me, even on his last flight he was working on the translation of *I and Thou*.[34]

Buber's own testimony indicates the central importance of this work.

Orientation versus realization

In *I and Thou* Buber is concerned primarily with man's twofold attitude toward reality, and especially with the dialogical attitude of I-Thou. While this concern receives its fullest expression in *I and Thou*, it was a problem which Buber had dealt with directly in an earlier book which he characterized later as one which is "obviously a book of transition." For Buber, his *Daniel*, published in 1913, ten years prior to *I and Thou*, was a work "in which there is already expressed the great duality of human life, but only in its cognitive and not yet in its communicative and existential character."[35] In *Daniel* the duality is that of orientation versus realization; and it is a duality which is expressed in highly poetical and imaginative language.

The power of realization, of grasping meaning, is inborn in every man, but does not attain its height because it is continually oppressed and degraded by the power of orientation. We live in an age in which orientation predominates; more than any other age of civilization, "ours is the age that does not realize." We need but consider how men live today:

> They have aims, and they know how to obtain them. They have an environment, and they have information about their environment. They also have spirituality of many kinds, and they talk a great deal. And all of this outside of the real. They live, and they do not realize what they live. Their experience is ordered without being comprehended. . . . To each of them eternity calls, "Be!" They smile at eternity and answer, "I have information." Their limitation is so closely cut to the body that they are glad and proud of it, and call it by elegant and pretentious names, such as culture, or religion, or progress, or tradition, or intellectuality: Ah, the unreal has a thousand masks.
>
> Orientation is their lord. . . . In the dead light of orientation, their destiny, which was summoned to experience living illumination in a living way and to become illuminated in itself, passes away. They walk as unreal men.[36]

Orientation tends to catalog all happenings in formulas and rules; this is useful in its own province, but it binds the happening and cuts it off from a freer existence. Realization relates each event "to nothing other than its own content and just thereby shapes it into a sign of the eternal." The man of realization receives that which befalls him as a "message"; he does whatever is necessary, aware that he has been commissioned. For the man of realization is one who has direction and meaning; he celebrates "an ever-new mystery in his realizing: to live so as to realize God in all things."

But again and again man desires security, and so he yields to orientation. In the contradictions and divisions which he experiences, he is gripped by fear. And in his fear the choice is ever before him: "To which will he give the power, orientation or realization? This is not a question of delivering himself wholly to one: neither can exist without the other; it is a question of mastery. Orientation promises him security. Realization has nothing to promise. It says: if you wish to become mine, you must descend into this abyss. What wonder is it if the choosing man hands himself over to the friendlier mistress and only now and then, in the rare hours of self-recollection, casts a melancholy glance at the other?"[37]

This choice of orientation rather than realization, when given its full existential character in Buber's later thought, becomes the choice of using and experiencing, rather than of standing in relation; the choice of possession, rather than of openness; it is basically the choice of I-It rather than I-Thou.

Man's twofold attitude

"To man the world is twofold, in accordance with his twofold attitude." With this assertion Buber begins his development of the meaning of I-Thou and I-It. I-Thou and I-It are the "primary words" that man speaks with his being; they express the attitude or relationship that man takes toward the world.

My life as a human being does not consist simply of activities which have some *thing* for their object. I see some *thing*, I touch some *thing*, I imagine some *thing*, I talk to some *one*, I like some *one*, I even "love" some *one*—but always the object is one among others. These, and other similar relationships, establish the realm of *It*. Every It is bounded by others, for It exists only through being bounded by others. "The primary word *I-It* can never be spoken with the whole being."

The realm of It is the realm of experience in which I extract knowledge of things. But the world is not presented to man by experience alone; this presents man only with a world composed of "*It* and *She* and *He*, and *It* again." Man is constantly experiencing and acquiring knowledge. "O, accumulation of information! It, always It!" This world of experience belongs to the primary word I-It.[38]

The realm of *Thou* has a different basis. When I say Thou, there is no *thing* for my object, for a thing exists only among other things, bounded by other things, and this is the realm of It. Thou has no bounds. "When Thou is spoken, the speaker has no *thing*; he has indeed nothing. But he takes his stand in relation." Man can speak the primary word "I-Thou" only "with the whole being." If I say Thou to another human being, he is not a thing among other things, he is not a He or a She hemmed in by every other He and She, not a He or She able to be "experienced and described"; rather, "he is *Thou* and fills the heavens." This does not mean that nothing else exists, but that everything else "lives in *his* light." The world of Thou is the world of relation.[39]

The world of relation

To say Thou to another means to take my stand over against him as such, to see him as present and to relate to him thus. "A being to whom I really say 'Thou' is not for me in this moment my object, about whom I observe this and that or whom I put to this or that use, but my partner who stands over against me in his own right and existence and yet is related to me in his life."[40] The relation to Thou is always direct. No system of ideas, no foreknowledge, no anticipation, no purpose can help man to say Thou. "Every means is an obstacle. Only when every means has collapsed does the meeting come about."

The relationship of It only brings me to aspects of an existing being, never to the being itself. I-It means that the existing being is always covered over by an aspect. Only I-Thou, "that which establishes essential immediacy between me and an existing being," brings me directly to the being itself; it brings me to the existential meeting but it does not permit me to view the other objectively in its being. "As soon as an objective viewing is established, we are given only an aspect and ever again only an aspect." In other words, as soon as I start to view the Thou objectively, it has already become It. The man who strains to hold fast to an afterimage after the cessation of the full I-Thou relation "has already lost the vision." I can specify of the one to whom I say Thou the color of his hair, the sound of his voice, his mannerisms, his goodness. I must certainly do this, and do it continually, "but each time I do it he ceases to be *Thou*."[41]

The relation to Thou is always in the present, never of the past. "The present arises only in virtue of the fact that the *Thou* becomes present." On the other hand, the *I* of the primary word "I-It" "has no present, only the past." Insofar as man remains satisfied in the things he experiences and uses, he lives only in the past; there is no present for him. "He has nothing but objects. But objects subsist in time that has been."[42]

In the direct, present relation of I-Thou, the I in no way becomes the other or possesses the other; rather, the I meets the other as something "that it is not and that it cannot become."

> Only then, when having become aware of the unincludable otherness of a being, I renounce all claim to incorporating it in any way within me or making it a part of my soul, does it truly become Thou for me. This holds true for God as for man.[43]

The twofold world

The world of It is the world of experiencing and using. I do not experience the one to whom I say Thou. Experience belongs to the realm of It. "In the act of experience *Thou* is far away." Thou is always apart from time and place. I can set the other in a particular time and place; I must continually do it: "but I set only a *He* or a *She*, that is an *It*" into the space-time categories, no longer my Thou. Whenever a man "singles out, observes, explores, applies, uses," he is in the world of It. The world of It is a reliable world, it is necessary for the growth and sustenance of human life; its organization can be surveyed and verified; it puts things in terms of categories and connections; it is comprehensible and orderable. In the world of It man makes himself understood with others, but he cannot meet others in it. The world of It is absolutely necessary for human life. "You cannot hold on to life without it, its reliability sustains you; but should you die in it, your grave would be in nothingness."[44]

The world of Thou is "always simply a *single* being." The being need not be a man: it can also be an object of nature, a work of art, an animal, God. Nothing is present for man in the meeting except the one being, but it "implicates the whole world." Regulation and control disappear. It is a world which is unreliable, continually taking on new appearances; "you cannot hold it to its word." If man tries to survey it, he loses it. It stirs within the depths of man, but if you try to remove it into your soul "you annihilate it."

> Between you and it there is mutual giving; you say *Thou* to it and give yourself to it, it says *Thou* to you and gives itself to you. You cannot make yourself understood with others concerning it, you are alone with it. But it teaches you to meet others, and to hold your ground when you meet them. Through the graciousness of its comings and the solemn sadness of its goings it leads you away to the *Thou* in which the parallel lines of relations meet. It does not help to sustain you in life, it only helps you to glimpse eternity.[45]

To add to the unreliability of the world of Thou, every Thou in our world, no matter how exclusively present it was, is destined to become It. This, for Buber, is the "exalted melancholy of our fate": that every Thou in the world is by its nature fated to become a thing. But one can say too that every thing is capable of becoming Thou to an I. "The particular *Thou*, after the relational event has run its course, *is bound* to become an *It*. The particular *It*, by entering the relational event, *may* become a *Thou*"—in Buber's words: "The *It* is the eternal chrysalis, the *Thou* the eternal butterfly."[46]

Moreover, the stronger that one responds to Thou, the more quickly does he bind up the Thou and turn it into an object. Only silence before the Thou leaves the Thou free; each response binds the Thou into the world of It. This indeed is "the melancholy of man, and his greatness."[47]

Thus man is continually making Thou into an object for himself to experience and use, but as he does this, he no longer confronts Thou. Man cannot live solely in the world of Thou; he needs the world of It in order to be a man. "And in all the seriousness of truth, hear this: without *It* man cannot live. But he who lives with *It* alone is not a man."[48]

The twofold I

Just as the attitude of man toward the world is twofold, so the I of the man who assumes these attitudes is twofold. For the I of the primary word "I-It" is not the same as the I of the primary word "I-Thou." In the first the I makes its appearance as an individual; in the latter the I makes its appearance as person. The individual makes its appearance "by being differentiated from other individualities." The person makes his appearance "by entering into relation with other persons."[49]

The word "person," for Buber, points to the underivable, it points to the mystery of creation, it points to the miracle that "is proclaimed to me by each newborn child to whose cradle I step, through his traits, gestures, sounds that never yet have been."

> And, God be thanked, I too am there, as the father, the grandfather, the great-grandfather, or perhaps only as a guest, gazing ever more deeply into the mystery. Human existence, even the most silent, is speech; and speech . . . is always address. What addresses you . . . is the underivable person, the now living new creature. The person becomes known in the I-Thou relation.[50]

Only the person is real; "individuality neither shares in nor obtains any reality"; rather, by experiencing and using it seeks to appropriate as much as it can. When a man says Thou with his whole being, he possesses nothing, but he enters into "the cradle of the Real Life." A man becomes I only when he says Thou. "I become through my relation to the *Thou;* as I become I, I say *Thou. All real living is meeting.*"[51]

> He who takes his stand in relation shares in reality. . . . All reality is an activity in which I share without being able to appropriate for myself. Where there is no sharing there is no reality. Where there is self-appropriation there is no reality. The more direct the contact with the *Thou,* the fuller is the sharing.
>
> The *I* is real in virtue of its sharing in reality. The fuller its sharing the more real it becomes.

This does not mean that the I that steps out of the relational event suddenly loses its reality. Rather, its sharing is somehow preserved in it in a living way: "the seed remains in it."[52]

Thus it is not a question of some men being real and others unreal, but whether reality or unreality, the person or individuality, dominates in man's life.

> There are not two kinds of man, but two poles of humanity.
>
> No man is pure person and no man pure individuality. None is wholly real, and none wholly unreal. Every man lives in the twofold *I.* But there are men so defined by person that they may be called persons, and men so defined by individuality that they may be called individuals. True history is decided in the field between these two poles.
>
> The more a man, humanity, is mastered by individuality, the deeper does the *I* sink into unreality. In such times the person in man and in humanity leads a hidden subterranean . . . existence—till it is recalled.
>
> The stronger the *I* of the primary word *I-Thou* is in the twofold *I,* the more personal is the man.[53]

Buber is clear and insistent on this point. Whenever one treats people and things around him as objects of observation, of reflection, of use, a different I is manifested, a different I exists, than when one stands with the whole of his being "over against another being and steps into an essential relation with him." Everyone who knows himself comes also to know both I's in himself.

> Both together build up human existence; it is only a question of which of the two is at any particular time the architect and which

is his assistant. Rather, it is a question of whether the I-Thou relation remains the architect, for it is self-evident that it cannot be employed as assistant. If it does not command, then it is already disappearing.[54]

The meaning of the word "I" is the key to understanding the meaning of mankind. We must listen to this word: "how discordant" is the I of the individual, "how lovely and how fitting" is the I of endless dialogue. Buber cites one example in particular of a man in whom the I-Thou relation is in complete command, an example of an I that is caught up totally in dialogue, in unconditional relation:

> How powerful, even to being overpowering, and how legitimate, even to being self-evident, is the saying of *I* by Jesus! For it is the *I* of unconditional relation in which the man calls his *Thou* Father in such a way that he himself is simply Son, and nothing else but Son. Whenever he says *I* he can only mean the *I* of the holy primary word that has been raised for him into unconditional being. If separation ever touches him, his solidarity of relation is the greater; he speaks to others only out of this solidarity. It is useless to seek to limit this *I* to a power in itself or this *Thou* to something dwelling in ourselves, and once again to empty the real, the present relation, of reality. *I* and *Thou* abide; every man can say *Thou* and is then *I*, every man can say Father and is then Son: reality abides.[55]

Love and suffering

One must pay dearly in order to be a genuine person and to share in reality. Man cannot say Thou except with his whole being, and this always implies risk; it is the risk of the "full acceptance of the present." To enter into relation means "being chosen and choosing, suffering and action in one"; any action of man's whole being is "bound to resemble suffering." It is the suffering of the man who believes in reality, who believes in destiny and believes that it stands in need of him and awaits him, who believes that he must go to it even though he does not know where it is to be found. He must go out "with his whole being," yet he knows the matter cannot turn out according to his decision, because one can have no prearranged decisions when he says Thou. There can be no possessing and using here.

He listens to what is emerging from himself, to the course of being in the world; not in order to be supported by it, but in order to bring it to reality as it desires, in its need of him, to be brought—with human spirit and deed, human life and death. I said *he believes*, but that really means *he meets*.[56]

The self-willed man "does not believe and does not meet." He knows only the frantic world outside and his frantic desire to use it. The self-willed man, the man of I-It, perceives nothing but "unbelief and self-will"; he thinks of nothing except establishing a purpose and devising a means. "Without sacrifice and without grace, without meeting and without presentness," he has a world cluttered with purposes; he is a man wholly "entangled in the unreal."[57]

Only the man who is open to others, who is present to others, can really know suffering and pain. To recognize the nature of suffering, one must know "the depth of the pain of other lives"; and this is achieved "not with 'sympathy,' which does not press forward to being, but with great love." Only then does one's own pain and suffering in its ultimate depth "light a way into the suffering of the world."[58]

Buber does not identify the I-Thou relation with love. But love without this genuine relation, love without real going to the other, reaching to the other, and companying with the other, such a love is called "Lucifer." No one, not even Jesus, has succeeded in loving every man he met; but even if Jesus did not love those who were hardened and intransigent against him and his message, he at least stood in direct relation to them, he was totally and completely turned to them with the fullness of his being.[59] And for the man who seeks always to stand in direct relation, who seeks to be a wholly a person, the cost is awesome.

Love bears the added note of responsibility for the other. Love is always *between* persons: "love is *between I and Thou.*" If a man does not know this, "with his very being know this," then he does not know love. He is confusing feelings and love. The man who loves can hold back nothing of himself; he assumes responsibility for the one to whom he says Thou.

> Love ranges in its effect through the whole world. In the eyes of him who takes his stand in love, and gazes out of it, men are cut free from their entanglement in bustling activity. Good people and evil, wise and foolish, beautiful and ugly, become successively real to him; that is, set free, they step forth in their singleness, and confront him as *Thou*. In a wonderful way, from time

to time, exclusiveness arises—and so he can be effective, helping, healing, educating, raising up, saving. Love is responsibility of an *I* for a *Thou*. In this lies the likeness—impossible in any feeling whatsoever—of all who love, from the smallest to the greatest and from the blessedly protected man, whose life is rounded in that of a loved being, to him who is all his life nailed to the cross of the world, and who ventures to bring himself to the dreadful point—to love *all men*.[60]

The metaphor Buber has chosen here is unmistakably clear in its meaning and reference: to strive for the "dreadful point" of loving all men is to bring oneself to the point of crucifixion. It implies the constant risk of one's whole being in gift to one's fellowmen. Buber's insight may help us to understand more clearly the command of that other Jew for whom Buber had such deep respect: "Love one another as I have loved you."

Need for a rebirth of I-Thou

Again and again throughout his writings Buber has pointed to the growing impersonalism between man and man and the increasing power of I-It. "It has become very rare for one person to open up spontaneously to another. He holds back, observes, calculates and criticizes." Today more than ever a type of man predominates who "prefers to observe and make use of the beings whom he encounters on his life way" instead of turning toward them the fullness of his being in meeting. Time and again the other becomes merely a "sum of qualities which are more or less useful to me; he is an aggregate of forces which I regard as excellent or poor prospects for my exploitation."[61]

The history of man is clear on at least one point: the progressive growth of the world of It, a growth that now threatens the very existence of man. In an address given in 1951, Buber noted:

In our age the I-It relation, gigantically swollen, has usurped, practically uncontested, the mastery and the rule. The I of this relation, an I that possesses all, makes all, succeeds with all, this I that is unable to say Thou, unable to meet a being essentially, is the lord of the hour. This selfhood that has become omnipotent, with all the It around it, can naturally acknowledge neither God nor any genuine absolute which manifests itself to men as of non-human origin. It steps in between and shuts off from us the light of heaven.[62]

Such, for Buber, is the nature of this hour. Man's increasing ability to experience and use and possess comes about "mostly through the decrease of man's power to enter into relation." As the influence of I-It grows in the world, the influence of the I-Thou relation decreases. And the power of this relation alone can enable man to live a truly human life. Unless, then, there is a "turning of man to his Thou, no turn in his destiny can come." Buber was vitally concerned that the life of man "be determined and formed" by the I-Thou relation. "For I believe that it can transform the world, not into something perfect, but perhaps into something very much more human, according to the created meaning of man, than exists today."[63]

We live in an era when the I-Thou relation has gone underground; "who can say with how much greater power will it step forth!" The prevalence of I-It has indeed shut us off from the light of heaven, but this is no cause for despair; "the eclipse of the light of God is no extinction; even to-morrow that which has stepped in between may give way."[64]

INSTITUTION AND COMMUNITY

In his personal life man cannot live without It; he needs It in order to be; yet if he knows only It, he is not a man. Only to the extent that he speaks the primary word "I-Thou" does he become a human person. So also in his communal life: man cannot live without structure and institution; there can be no communal existence without structure and institution. "The communal life of man can no more than man himself dispense with the world of *It.*"[65] But structure does not produce community. Community is had only among those persons who can say not only Thou, but We. An understanding of the relationship between community and institution is of great importance for the purpose of this work, and of vital importance for the very existence of man.

Institution and feelings

A man who takes his stand in the shelter of the primary word, "I-It" divides his life with his fellows into two distinct areas: one of institutions, the province of It, and one of feelings, the province of I. Institutions are "outside" man, where all kinds of affairs are pursued, where a man "works, negotiates, bears influ-

ence, undertakes, concurs, organizes, conducts business, offici-
ates, preaches." Institutions are the rather well-ordered and
harmonious structures in which man's affairs are carried on.
Feelings, on the other hand, are "within" man, where man lives
his life and recovers from institutions.

Neither institutions nor feelings know man; they know only a
specimen or an object, but never the person or mutual life.
Neither of them knows the present, neither of them has access to
real life. "Even the most up-to-date institutions know only the
lifeless past that is over and done with, and even the most lasting
feelings know only the flitting moment that has not yet come
properly into being."[66]

More importantly, institutions of themselves yield no "public" or communal life, a fact "realized by increasing numbers,
realized with increasing distress." Many of those who suffer
such distress want to loosen and burst asunder the rigid structures by introducing into them a "freedom of feeling." For
them, the institution too often links its members together without establishing or promoting a real "being together." The institution should thus be replaced by the "community of love"
which will come about when people, out of their feeling for one
another, wish to live with one another. But Buber sees a subtle
and corrosive error at work here, for communal life cannot be
rooted simply in personal feelings.

> The true community does not arise through peoples having feel-
> ings for one another (though indeed not without it), but through,
> first, their taking their stand in living mutual relation with a
> living Centre, and, second, their being in living mutual relation
> with one another. The second has its source in the first, but is not
> given when the first alone is given. Living mutual relation in-
> cludes feelings, but does not originate with them. The commu-
> nity is built up out of living mutual relation, but the builder is the
> living effective Centre.[67]

The insight in this passage of Buber's, written in 1923, is so often
lost sight of today in man's search for community. Community
cannot be rooted in personal feelings; no desire of a people to
live together, no matter how strong it may be, is sufficient for
building genuine community. The builder of community is not
personal feelings, but rather "the living effective Centre."

The mastery of It

Buber raises the objection once more that he is too idealistic. Institutional life, especially the political and economic life of man, is of necessity rooted in the world of It; the communal life of man can know no other basis than the world of It; the whole development of modern society has its source here. If we deny its rootedness in It, then the "enormous and nicely balanced apparatus of this civilization," which alone makes life possible for vast numbers of men, would simultaneously be destroyed.

Buber sees this objection as touching on the heart of the problem. Men originally adapted the apparatus of economic and political institutions to suit the circumstances of their milieu; now it has become necessary for men to suit themselves to the apparatus. A structure was established to aid men in their common life, but now the reverse is true: men must adapt their communal life in order to suit the structure. Man is beginning to realize that he has inherited nothing except the "tyranny of the exuberantly growing *It*, under which the *I*, less and less able to master, dreams on that it is the ruler."[68]

It would be wrong to conclude from this that the world of It is to be categorized as evil. It becomes evil only when man lets it have mastery over him, when he lets it overwhelm him and rob him of the "reality of his own I." In his communal life man cannot dispense with the world of It, but he must recognize above this the presence of the Thou which moves "like the spirit upon the face of the waters." Loosening or destroying structures cannot compensate for the lack of Thou: "No disturbance on the periphery can serve as a substitute for the living relation with the Centre." This is not to say that structures should not be loosened or changed; but this alone cannot rescue man's communal life. Communal life can develop only in that structure "over which the presence of the *Thou* broods." Only from the presence of spirit "can meaning and joy stream into all work, awe and sacrificial power into all possession"; only from the presence of spirit can everything which is used and possessed, even while retaining its adherence to the world of It, be transfigured into "what is over against man—into the representation of the *Thou.*" Only when the spirit which can utter Thou permeates and transforms the world of It, will man's communal life be saved from destruction.[69]

Need for real persons

Genuine community presupposes the existence of an essential or genuine We. The essential We connotes the relationship existing among a host of men which corresponds to the essential Thou on the level of the individual person. Just as a person who is treated as an object is not a Thou, but a He or a She, so also a group that is treated as an object is not a We, but a nameless, faceless crowd. But just as there is a Thou, so also there is a We.

> By *We* I mean a community of several independent persons, who have reached a self and self-responsibility, the community resting on the basis of this self and self-responsibility, and being made possible by them. The essential character of the *We* is shown in the essential relation existing . . . between its members. . . . The *We* includes the *Thou* potentially. Only men who are capable of truly saying *Thou* to one another can truly say *We* with one another.[70]

Community exists only where there are real persons. A group of men cannot say We unless they are first capable of saying Thou to each other. Communal life exists only when there is throughout the community, among those led as among those who lead, "the element of the person, the sphere of the person, the freedom and responsibility of the person." Whatever destroys personal life destroys also the life of a people. The spirit of solidarity and community remains alive only to the extent that "a living relationship obtains between human beings."[71]

Most men have experienced at least some type of transient form of We—for example, the real union that exists among a people when an important and beloved leader dies, even though the relationship lasts only a few days; or that which takes place when a group of people are faced with inevitable doom, as they withdraw from all idle talk and routine and each becomes open to the other as they anticipate "in a brief common life, the binding power of a common death"; or in time of political persecution when the heroic ones, standing in opposition and hitherto strangers to one another, "perceive that they are brothers and meet not as members of a party but in genuine community."[72]

The genuine We can be recognized by the fact that, from whatever aspect it is regarded, an essential relation between person and person, between I and Thou, is always evident. The

We receives its life from the element of speech, the communal speaking "that begins in the midst of speaking to one another." It is this communal speaking that ultimately constitutes the genuine We.

> Speech in its ontological sense was at all times present wherever men regarded one another in the mutuality of I and Thou; wherever one showed the other something in the world in such a way that from then on he began really to perceive it; wherever one gave another a sign in such a way that he could recognize the designated situation as he had not been able to before; wherever one communicated to the other his own experience in such a way that it penetrated the other's circle of experience and supplemented it as from within, so that from now on his perceptions were set within a world as they had not been before. All this flowing ever again into a great stream of reciprocal sharing of knowledge—thus came to be and thus is the living We, the genuine We, which, where it fulfills itself, embraces the dead who once took part in colloquy and now take part in it through what they have handed down to posterity.[73]

The flight from We

In the realm of We, the realm of authentic speech, a response is demanded, and "response is responsibility." Man today flees this responsibility; he acts as if speech were nothing but temptation to falsehood and convention, instead of being also "our great pledge of truth." Man flees the genuine We because he is afraid of "responsible personal existence," because he is not willing to answer for the "genuineness of his existence." The typical man today takes refuge either in the general collective which takes from him his responsibility, or in the attitude of an individual self who has to account to no one but himself.[74]

Perhaps the greater temptation is simply to yield to a higher authority. Man is all too willing to be deprived of personal responsibility; he only wants to obey. And so the "most valuable of all goods—the life between man and man—gets lost in the process; the autonomous relationships become meaningless, personal relationships wither; the very spirit of man hires itself out as a functionary." Man becomes a cog in the machine; he becomes insensitive to real community "just when he is so full of the illusion of living in perfect devotion to his community."[75]

This is why real communal life is so rare today. Man finds it too difficult really to listen to the voice of another. The other is no longer the man met in relation whose claim stands over against his own in equal right; the other is simply an object. And so the whole basis for community is lacking: "He who existentially knows no Thou will never succeed in knowing a We."[76]

Man's primary aspiration

Yet the genuine We is needed for human existence; without it, man may cease to exist at all.

> In our age, in which the true meaning of every word is encompassed by delusion and falsehood, and the original intention of the human glance is stifled by tenacious mistrust, it is of decisive importance to find again the genuineness of speech and existence as We. This is no longer a matter which concerns the small circles that have been so important in the essential history of man; this is a matter of leavening the human race in all places with genuine We-ness. Man will not persist in existence if he does not learn anew to persist in it as a genuine We.

For Buber there is simply no salvation in sight for mankind "if we are not able to 'stand before the face of God' in all reality as a We."[77]

The primary aspiration of all history is precisely this: "a genuine community of human beings." Man's primal hope depends upon a "genuine, hence thoroughly *communally disposed* community of the human race."[78] But community is a living form, not a rigid principle; it should always satisfy a given situation rather than an abstraction. Hence any particular form of community must always be temporary: "The realization of community, like the realization of any idea, cannot occur once and for all time: always it must be the moment's answer to the moment's question and nothing more." All sentimentality, all over-enthusiasm, all emotionalism must be kept far from our thinking about community. Communal life cannot be rooted in feeling. Community involves toil and tribulation before there can be a real community of spirit. Even the so-called religious communities are community only if they serve their Lord in the midst of simple, unexalted, unselected reality; they are community "only if they prepare the way to the Promised Land through the thickets of this pathless hour."[79]

The essence of community

The essence of community is to be found in its relation to a center.

> The real essence of community is undoubtedly to be found in the—manifest or hidden—fact that it has a center. The real origin of community is undoubtedly only to be understood by the fact that its members have a common relationship to the center superior to all other relations: the circle is drawn from the radii, not from the points of the periphery. And undoubtedly the primal reality of the center cannot be known if it is not known as transparent to the divine. But the more earthly, the more creaturely, the more bound a character the circle takes, so much the truer, the more transparent it is.

It is precisely in the world, in man's relationships to other men and to things, that the truth of the center is proved. Some of the early Christians fled the world and went into the desert so as to have no community save with God. But it was shown to them that God does not wish man to be alone with him; so above the holy solitude of the hermit, there rose the brotherly order; and finally, going beyond Saint Benedict, Saint Francis entered into alliance with the whole of creation.[80]

A real community does not require people who are always together, but it does require people who, precisely because they are comrades, "have mutual access to one another and are ready for one another." A real community is one which in every aspect of its being possesses "the whole character of community." Community is no union of like-minded people; it is not something which binds men together on a minimal basis; it is not simply living in tolerance and neutrality. Rather, it is a genuine coming together of men of differing minds, it is a solidarity and a mutuality, a "living answering for one another" and a "living reciprocity." It does not seek to efface the boundaries between different groups and parties, but rather it promotes "communal recognition of the common reality and communal testing of the common responsibility." Community, in Buber's mind, is "the overcoming of *otherness* in living unity." It is indeed the primal hope of all history.[81]

THE NARROW RIDGE

Buber often warned his readers that if they sought certitude and security, his life of dialogue would be of little help to them. The road to reality, to realization, is filled with risk and insecurity. The man who engages in dialogue risks his whole being; he finds himself in the same situation which Buber described as his own: the "narrow ridge." "I wanted by this to express that I did not rest on the broad upland of a system that includes a series of sure statements about the absolute, but on a narrow rocky ridge between the gulfs where there is no sureness of expressible knowledge."[82] Man too often seeks a once-for-all type of security; he wants to possess absolute truths that would never upset his ways or disappoint him; he seeks "objective" criteria that would serve as an unchanging guide.

Buber offers no such criterion; such a criterion is not even conceivable for him. "I have never concealed the fact that he who wishes to live securely would do better to stay far away from the way which I have indicated." Buber calls upon man to "exist without guarantees," to live by faith and trust and risk, without "objective" criteria, to embrace a life of insecurity: "I would have to be untrue to my basic experience, which is an experience of faith, if I should seek to establish such "objective" criteria. I do indeed mean an "insecurity," insofar as criteria are concerned, but I mean—I say it once again—a holy insecurity."[83]

An I-Thou knowledge that can be "held fast, preserved, factually transmitted" does not really exist. That which is disclosed from time to time in the I-Thou relationship can only become such a knowledge by being transposed into the I-It sphere. And so the more man gives himself to the life of dialogue, to a life of genuine relation, the less does he possess factual and objective "guarantees," and the more he finds himself on Buber's narrow ridge, living a life of "holy insecurity."

Trust and meaning

To pursue a life of "holy insecurity" demands courage and trust on the part of man. If he lacks courage, he must be educated for it. "How does one educate for courage? Through nourishing trust. How does one nourish trust? Through one's own trustworthiness."[84] Man can be educated to trust through his relationship to another, by the fact that this other exists and stands over against him. Because the other exists and is present to him, man is brought to trust in the world. "Because this human being exists, meaninglessness, however hard pressed you are by it, cannot be the real truth. Because this human being exists, in the darkness the light lies hidden, in fear salvation, and in the callousness of one's fellow-men the great Love." Or, as Buber wrote elsewhere, what does a man have a right to expect when he seeks to meet another? "Surely a presence by means of which we are told that nevertheless there is meaning."[85]

It is through our openness and trust in the other that meaning is given to us. It is not a knowledge that can be grasped and held on to and cataloged, but simply the existential assurance that meaning exists. It cannot be expressed in a formula or rule; it cannot be passed on to others as something to be learned. Only by being really present to another can a man give him a sense of meaning. "Only he can educate who stands in the eternal presence; he educates by leading others into it."[86]

Some final remarks

Perhaps this explains the widespread and enduring influence of Martin Buber: he was a man who stood in the eternal presence and has led, and continues to lead, others into it. He offers neither arguments nor proof for his position:

> I can neither prove nor wish to be able to prove. I offer the philosophical expression of an experience to those who know this experience as their own or are ready to expose themselves to it. More than this I cannot do; but I venture to believe that in this "not" I am faithful to my task.[87]

More than this we cannot ask. He remained faithful to his task and faithful to his experience. He makes a constant appeal to experience, to openness, to presence: "A silent understanding is again and again established between me and those of my readers who are ready without holding back to make their own the experiences that I mean."[88]

This understanding is, above all, based on the experience of the Thou in the fullness of its dimension. Only a partial aspect of this experience has thus far been treated: the dialogue between man and man. There is another and richer aspect of this same experience: the dialogue between man and God. For every Thou in this world points to the *eternal Thou*. It is to this dimension of man's experience of Thou that we now turn.

THE DIALOGUE BETWEEN MAN AND GOD

Martin Buber was a man of deep faith. He possessed a living faith in the God who revealed Himself to Moses, and who continues to be present to His people. For such a man of faith the world becomes a great arena where God addresses man and man is called upon to respond. For such a man of faith a continual dialogue between God and man takes place within the world, if only man be present and attentive. The man of faith, the man who knows God, knows also remoteness from God, but he does not know the absence of God: "It is we only who are not always there." God is never absent; it is man who is not always present.[1]

The man who is really present to the world is somehow present also to God. Man is present in a genuine way only when he says Thou. But by its nature every created Thou is destined to become an It. Man cannot always say Thou; so also he cannot always be really present. But God is always present to man, even though man is not always present to God. Hence, for Buber, God is the eternal Thou; he is eternally Thou, but our human nature compels us constantly to draw the eternal Thou into the world of It and into the talk of It.[2] It is this task, of its nature a paradox, that we set forth for ourselves in this chapter.

THE ETERNAL THOU

Every time man utters the primary word "I-Thou," he is also addressing the eternal Thou. Every Thou points to the eternal Thou. The lines of relation, extended beyond each particular Thou, meet at the center, the eternal Thou. "Every particular *Thou* is a glimpse through to the eternal *Thou;* by means of every particular *Thou* the primary word addresses the eternal *Thou.*"

In no matter what sphere man enters into relation, whether

it be the world of nature or of animals or of man, there is in some way a confrontation with the eternal Thou: "In every sphere in its own way, through each process of becoming that is present to us, we look out toward the fringe of the eternal *Thou;* in each we are aware of a breath from the eternal Thou; in each *Thou* we address the eternal *Thou.*"3

Of the various spheres of relation, our life with man stands out. When I turn toward another human being in openness, I receive the world in him. When the other turns and faces me in the fullness of his existence, he brings "the radiance of eternity" to me. When two men say to one another, "It is Thou," the indwelling of the Present Being is between them. In man's being with man, "God is truly present when one man clasps the hand of another."4 Here alone is the full reality of the Thou; here alone the word that is spoken receives its response. Man's relation with man is the real simile of man's relation with God: "In it true address receives true response."5

Man's relation with the eternal Thou is what Buber calls "pure" or "absolute" relation. This alone can satiate man's drive for relation.

> He who enters on the absolute relation is concerned with nothing isolated any more, neither things nor beings, neither earth nor heaven; but everything is gathered up in the relation. For to step into pure relation is not to disregard everything but to see everything in the *Thou,* not to renounce the world but to establish it on its true basis.6

In every relation man seeks this endless Thou, but his inborn sense of Thou is consummated only by that Thou which "by its nature cannot become *It.*" Man possesses an inborn drive for the presence of the eternal Thou: "His sense of *Thou,* which cannot be satiated till he finds the endless *Thou,* had the *Thou* present to it from the beginning; the presence had only to become wholly real to him in the reality of the hallowed life of the world."7 By being present to the world, man is ultimately present to God.

God cannot be expressed

The eternal Thou never enters into the world of It; it is always Thou. If we are to understand Buber's thought, we must never lose sight of this crucial point:

The eternal *Thou* can by its nature not become *It;* for by its nature it cannot be established in measure and bounds, not even in the measure of the immeasurable, or the bounds of boundless being; for by its nature it cannot be understood as a sum of qualities, not even as an infinite sum of qualities raised to a transcendental level; for it can be found neither in nor out of the world; for it cannot be experienced or thought; for we miss Him, Him who is, if we say "I believe that He is"—"He" is also a metaphor, but "Thou" is not.[8]

Buber does not try to prove God's existence; he does not posit God's existence from any inference or from any argument. Rather, he simply affirms that God is the "wholly Present," he is "nearer to me than my *I.*" God is "the Being that is directly, most nearly, and lastingly, over against us, that may properly *only be addressed, not expressed.*" Man can only address God, he can only meet God by saying Thou; hence, in absolute contrast to all other existing beings, one can say of God that "*no objective aspect* can be attained."[9] The importance of this insight must not be overlooked. Man can in no way bring God validly into the world of It; God is the eternal Thou, "eternally *Thou.*" Man can only address God; he can never express God; he can never talk about God. Language *about* God belongs to the world of It; God, the eternal Thou, can never become It. God can be reached only when man no longer says "He," but "Thou."

Men have addressed their eternal Thou by many different names, but always they had the Thou in mind. Gradually, the names became encrusted in the language of It; more and more men came to think of and to address their eternal Thou as an It. But all of God's names remain hallowed for in them he is not merely "spoken about, but also spoken to." Yet because the name has been so misused, men have wanted to reject the name "God." Buber strongly defends its use:

It is indeed the most heavily laden of all the words used by men. For that very reason it is the most imperishable and most indispensable. What does all mistaken talk about God's being and works (though there has been, and can be, no other talk about these) matter in comparison with the one truth that all men who have addressed God had God Himself in mind? For he who speaks the word God and really has *Thou* in mind (whatever the illusion by which he is held), addresses the true *Thou* of his life,

which cannot be limited by another *Thou*, and to which he
stands in a relation that gathers up and includes all others.

But when he, too, who abhors the name, and believes himself
to be godless, gives his whole being to addressing the Thou of his
life, as a *Thou* that cannot be limited by another, he addresses
God.[10]

Here Buber emphasizes the importance of man addressing his
whole being to the "*Thou* of his life"; no matter what name he
calls the Thou, he is addressing God. And here too Buber
reaffirms his position that all talk *about* God's "being and
works" is necessarily "mistaken" talk; it is impossible for man
to speak accurately *about* God.

The desire to possess God

In accord with our human nature we are continually making
the eternal Thou into an It, we are continually making God into
a *thing*. This is the way it must be: a continual passage away
from the living God and back again to Him. A serious problem
arises, however, in man's desire to possess and hold on to God.
Man desires "a continuity in space and time of possession of
God." Man is not satisfied with that "inexpressible confirmation
of meaning" which is his when he addresses the eternal Thou.
He wants to bring this confirmation into the world of It, into the
world of space and time, where it can be continually taken up
and handled, and where it will provide security for his life "at
every point and every moment."[11] Man's thirst for security is
unsatisfied by the coming and going of pure relation. He longs
for extension in time; he longs for duration and stability; and
thus God becomes an object of faith. Certainly faith is necessary; it completes the acts of relation, of man's presence to the
eternal Thou. For the man who genuinely believes, the "latent"
Thou is unmistakable: "Even when he is not able to turn to God
with collected soul, God's presence, the presence of his eternal
Thou, is primally real." But the man of genuine belief is rare.
More often than not, man's faith—that is, his belief in God as an
object of faith—replaces those acts by which he addresses himself to the eternal Thou. "Resting in belief in an *It* takes the
place of the continually renewed movement of the being towards concentration and going out to the relation." In other
words, man finds it much more convenient to believe in a "He"
than to take upon himself the responsibility of going forth here

and now to the meeting with the eternal Thou. And so the living faith of the embattled believer, who knows remoteness from as well as nearness to God, is more and more completely transformed into the certainty of him who enjoys security, for "nothing can happen to him, since he believes that there is One who will not let anything happen to him." It is the security of the man who thinks he possesses God because he believes in God.[12]

Replacing genuine relation

Furthermore, man is not satisfied with the "solitude" of the I before the Thou; he is not satisfied with approaching and meeting God as an individual person. He longs for those acts by which the community of the faithful is united with its God. Thus God becomes the object of a cult. Cult, like faith, is necessary; it too completes the acts of relation, expressing the living prayer of the community. But gradually it too replaces the acts of relation; personal prayer is no longer supported but replaced by communal prayer; the act of the being in going forth to the meeting is replaced by "ordered devotional exercises."[13]

In all this there is a movement away from genuine cult and sacrifice, from genuine faith and prayer, to a type of religious magic. What is the difference? Magic tries to obtain its effects without entering into relation, and so it "practices its tricks in the void." Genuine cult and sacrifice, genuine faith and prayer, are set before the face of God: "They speak the *Thou*, and then they hear."[14] Buber again and again condemns this tendency toward magic which appears so often in man's religious strivings. He speaks out against the man who imagines that he possesses and controls God; such a man simply holds and possesses a phantom that he calls God. In solemn tones, Buber warns us that God, the eternal Presence, does not permit Himself to be held: "Woe to the man so possessed that he thinks he possesses God!"[15]

DIALOGUE AND REVELATION

The man who is true to the life of dialogue and who takes upon himself the responsibility of response is somehow meeting and responding to the eternal Thou. He meets God in the word that is spoken to him, the word which presses in on him and stirs him to the very depths of his being. "A man can ward off with all his strength the belief that 'God' is there, and he tastes him in the strict sacrament of dialogue." And this address of God to man is not something that occurs solely alongside or above the everyday.

> God's speech to men penetrates what happens in the life of each one of us, and all that happens in the world around us, . . . and makes it for you and me into instruction, message, demand. Happening upon happening, situation upon situation, are enabled and empowered by the personal speech of God to demand of the human person that he take his stand and make his decision. Often enough we think there is nothing to hear, but long before we have put wax in our ears.

This existence of mutuality between man and God cannot be proved, any more than the existence of God can be proved. "Yet he who dares to speak of it, bears witness, and calls to witness him to whom he speaks."[16]

The Lord of the voice

Yet it is of no avail to say that it is God who speaks to us in these everyday happenings if we mean by God some preconceived notion of a supreme being that belongs to the world of It. The act by which we recognize that it is the living God who speaks can only be rooted in that "decisive hour of personal existence" in which we had to forget "everything we imagined we knew of God," in which we dared to keep nothing "handed down or learned or self-contrived," in which we held on to no shred of knowledge and "were plunged into the night." It is the hour of the "fear of God" when, in trembling, we become aware of his incomprehensibility. The fear of God is the experience of that darkness out of which God reveals himself. It is the portal of darkness through which man must pass if he is to enter into the love of God. Too often man prefers to avoid this darkness and to rest in the security of an "It-God."

> He who wishes to avoid passing through this gate, he who begins to provide himself with a comprehensible God, constructed thus and not otherwise, runs the risk of having to despair of God in view of the actualities of history and life, or of falling into inner falsehood. Only through the fear of God does man enter so deep into the love of God that he cannot again be cast out of it.

But fear of God, the darkness, is just a gate; it is not a house in which one could comfortably settle down. "God is incomprehensible, but he can be known through a bond of mutual relationship."[17]

And what can be known of him who addresses us? We can only know what we experience from time to time in the signs of address; we know only the God of this moment, a "moment-God." But the signs of address complete and confirm one another. For the man who is true to the life of dialogue, there arises from the givers of the signs, from the words addressed in lived life, the one God of single identity; for the man who attentively listens there arises from the moment-Gods the single "Lord of the voice."[18]

Revelation in the meeting

The meeting of man with the eternal Thou, his recognition of the Lord who speaks, is in reality the revelation of God to man. Buber recognizes no other revelation than this *"meeting of the divine and the human."* Revelation always comes to man as a force from without; it seizes the human elements that are at hand and recasts them: "It is the *pure shape of the meeting."* From this point of view, then, revelation is continual, and everything is fit to become a sign of revelation, for everything can be a sign by which the Lord addresses man.[19]

In revelation something happens to man; he does not pass from this moment of supreme meeting as the same being who entered into it. This moment of meeting, of revelation, is not an "experience" of perfect bliss; its effect on man is variable: "At times it is like a light breath, at times like a wrestling bout, but always—it *happens."* The man who emerges from this act of pure relation is somehow different; something has grown in him. The reality of revelation is that we receive what we did not hitherto have, and that we receive it in such a way that we know it as gift, as something that has been given to us. Revelation demands openness and presence.[20]

The confirmation of meaning

That which is disclosed to us in revelation has nothing to do with God's essence as it exists in itself, but rather it concerns "his relationship to us and our relationship to him." We do not receive a specific "content," but rather "a Presence, a Presence as a power."

There are three aspects of this gift of Presence which Buber considers. First, there is the fullness of being raised and bound up in relation. Man can give no account of how this takes place; it in no way eases his burden; rather, "it makes life heavier, but heavy with meaning." Second, this Presence bestows on man the "inexpressible confirmation" of meaning: "Meaning is assured. Nothing can any longer be meaningless." The question about the meaning of life is no longer there, even though it has not been adequately answered. "You do not know how to exhibit and define the meaning of life, you have no formula or picture for it, yet it has more certitude for you than the perceptions of your senses." It is not a meaning that can be explained by man, but only accomplished by man. Finally, this meaning does not deal with "another life" or with a world "beyond," but simply with *this life* and *this world;* it receives its confirmation in this life and in relation with this world. Buber sums up the meaning revealed to man by this Presence:

> This meaning can be received, but not experienced; it cannot be experienced but it can be done, and this is its purpose with us. The assurance I have of it does not wish to be sealed within me, but it wishes to be born by me into the world. But just as the meaning itself does not permit itself to be transmitted and made into knowledge . . . , so confirmation of it cannot be transmitted as a valid Ought; it is not prescribed, it is not specified on any tablet, to be raised above all men's heads. The meaning that has been received can be proved true by each man only in the singleness of his being and the singleness of his life. As no prescription can lead us to the meeting, so none leads from it. As we reach the meeting with the simple *Thou* on our lips, so with the *Thou* on our lips we leave it and return to the world.[21]

The mystery before which man lives remains what it was. It has become present to us, we have "known" it, but we have acquired no knowledge which would lessen the mystery. "We have come near to God, but not nearer to unveiling being or solving its riddle." We have discovered no solution; we cannot tell others what they must do; we can only go and confirm the truth of this meeting. In this consists the revelation of God to man, and thus it has always been:

This is the eternal revelation that is present here and now. I know of no revelation and believe in none whose primal phenomenon is not precisely this. I do not believe in a self-naming of God, a self-definition of God before men. The word of revelation is *I am that I am.* That which reveals is that which reveals. That which is *is,* and nothing more. The eternal source of strength streams, the eternal contact persists, the eternal voice sounds forth, and nothing more.[22]

Buber insists that there is no revelation of what God is in Himself, but only of His relation to men; revelation does not imply an "unveiling of the mystery." Finally, both the "mighty revelations," to which the religions appeal and which stand at the origins of great communities, and the "quiet revelations" that are to be found "everywhere and at all times" are alike in being; both are of the eternal revelation. In both cases it is a question of man's being caught up in pure relation, of his being seized by the presence of the eternal Thou.[23]

ROOTEDNESS IN THE WORLD

The revelation of God to man deals with *this* life and with *this* world; it is confirmed by man's life in the world, not by his concerns with a world beyond this one. Buber records the interesting tale of a God-inspired man who, after wandering through the creaturely wastes, knocks on the gates of the mystery:

From within came the cry: "What do you want here?" He said, "I have proclaimed your praise in the ears of mortals, but they were deaf to me. So I come to you that you yourself may hear me and reply." "Turn back," came the cry from within. "Here is no ear for you. I have sunk my hearing in the deafness of mortals."

Thus it is that true address from God again and again directs man into the place of "lived speech," into the world of the deafness of men. "The word of him who wishes to speak to men without speaking with God is not fulfilled; but the word of him who wishes to speak with God without speaking with men goes astray."[24]

Embracing the world

Man's primary concern is with his fellowmen and with the world. Buber again and again stresses this point. It is through the world that man comes to God, and from his meeting with God he is sent forth anew into the world. It is basic to Buber's thought that the man who believes in the world and who gives himself in relation to the world cannot remain godless. Man will not find God when he stretches his hands forth beyond creation. He must put his arms around the world and only then will his fingers "reach the realm of lightning and grace." We must really love the world; if only we dare surround it with the arms of our spirit, "our hands will meet hands that grip them. I know nothing of a 'world' and a 'life in the world' that might separate a man from God. What is thus described is actually life with an alienated world of *It*, which experiences and uses. He who truly goes out to meet the world goes out also to God."[25]

It is from this point of view that Buber strongly criticized Kierkegaard's decision to renounce his fiancée, Regina Olsen, because he considered her an obstacle to his love of God. In Buber's eyes, such a decision is rooted in a sublime misunderstanding of God. It was Jesus himself who, by his twofold commandment of love of God and love of men, brought to life the Old Testament truth that God and man are *not* rivals. An exclusive love of God is in fact, *"because he is God,"* an inclusive love, ready to accept and include the whole of creation. Men cannot love God in truth without also loving the world He has created. Men who love one another in holy love "bring each other toward the love with which God loves His world." Creation should not become a hurdle on the road to God; rather, "it is the road itself." Men are created with one another and directed to a life with one another. Creatures are placed in man's way so that "by means of them and with them" he may find his way to God. A god reached by the exclusion of creation would not be the God of all the living in whom all life is fulfilled; such a god would simply be an object artificially produced from the abundance of the human spirit, and such a love would have its being "in the void." Addressing himself to the position of Kierkegaard, Buber says simply: "God wants us to come to him by means of the Reginas he has created and not by renunciation of them."[26]

Man will meet God not by denying this life, but by hallowing this life.

> To look away from the world, or to stare at it, does not help a man to reach God; but he who sees the world in Him stands in His

presence. "Here world, there God" is the language of *It;* "God in the world" is another language of *It;* but to eliminate or leave behind nothing at all, to include the whole world in the *Thou,* to give the world its due and its truth, to include nothing beside God but everything in him—this is full and complete relation.

Men do not find God if they stay in the world. They do not find Him if they leave the world. He who goes out with his whole being to meet his *Thou* and carries to it all being that is in the world, finds Him who cannot be sought.

The man who denies this life stands before nothingness; the man who hallows this life meets the living God.[27]

God cannot be sought

If man endeavors to seek God, he will not find Him, for God cannot be sought. The finding of God is a "finding without seeking." How foolish the man who turns aside from the course of his life in the world in order to seek God; even though he should gain "all the wisdom of solitude," he would miss God. Actually, "there is no such thing as seeking God, for there is nothing in which He could not be found." And so man should simply go his way in the world with reverence and openness and wish that it might be the way. Every Thou he utters affords him a glimpse into the "consummating event," and when he enters the absolute relation, his heart is in no way turned from the world; rather, the eternal Thou becomes really present to him in the reality of the "hallowed life of the world."[28]

Man cannot have a relation of I-It with the world and a relation of I-Thou with God; human life cannot be divided in this manner. The man who is completely caught up in using and experiencing this world cannot find God: "You cannot both truly pray to God and profit by the world."

> He who knows the world as something by which he is to profit knows God also in the same way. His prayer is a procedure of exoneration heard by the ear of the void. He—not the "atheist," who addresses the Nameless out of the night and yearning of his garret-window—is the godless man.[29]

Again, Buber stresses the point that genuine human life in the world can never be godless; in the very effort to be truly human, man addresses God.

Responsibility for the world

The man who enters the consummating event, who "approaches the Face," is in no way turned away from the world; rather, he is drawn closer to it and he assumes a peculiar responsibility for it. He is beyond duty and obligation, because love is beyond duty and obligation. The man who is drawn into the Presence is drawn also into God's love for men and for the world. For him, there is no longer a tension between the world and God, "but only the one reality." He has now the grave responsibility of love for the whole of creation as it exists before the face of God. The "evil" man is not to be shunned; instead, he is one for whom greater responsibility must be assumed, for he is one "more needy of love." For Buber the man who approaches the face of God knows not only that he needs God more than everything, but also that God needs him.

> How would man be, how would you be, if God did not need him, did not need you? You need God, in order to be—and God needs you, for the very meaning of your life. . . . The world is not divine sport, it is divine destiny. There is divine meaning in the life of the world, of man, of human persons, of you and of me.[30]

The man who has shared in this revelation of God can do justice to it only if he "realizes God anew in the world according to his strength and to the measure of each day." This implies living a life of genuine relation insofar as this is possible. Pure relation can be fulfilled only in the growth and rise of beings into Thou, for in every Thou the "holy primary word makes itself heard." In other words, the meeting with the eternal Thou imposes upon man the responsibility to enter into genuine relation with other beings, as much as this is possible in his life. In this way human life, although it neither can nor ought to overcome its connection with It, moves toward a fullness of reality, for life becomes so penetrated with relation that relation achieves in it a "shining streaming constancy." And the moments of supreme meeting are not, then, like lightning flashes in the darkness, but like the "rising moon in a clear starlit night."[31]

Summons and sending

Each supreme meeting confers on man deeper meaning and deeper realization and sends him forth into the world. The

world leads man to God, and God in turn sends man into the
world.

> Meeting with God does not come to man in order that he may
> concern himself with God, but in order that he may confirm that
> there is meaning in the world. All revelation is summons and
> sending. But again and again man brings about, instead of reali-
> zation, a reflexion to Him who reveals: he wishes to concern
> himself with God instead of with the world. Only, in such a
> reflexion, he is no longer confronted by a *Thou*, he can do noth-
> ing but establish an It-God in the realm of things, believe that he
> knows of God as of an *It*, and so speak about Him. Just as the
> "self"-seeking man . . . reflects about his perspective or reflective
> *I*, and thereby misses the truth of the event, so the man who
> seeks God . . . , instead of allowing the gift to work itself out,
> reflects about the Giver—and misses both.
>
> God remains present to you when you have been sent forth;
> he who goes on a mission has always God before him: the truer
> the fulfillment the stronger and more constant His nearness. To
> be sure, he cannot directly concern himself with God, but he can
> converse with Him. Reflexion, on the other hand, makes God
> into an object.

"Summons and sending": this is at the heart of God's revelation
to man—a summons from the world and a sending to the world.
At the same time Buber points to the great weakness of man:
he wants to concern himself with God instead of with the world.
He prefers to "unveil" the mystery, to seek security in knowledge about God, rather than incur the risk of realization
through the depths of his decisions made ever anew.[32]

This is the great paradox of religious man. Buber has often
referred to it in one way or another in his biblical and Hasidic
writings and in his studies on the meaning of Judaism. It is, in
its root meaning, the tendency to gnosis and magic, the attempt
to know God and thus to control Him. The more man enters
into relation with the world, the more likely he is to reach the
absolute relation with the eternal Thou; and the more he is
summoned into this absolute relation, the more likely he is to
rest there and to reflect on God rather than to realize Him in
the world. One might almost say that the more human man
becomes, the greater his risk of becoming inhuman; the more
"religious" a man becomes, the greater his risk of becoming
irreligious; the more man enters into the absolute relation, the
greater the obstacles to his living a life of relation. Buber warns

us: "Those who may be called true human beings are time and again in danger of slipping into inhumanity."[33]

In speaking of man's religious situation, of his *"being there* in the Presence," Buber says it is characterized by an "essential and indissoluble" paradox. If man tries to think out a synthesis he destroys "the significance of the situation." If he tries to work out the paradox "other than with his life," he transposes the significance of the situation. For the significance of the situation lies precisely in the fact that it is to be "lived, and nothing but lived, continually, ever anew, without foresight, without forethought, without prescription," in the fullness of its paradox.[34] More will be said on this aspect of Buber's thought in the next chapter.

Prayer and solitude

If man reaches God only through his relation to the world, if man must love the world in order to love God, if he is to concern himself not with God but with the world, one might well ask if man can ever love God without this love being at the same time a love of a creature. Does Buber admit a direct relation of man to God which does not necessarily come through man's relation to a creature?[35] Does not man also need solitude in his life with God?

When Buber tells us of the dangers of man approaching God by the exclusion of creatures, when he says that God wants us to come to Him by means of His creatures and not by their exclusion, he is speaking of man's *habitual* attitude, not of *particular moments* in the life of man.

> When I speak of the exclusion of the world from the relation to God, I do not speak of the *hour* of man, but of his *life.* I regard it as unqualifiedly legitimate when a man again and again, in an hour of religious fervor, adoring and praying, enters into a direct, "world-free" relation to God; and my heart understands as well the Byzantine composer of hymns who speaks as "the alone to the Alone," as also that Hasidic rabbi who, feeling himself a stranger on earth, asks God, who is also, indeed, a stranger on earth, to grant him, just for that reason, his friendship. But a "life with God" erected on the rejection of the living is no life with God. Often we hear of animals who have been loved by holy hermits, but I would not be able to regard anyone as holy who in the desert ceased to love the men whom he had left.[36]

Prayer, for Buber, implies that man is directly turned to God; it is the speech of man to God which ultimately asks for "the manifestation of the divine Presence, for this Presence's becoming dialogically perceivable." The single prerequisite for genuine prayer is "the readiness of the whole man for this Presence, simple turned-towardness, unreserved spontaneity." Prayer demands that man be wholly and fully turned toward God.[37]

And Buber certainly admits the need for solitude in man's life —not the solitude of a man who turns his back on relation with the world, but the solitude of the man who wants to free himself from the world of using and experiencing, and a solitude of purification even for the man whose life is bound up in relation. The solitary man who has been forsaken by those to whom he has spoken the genuine Thou will be raised up by God. The solitary man who seeks isolation from creatures can never find God; he may advance to the point where he imagines he has God in himself and is speaking to Him; but truly, "though God surrounds us and dwells in us, we never have Him in us." We begin to speak to God only when speech dies within us.[38]

FAITH AND RESPONSIBILITY

The man who enters the pure relation with the eternal Thou is certainly a man of faith. But it would be very difficult, if not impossible, to define the meaning of faith in Buber's thought. Faith does not belong to the category of things that can be defined. Real faith begins only "when the dictionary is put down"; it is not something discovered once for all. Real faith is not a conviction or certainty that something is; it is not something that can be explained or interpreted or displayed; faith is simply not a *what* at all. Nevertheless, we can gain some insights into its meaning.[39]

Openness to the mystery

Real faith is not knowledge with a content, but rather it is "factual event"; it is life lived in dialogue. Real faith means "being addressed by word and sign, answering by doing and not-doing, by holding one's ground and being responsible in the lived everyday."[40] Faith is the word spoken into my very life; it is not an experience that can be regarded independently of the concrete situation; it is the address of the moment and cannot be isolated.

One cannot lead another to real faith but he can show him the face of real faith, and he can show it to him so deeply and so clearly that he will never confuse faith with its artful imitation, "religious" feeling. The man who really believes does not teach another *what* he believes but rather *with what* he believes, namely, "with the lived moment and ever again with the lived moment."[41] Buber's idea of faith is deeply rooted in his preference of the Hebraic notion of faith—unconditional trust before the Lord—to what he calls the Pauline notion of faith—belief in a proposition as true. In one of his clearest expositions on the meaning of faith, he writes:

> Real faith does not mean professing what we hold true in a ready-made formula. On the contrary: it means holding ourselves open to the unconditional mystery which we encounter in every sphere of our life and which cannot be comprised in any formula. It means that, from the very roots of our being, we should always be prepared to live with this mystery as one being lives with another. Real faith means the ability to endure life in the face of this mystery.[42]

It is difficult and costly to live in the face of mystery without trying to control or possess it. And the forms under which the mystery approaches us are simply our daily, everyday experiences. It is always in the lived moment here and now that a man gives testimony to his faith.

Totality of life

One may speak readily of belief in a cause, in a people, in a party, in a leader. But for Buber these are all metaphors; genuine faith means personal relationship with the "one existing God." And this relationship of faith to the eternal Thou is perverted into semblance and self-deceit if it is not an all-embracing relation. A man may think that he need only join a particular group or community and he is no longer responsible for his decisions. He may think that everything is decided, that he no longer stands at the crossroads where he must answer, situation by situation, for the choice he makes; he may think that the community or the institution has relieved him of this responsibility. If a man of faith embraces this attitude it means ultimately "his fall from faith," even though he could not be persuaded of this.

Man may look on "religion" as one compartment of life among others, even as having its own law and manner of behavior; but once he has done this, he has already perverted the relation of faith. Genuine faith embraces the totality of lived life; anything less than this is ultimately a denial of the sovereignty of God.

> To remove any realm basically from this relation, from its defining power, is to try to remove it from God's defining power which rules over the relation of faith. To prescribe to the relation of faith that "so far and no further you may define what I have to do; here your power ends and that of the group to which I belong begins" is to address God in precisely the same way. He who does not let his relation of faith be fulfilled in the uncurtailed measure of the life he lives, however much he is capable of at different times, is trying to curtail the fulfillment of God's rule of the world.[43]

Faith calls upon me to answer for *this* hour: it does not provide me with a "book of rules" to tell me what I must do. What God demands of me in this hour, I learn, insofar as I can learn it, in this hour and not before it. I learn it only when I realize that I am answerable before God for this hour as *my* hour, and when I carry out responsibility for this hour before God insofar as I can. What approaches me now, the unforeseen and the unforeseeable, is word from Him, a word that stands in no dictionary, and what it demands is my answer, my choice, my decision, my action. I answer the word, I answer for my hour. This responsibility no one can take from me: no group, no individual, no institution. I must not let anyone take it from me. Otherwise I pervert my relation of faith: I separate the authority of the individual or the group or the institution from God's sphere of power by yielding to them a responsibility I owe only to God.[44]

No substitute for personal decision

This is not to say that my community or group does not concern me when I face the decision of this hour. It concerns me greatly because in my decision the world concerns me greatly; and before all else in the world, it may be the group or community to whose welfare I cling which is of concern to me. But no program and no command and no resolution can tell me how I, as I decide before the face of God, must do justice to my group or community or to some other interest. Buber thus describes the grave responsibility of the man of faith in coming to a decision in those things which concern his community:

> It can be that I may serve it in the way that program, resolution, command have ordered. It can mean that I shall serve it otherwise. It can even be . . . that I shall mercilessly oppose the success of its program because I have become aware that God loves it otherwise than for this success. What matters is only this: that I open my ear to the situation as it presents itself to me as to the word directed to me unto the ground where hearing flows into being, and hear what is to be heard, and answer what is heard. He who prompts me with an answer in such a way that he hinders me from hearing is the devil, whatever else he may be.[45]

Buber does not mean that the man of faith is all alone, that he should seek no advice or help in his decision. Quite naturally the wisdom of those in authority, whether the authority be political or religious or whatever, is going to enter into the decision I make. Certainly the advice of friends, of those who really know me, will aid me in the decision. But it must remain *my* decision; none of these things may *replace* my decision; it is a question of personal responsibility; "no substitute is acceptable." The man of faith may entrust himself to one in authority, but only his bodily person; he can never entrust his responsibility to another. He will approach the moment of decision armed with all the "oughts" forged by his group, but when he hears the word addressed to him in this hour by this situation, "all armor will fall away from him." One cannot expect an answer to come from God. "God presents me with the situation which I must answer; that he presents me with anything of my answer I must not expect. Certainly in answering I am in the hands of his grace; but I cannot measure the share of what comes from above, and even the most blessed feeling of grace can deceive." Thus the man of faith has no guarantee that his decision is right in any but a personal way; his certainty is only a "personal certainty," hence it is an "uncertain certainty," but it is a certainty that springs from the very being of this person who is addressed and who answers before the face of God.[46]

Opposed to individualism

This insistence on the personal responsibility of the man of faith has nothing to do with "individualism." Buber is insistent on this point: "I hold the individual to be neither the starting point nor the goal of the human world. But I hold the human person to be the irremovable central place of the struggle between the movement of the world away from God and its movement to God." This struggle is going on constantly; it takes place to a large extent in the area of public life, but its decisive battles are fought out in the depths of the person.

One generation's mad search for bondage is followed by another's craze for freedom; in both cases there is an extreme, in both there is infidelity to the given situation in which man is addressed and called to respond. The man of faith must accept responsibility by avoiding the extremes of a flight into a protective "once for all" and the wild urge of a blind freedom that seeks only more freedom. Too often man does not want to listen to the word that is spoken to him here and now. It is in this sense that we should understand Buber's remark: "Only he who knows himself bound to the place where he stands is true to the One Existing and just from that point free for his own responsibility." Only men who are thus bound and thus free can form a true community. Even at this point the man of faith must continue to submit his whole life, and thus his whole communal life, to the One who is his Lord. There is no certainty of "finding what is right" in this life of faith; there is always chance of error. The risk of faith does not insure the truth for us; but it, and it alone, leads us to where the breath of truth is to be felt.[47]

Freedom and responsibility

It is obvious that the capacity of the man of faith for personal and essential decision is continually threatened by collective decisions. Every group to which he belongs threatens to erode the ground of personal responsibility. He must constantly guard against this danger and search for the freedom needed for responsible decision. But the man of faith must also guard against the danger of freedom for its own sake. No human endeavor succeeds without freedom; freedom cannot be dispensed with, yet it cannot be made use of in itself; no endeavor succeeds simply because it is free. Freedom is "the run before the jump, the tuning of the violin," but it is not the ultimate goal. This, for Buber, would be sheer folly.

> Freedom—I love its flashing face: it flashes forth from the darkness and dies away, but it has made the heart invulnerable. I am devoted to it, I am always ready to join in the fight for it, for the appearance of the flash, which lasts no longer than the eye is able to endure it . . . I give my left hand to the rebel and my right to the heretic: forward! But I do not trust them. They know how to die, but that is not enough. I love freedom, but I do not believe in it. How could one believe in it after looking in its face? It is the flash of a significance comprising all meanings, of a possibility comprising all potentiality. For it we fight, again and again, from of old, victorious and in vain.[48]

It is easy to understand that in a time when traditional bonds are deteriorating and their legitimacy is questioned, the tendency of freedom is exalted; freedom is sought for its own sake, "the springboard is treated as the goal." When an individual or community has lost its sense of direction, there will certainly be any number of 'experiments in freedom.' People may well risk their lives in the search for some new kind of of existence; but they must not make freedom the basis of their program. Freedom is not to be sported like a feather in one's cap. It is much too serious a matter, much too heavily laden with responsibility. In a penetrating insight into the "risk" of freedom, Buber writes:

> To become free of a bond is destiny; one carries that like a cross, not like a cockade. Let us realize the true meaning of being free of a bond: it means that a quite personal responsibility takes the place of one shared with many generations. Life lived in freedom is personal responsibility or it is a pathetic farce.[49]

If the free man does not assume personal responsibility, he soon destroys the freedom he cherishes, and ultimately he destroys himself. Freedom demands responsibility; only when man is responsible is he genuinely free. These words may well serve as a warning to all of us, especially when we consider the direction of world events in the few short years since Buber's death: "Life lived in freedom is personal responsibility or it is a pathetic farce."

This for Buber is the awful and sometimes terrifying responsibility of the man of faith. He is is called upon to listen and to

be attentive with the "unreserved effort" of his whole being.
And he is called upon to respond in this, his hour. In *this* hour
we are addressed, in *this* hour we are to respond. But if we are
not attentive, if we do not listen, if we do not respond, then the
voice that speaks echoes in the void, the word passes us by and
is lost irrevocably; in Buber's simple expression, our omission
"will persist in eternity."[50]

DRIVE FOR SECURITY

One of the great obstacles that prevents man from being
attentive to the present moment with the fullness of his being
is his drive for security. Security is opposed to a life of faith and
responsibility. This has already been pointed out earlier, but it
would be helpful to treat here more fully Buber's consideration
of this problem. One of his earliest, yet certainly one of his
clearest, treatments of the problem of security as opposed to
risk appeared in his *Daniel*. We must remember that this work,
published in 1913, possesses a poetic character strongly influenced by German romanticism. Here the man of realization,
of genuine relation, is the man of faith, while the man of orientation, of experience and use, is the man who cannot live before
the face of God. All living with the whole being means danger;
he who lives a life of genuine faith must constantly begin anew,
and constantly risk all. He who seeks an all-embracing knowledge, a once-for-all security, cannot know God; he is thoroughly
godless.[51]

Seeking a weltanschauung

Buber describes the drive for security by using the metaphor
of a man lost in the midst of a strange city, surrounded by
darkness and shadows. Everything around him seems to be a
threat; no step is heard in the street, no sound; its silence seems
treacherous, its loneliness like something lying in wait. In his
anxiety, the wanderer is seized by a single powerful longing, the
longing for security. And the secret of security rests in one thing
above all: he must "know his way about." Within he asks himself: What sort of place is this? Where does the street lead? How
do I get out of here? "To know one's way about—that is the key
to salvation and health, to security itself."
Such is the longing of the man who, "seized by the shudder

of the boundless," only wishes to protect himself. The mystery presents itself to such men, but they are not ready to withstand it. The irrational fills them with anxiety. Instead of turning their whole being toward the mystery, they strive only "to guard their security." They fear that their stability will be shattered; they avoid the danger and risk of living with the fullness of their being, they are afraid to live a life of faith. "They want security, and security once for all." They want a world view as a security against the responsibility of really looking at the world here and now:

> They want to know where they are; they do not want to be under way but at home; they want to be provided for and insured; want a solid general truth that will not let itself be overturned; want only to know their way about, want only to *orient* themselves in the world, that is, protect themselves in the world. So they build their ark or have it built, and they name the ark *Weltanschauung*, and seal up with pitch not only its cracks but also its windows. But outside are the waters of the living world.[52]

But set a man of genuine faith in the same place and in the same circumstances, and let the same hour envelop him. He does not seek to know his way about; he is fully alive and sensitive and open to the given moment. He wants only to live this hour and to face the mystery so completely that it becomes for him "reality and message." He does not find himself in a sinister position: "Does not the indefinite proclaim existing being just as faithfully as the definite?" Is the reliable more of a testimony to the mystery than the unreliable? This man knows danger and will meet it when necessary; he has a strong wrist and is able to defend himself; but what would life be if it did not everywhere approach the brink and "threaten to capsize"? The script of life is so unspeakably beautiful to read "because death looks over our shoulder."[53]

The security of religion

Such is the way of the man of faith who forgets himself in order to realize the present moment here and now according to his strength. He does not want to know where he is, for he is never at the same place; he does not need the security of knowing his way about; he is ever before the face of God. The way of security, the way of orientation, is "thoroughly godless."

But security, too, is often the aim of theology and religion, and in so far as they seek to provide orientation, they too must be classified as godless:

> Godless also is the theologian who fixes his God in causality, a helping formula of orientation, and the spiritualist who knows his way about in the "true world" and sketches its topography; all religiousness degenerates into religion and church when it begins to orient itself: when instead of the one thing needful it provides a survey of what one must believe in this life and the beyond, and promises having instead of becoming, security instead of danger.[54]

Buber then issues a strong attack against the "churches" and opposes to them the man of "realization" and "direction" who becomes in his later writings the man of genuine faith:

> All security which is promised, all security which is longed for and acquired, means to protect oneself. It is that which is promised and allotted to the believers of all old and new churches. But he who loves danger and practices realization does not want to protect himself but to realize himself. He is the unprotected in the world, but he is not abandoned; for there is nothing that can lead him astray. He is not at home in the world, yet he is at home at all times; for the ground of each thing wishes to harbor him. He does not possess the world, yet stands in its love; for he realizes all being in its reality. He knows no security yet is never unsure; for he possesses steadfastly that before which all security appears vain and empty: direction and meaning.[55]

It should be noted that here "religion" and "church" represent for Buber a degeneration of man's religious spirit, and insofar as a church aims at providing security in the sense of knowing one's way about the mystery, it is an obstacle to the man of realization, to the man of faith. More on this point will be said later.

The man who has direction does not have information; but when he acts he accomplishes what he is called upon to do, he responds to the word addressed to him, he chooses with his whole being; he feels himself free and acts as a free man; he takes upon himself the full responsibility for what he chooses. Over this man, and over those like him, "the star shines down *meaning* and sends its beam into all happening." Almost thirty years later Buber was to point to the lack of direction and responsibility as the cause of rebellion, particularly by the young, against the "collective"—and, one might add, against the religious collectives, against the "churches." The young especially are beginning to feel that "because of their absorption by the collective, something important and irreplaceable is lost to them—personal responsibility for life and the world." Maybe they do not yet realize that their blind devotion to the collective was far from being a genuine "act of their personal life," or that it was rooted in their fear of being left to decide for themselves, at a time when their self was no longer receiving its direction from eternal values. Maybe they do not yet realize that this devotion was in reality an escape. But they are beginning to notice that he "who no longer, with his whole being, decides what he does or does not, and assumes responsibility for it " becomes empty and sterile. And a man who is empty and sterile soon ceases to be a man.[56]

Holy insecurity

One of the themes which marks Buber's thought throughout his life is his espousal of "holy insecurity."[57] It is in these terms that Buber's *Daniel* describes the kingdom of God: "This is the kingdom of God . . . : the kingdom of danger and of risk, of eternal beginning and of eternal becoming, of opened spirit and of deep realization, the kingdom of holy insecurity." Man may well live for a time in a certain security, protected from dangers or never taking notice of them. But eventually there comes "the hour of awakening." An abyss suddenly looms at man's feet, an abyss of "contradiction and of opposition;" it calls to man out of the depth, and man knows that he must answer from the depths of his own being; and he is afraid. His choice is either the security of orientation, with its rules and laws and formulas, or the risk of realization and responsibility, which offers him nothing save the invitation to step into the abyss; man must choose which of the two will master his life. It is truly an awesome choice. But in Buber's *Daniel* there is no doubt which is the choice of the man of faith: it is the one choice which embraces "God and danger." Danger is the door to the depths of reality, and reality is "the highest price of life and God's eternal birth."[58] A life which is truly human is a life lived constantly in the face of danger and risk; danger is to be found everywhere for the man who is attentive. And danger makes life beautiful.

And if the poets of the age should surround me and each ask me: "Have I not imagined the most beautiful life?" then I would answer: The most beautiful life that has been imagined is the life of the knight Don Quixote who created danger where he did not find it. But more beautiful still is the lived life of him who finds danger in all the places where it is to be found, and it is to be found in all places. All creation stands on the edge of being; all creation is risk. He who does not risk his soul can only ape the creator.[59]

The man who is open and attentive and responsible will have no security, but he will have direction and meaning. God will be near him at all times. He will have a genuine religious comprehension of the world; he will hear in the situation of this hour God's address to him; and he will answer responsibly and strive for the hallowing of all things in the everyday. He will not be afraid to descend into the abyss. Here he will find his task; he will be sharing in the work of creating and redeeming; he will know himself to be the center of the world's movement away from and toward God; he will know that here his task is endless, and that here a "once for all" is of no value: "You must descend ever anew into the transforming abyss, risk your soul ever anew, ever anew vowed to the holy insecurity."[60]

THE COMMUNITY OF FAITH

One final point should be treated in this area of man's dialogue with God, namely, what may be called the community of faith, the community that stands before God. True community can only be realized by men of genuine faith who take upon themselves the responsibility of life lived before the face of God. It is not a community which enters into the "dialogue of the ages" which God conducts with mankind; it is always the individual person. But it is from such persons, from those who strive for "an unemphatic and sacrificial realization of faith in life," that a true community is formed.[61]

The cry for community

The great urge of man, his primal hope, is to form true community. But time and again the effort is thwarted by those who shut themselves in the fortress of the spirit, by those who are "enthroned in withholding" and refuse to give themselves to others, by those who admit no one "who does not know the password" and who recognize only the "fellow-conspirators of the secret alliance." These men are beginning to fear the "crowd." But who has made the crowd so great? It is precisely those who have turned their back on the crowd: "He who hates it and he who despises it, he who is horrified by it, he who is disgusted by it, each indeed who says, "the crowd!"—all of them have made it so great that it now wants to surge up to your spiritual fortresses and your secret alliances."[62] Those who have held themselves aloof from "the crowd" must begin to break down the divisive barriers they have erected.

Buber appeals to such men: "Make the crowd no longer a crowd!" Men have it within their power to shape the shapeless crowd into true community: "Break the withholding, throw yourself into the surging waves, reach for and grasp hands, lift, help, lead, authenticate spirit and alliance in the trial of the abyss, make the crowd no longer a crowd!" The cause of community is never hopeless: "When it no longer horrifies you and no longer disgusts you, when you redeem the crowd into men and strike even the heart of the crude, the greedy, the stingy with your love, then and then alone is there present . . . the new beginning." Men must insert themselves into the crowd as seeds of true community; they must realize that true community is had no longer through exclusion but only by inclusion; a true community must be without barriers, for faith and love can know no barriers.[63] It is man's failure to achieve true community that has caused the appearance on the horizon of human history "a great dissatisfaction which is unlike all previous dissatisfactions." Men will no longer rise in rebellion against a dominating power, but rather against the "false realization of a great effort, the effort towards community." Men will rise against this distortion, they will fight for the "vision of the believing and hoping generations of mankind," for the genuine realization of genuine community.[64]

One might easily apply Buber's words here to those efforts of the religious communities, the communities of faith, the churches. One could say that the dissatisfaction manifested within the churches today is aimed precisely against the false realization of a great effort; men are rising now to overthrow this distortion; they will not be satisfied with anything less than the attempt at genuine realization of a real community of faith. Above all, this community of faith must be a community without walls, where men no longer recognize privileged membership and secret alliances as the source of union, but rather see

in openness and responsibility and love before the divine Presence the real bond of the community of believers.

At the same time it is important to recall in this matter Buber's remark that efforts at community are ever again destined
to miscarry. The disappointments and failures of those striving
to form community belong to the very nature of this effort.
"There is no other way than that of this miscarrying. That is the
way of faithful faith."[65] Those who are called to form community are called to an undertaking which is destined, in one way
or another, to failure; but in their failure and in their fidelity,
such men and women of faith are fulfilling their responsibility
before God.

Rooted in the eternal Thou

A genuine community is made one by its center. It would
appear that in Buber's mind a genuine community can be none
other than a community of faith, that is, a community rooted in
God. We have already pointed out Buber's emphasis on this
point, but it is a prerequisite that is repeatedly mentioned. He
insists that we must not put community first; what precedes
community, and is a necessary condition for community, is
man's relation to the eternal Thou: "It is not the periphery, the
community, that comes first, but the radii, the common quality
of relation with the Centre. This alone guarantees the authentic
existence of the community."[66]

Furthermore, what Buber says of every great national culture
can be said also of every great religious faith and of every great
religious community, namely, that it rests on "an original relational incident, on a response to the *Thou* made at its source."
The culture or the community retains its living strength as long
as each member makes the original relational event his own;
each is called upon, "in action and suffering in his own life," to
enter into relation. "If a culture ceases to be centered in the
living and continually renewed relational event, then it hardens
into the world of *It*, which the glowing deeds of solitary spirits
only spasmodically break through." When this happens, the
culture can be renewed and given new life only by "a new
event of meeting," by a new response of man to his Thou.[67]

This is especially true of the religious culture or community.
The forms of religion, especially belief and worship, are valid

expressions of man's openness to his eternal Thou, as long as man does not remove them from the relational event. It is through the true prayer of men of faith that belief and cult enter into the "living relation." Without true prayer, the religious community must necessarily degenerate; its practices become encrusted in the world of It and they no longer lead man toward the relational event. Rather, such religious practices become a barrier because man can become all too easily satisfied with an It-religion and an It-God. What is required above all is genuine prayer, the turning of man's whole being to his eternal Thou:

> The fact that true prayer lives in the religions witnesses to their true life: they live so long as it lives in them. Degeneration of the religions means degeneration of prayer in them. Their power to enter into relation is buried under increasing objectification, it becomes increasingly difficult for them to say *Thou* with the whole undivided being, and finally, in order to be able to say it, man must come out of the false security into the venture of the infinite—out of the community . . . into the final solitude.[68]

When a religion becomes overimmersed in the world of It, man must in some way depart from this community in order to face his God. Buber is not here appealing to "subjectivism" in religious matters; he reminds us that "life face to face with God is life in the one reality, the only true 'objective,' " and the man who turns to this life desires to save himself from the seduction of all that is apparent and illusory in a religion which is weighted down by empty and formalistic practices. It is by no means an outright condemnation of religion and of religious practices: "God is near His forms if man does not remove them from Him. But when the expanding movement of religion suppresses the movement of turning and removes the form from God, the countenance of the form is obliterated, its lips are dead." When a religion becomes submerged in It, God no longer recognizes it; its practices become a sham, and the fact that man does not realize this, the fact that he no longer sees what is taking place, this is itself "a part of what has then taken place."[69]

When this happens, it marks the "disintegration of the Word." The word that is revealed to man takes hold on men through the various religious forms which spring from this revelation, and the word becomes current or popular only when the now-dead forms dominate man's religious life; this latter is the stage of disintegration. Buber speaks of this problem at the conclusion of *I and Thou:*

> The times in which the living Word appears are those in which the solidarity of connexion between *I* and the world is renewed; the times in which the effective Word reigns are those in which the agreement between *I* and the world are maintained; the times in which the Word becomes current are those in which alienation between *I* and the world, loss of reality, growth of fate, is completed—till there comes the great shudder, the holding of the breath in the dark, and the preparing silence.
>
> But this course is not circular. It is the way. In each new aeon fate becomes more oppressive, turning more shattering. And theophany becomes ever *nearer,* increasingly near to the sphere that lies *between beings,* to the Kingdom that is hidden in our midst, there between us. History is a mysterious approach. Every spiral of its way leads us both into profounder perversion and more fundamental turning. But the event that from the side of the world is called turning is called from God's side redemption.[70]

God is always present to the world; He is present to religious forms unless man removes them from His sight; He is present to man; but again and again, it is man who is not always present to God.

A concluding remark

Perhaps we should stop at this point. Enough has been said in these pages to indicate the lines of Buber's criticism of organized religion. Buber was a man of deep faith who recognized the importance of religion and of the religious community; he recognized above all the need for man's personal turning to God, for genuine prayer, for awareness of His presence and of His address. He was a man who saw also the dangers intrinsic to religion, especially the tendency to isolate and objectify cult and faith from the living relational event. Like the prophets of old whom he admired so much, he did not hesitate to speak out clearly and forcefully against the dangers as he saw them, calling to account the great religions of man, and perhaps more importantly, calling to account man himself.

It is to this critique of religion that we now turn.

THE CRITIQUE OF RELIGION

6

THE DANGERS OF RELIGION

When Martin Buber speaks of religion, he uses the word in two primary meanings. At one time it is a system or structure which obscures man's vision of God, it is something which stifles man's openness to his eternal Thou, it is a hindrance to man's relationship with his Lord. At other times the word "religion" is used to express man's turning toward God, it is the sum of all those things by which man reaches out to his God, it means simply that man is caught up with God. In the latter case, religion *(die Religion)* is equated with religiosity or religiousness *(die Religiosität)*, which Buber uses more frequently to express man's openness to God. In most cases Buber uses the word "religion" to express a hindrance between man and God—in this sense, religion is opposed to religiousness.

Thus in speaking of the dangers of religion one can mean the threat which religion presents to man's relation to God, and one can also mean the dangers which threaten to corrupt the genuine meaning of religion. Buber treats both aspects of this problem. In each case it should be quite clear in what sense Buber is using the term "religion," and what it is that he is criticizing. Above all, his is a criticism of those forms and acts of religion which have hardened into rigidity and which block the personal relationship between man and God.

In this chapter we will be primarily concerned with that understanding and criticism of religion which is based more or less directly on Buber's personalism, on his approach to God as the eternal Thou; much of the criticism will be negative, centering on the dangers which religion should avoid and the dangers which religion presents to man. In the following chapter we will attempt to give a more positive criticism of religion drawn from Buber's writings, with special emphasis on man's need for religion, even for a structure or system of religion.

RELIGION VERSUS PHILOSOPHY

When Buber opposes religion to philosophy, he uses religion in the sense of religiosity or religiousness. Religion in this case is essentially the "act of holding fast to God"; it does not mean that massive fullness of "statements, concepts, and activities" that one ordinarily describes by the name "religion" and which men sometimes long for even more than they long for the living God. Religion, in this sense, does not mean simply "holding fast to an image that one has made of God, nor even holding fast to the faith in God that one has conceived. It means holding fast to the existing God."[1] Religion here is not human thought about the divine; religion becomes this only insofar as it becomes theology, for theology is a religion's thought about the divine. Religion is rather the relationship of the human to the divine.[2]

This concept of religion is opposed to a philosophy which makes God and all absoluteness appear as unreal. Buber describes such a philosophy as the process of thought and reflection which has as its final stage man's intellectual dismissal of God. It had its prephilosophical beginnings when man pictured the living God, whom he had previously only addressed, as a "Something, a thing among things, a being among beings, an It." Philosophy begins by changing this "Something" from an object of imagination and feelings and desires to an object that is "conceptually comprehensible," to an "object of thought." And this process ends when man annihilates conceptually "the absoluteness of the absolute" and conceptually lets go of God. Not all philosophy arrives at this last stage, but Buber indicates that all philosophy which presumes to encompass God in its system of thought must ultimately arrive at the denial of the Absolute.[3]

The God of philosophy and the God of Israel

The cryptic cry of Pascal, "God of Abraham, God of Isaac, God of Jacob—not of the philosophers and scholars," can help clarify Buber's distinction between religion and philosophy, and even between religion and theology. For Buber, this cry represents Pascal's change of heart from the God of the philosophers, the God who occupies "a definite position in a definite system of thought," to the God in whom Abraham believed and whom Abraham loved, a God who cannot be introduced into a system of thought "precisely because He is God." The God of Israel, the God who can only be addressed, not expressed, is beyond each and every philosophical system "absolutely and by virtue of His nature." And insofar as theology places God within a system too, then the God of the theologians is also a "logicized God"; he becomes an object among objects; he is not the God to whom man says Thou.[4]

What philosophers describe by the name of God is no more than an idea. But the God of Abraham, the living God, is not an idea; He is not an object; He is always Thou, the eternal Thou. In replacing God by an idea, "the image of images," philosophers remove themselves as well as the rest of us further from the existing God. For Buber, man is left with no alternative but to choose, as Pascal had to choose, between the God of the philosophers and the God of Israel, no matter what name one might give to the living God. The philosopher who chooses the God of Israel would be compelled to renounce the attempt to include God in his system under any conceptual form. Instead of including God as one theme among others, such a philosopher would be compelled simply "to point toward God, without actually dealing with Him" within his philosophical system.

> This means that the philosopher would be compelled to recognize and admit the fact that his idea of the Absolute was dissolving at the point where the Absolute *lives;* that it was dissolving at the point where the Absolute is loved; because at that point the Absolute is no longer the "Absolute" about which one may philosophize, but God.[5]

Buber insists that the living God can be encompassed in no system of philosophy or theology.

Religion rooted in the Thou

Genuine religion springs from man's encounter with Thou. We must point out once again Buber's emphasis on man's twofold attitude toward the world about him. The other becomes for me either face-to-face being, or it becomes a passive object.

> The child that calls to his mother and the child that watches his mother . . . the child that silently speaks to his mother through nothing other than looking into her eyes and the same child that looks at something on the mother as at any other object—show the twofoldness in which man stands and remains standing.

This twofold attitude expresses the two basic modes of human existence: I-Thou and I-It. The relation of I-Thou finds its highest expression and intensity in "religious reality, in which unlimited Being becomes, as absolute person, my partner." The relation of I-It finds its "highest concentration and illumination in philosophical knowledge."[6]

Thus religion is founded on the "duality of I and Thou," philosophy is founded on the "duality of subject and object." The duality of subject and object sustains the philosophical enterprise, while the duality of I and Thou finds "its fulfillment in the religious relationship." Religion arises out of man's living before "the face of Being, turned toward him as he is turned toward it." Religion is caught up in lived concreteness; the religious relationship is in its essence nothing other than "the unfolding of the existence that is lent to us."[7]

Genuine religion, then, is directed to the Thou; it practices the "living relationship of I-Thou"; it is only in the relationship of I-Thou that man meets God.[8] Religion, or the genuine religious spirit of man, is rooted in the direct relation of man and God; while philosophy, and to a great extent theology, are ultimately rooted in the relation of I-It. Religion without the absolute relation, religion without this encounter, religion without prayer is but a counterfeit, and will be ultimately rejected by the man of real faith.

Two types of knowledge

Buber also expresses the difference between philosophy and religion in terms of the two general types of knowing. To know in the customary sense means to regard a thing as an object; it is based on the duality of subject and object. But to know in the biblical sense is to stand in relation to the other, it is the real knowing of I and Thou. The first type of knowing is the basis of philosophy; the second type is the basis of religion.[9] Buber oversimplifies this twofold division for the sake of his explanation; yet his basic argument remains quite clear.

Philosophy must split apart the relationship of I-Thou into two entirely distinct modes of existence, "one which is able to do nothing but observe and reflect and one which is able to do nothing but be observed and reflected upon."[10] Philosophical man begins "by looking away from his *concrete situation*."

Philosophy begins ever anew with man turning from the lived concrete; it begins with "the primary act of abstraction." And the lived concrete, which is the starting point of philosophy, cannot be again reached by way of philosophical abstraction; "it is irrecoverable."[11]

Yet at the same time religion, even in the face of a philosophy arrogant with pride and triumphalism, cannot deny the greatness of the philosophical enterprise. Religion must recognize that philosophical knowledge is not only a need but also an obligation of man. Buber writes that this knowledge is "an indispensable necessity and duty of human existence. It guarantees the continuity of thought through which man has acquired his special position in nature; it lays the foundation for the cohesion of the experience and of the thought of mankind." But philosophical knowledge is purchased at a great price: it renounces the I-Thou relationship, the original relational bond, the spontaneity of the moment. And only because philosophy has abandoned this relation with the concrete has it been able to construct its amazing "thought-continuum"; it assures the connection and communication of human thought; it assures that men understand one another in conceptual speech.[12]

A content of being is objectively communicable only "in and through philosophy," that is, only by elaborating on a situation in an objective manner. A religious communication of a content of being is a paradox, for religion is rooted in the I-Thou relation, and this relation knows no "content" of being. Any such content belongs to the world of It, and hence it is outside the religious in the strict sense of the term as employed by Buber here. Religion cannot demonstrate its assertions; if theology pretends to do this, it becomes for Buber a "questionable type of philosophy." Rather, religion can only point toward the "hidden realm of existence" of the hearing man himself and toward that which can be experienced "there and there alone." A religious statement, an assertion of religious truth, is valid to the extent that it witnesses to a living dialogue between I and Thou.[13]

Limitations of philosophy

In renouncing the bond between I and Thou, philosophy becomes incapable of forming community, either between man and man or between man and God. Unlike religion, philosophy demands no personal involvement in life. In the act of looking away from the lived concrete, philosophical knowledge tears asunder "not merely the wholeness of the concrete person but also God and man from each other." Religious knowing involves a person wholly and completely; a man is able to live religiously only as a unified being; only with the fullness of his being is he able to stand in relation to the Other. This fullness of being naturally includes thought, but not as a province which strives to make its autonomy absolute. Genuine philosophy involves a man totally, but it does not unify man. Instead, thinking "over-runs and overwhelms" all the faculties of the person. "In the great act of philosophizing even the finger-tips think—but they no longer feel."[14]

Thus, if a man remains strictly within the limits of a philo-sophical mentality, he cannot address God as Thou. Philosophy cannot be the meeting place between man and God, for when a man says Thou, he is no longer standing within the realm of philosophy. And insofar as theology shares this philosophical attitude it too shares the limitations of philosophy, limitations which must be kept clearly in mind. Otherwise philosophy and theology become, not paths by which man is led to the meeting with the eternal Thou, but an endless maze in which man wand-ers in his search, lost and dazed, saying "He, He" but never "Thou, Thou."

THE ROLE OF IMAGES

One of the dangers which threaten the genuine relation of man with God are the images and symbols which he employs to express his encounter with the divine. Symbols are always needed; but there is the constant danger that the symbol and the image may be confused with the reality. One of the impor-tant roles that philosophy should play in the service of religion is to point out this confusion and to urge man to create ever again new and more faithful images and symbols of the divine.

In his experience of the unconditional as the Thou set over against him, man creates symbols and images so that his mind may comprehend that which in itself remains always incompre-hensible. In the great ages of man these images are seen in their inadequacy; the divine "outgrows old symbolisms and blossoms forth in new ones." It is not God who changes, but rather the manifestation of God in human symbols. "In the search for the living God one must now and again destroy the images that have become unworthy in order to create room for a new one." This process will continue until ultimately no symbol is adequate any longer and none is needed; life itself becomes the symbol of God's presence to man.[15]

Confused meaning of "religious"

One of the great problems of religion which Buber confronted over the last forty years of his life, and which continues to confront man today, is the misinterpretation of the term "religious." Too often it is looked on as something which takes place entirely within man rather than between man and God. In his preface to *Reden über das Judentum,* published in 1923, Buber wrote that

> today we describe as "religious" essentially something that takes place in man's inner life, as well as the expressions of this something insofar as they reflect this inner life. I, however, am referring to something that takes place between man and God, that is, in the reality of their relationship, the mutual reality of God and man.[16]

This confusion over the meaning of "religious" has its parallel in the confusion over the meaning of the term "God." If God is considered primarily as a psychic projection, then obviously religion becomes an affair of man's inner life; God becomes a being *possessed* by man but not *encountered* by man. Thus Buber continued in the above-mentioned preface:

> by the term "God" I mean not a metaphysical idea, nor a moral idea, not a projection of a psychic or social image, nor anything at all created by, or developed within, man. I do mean God, whom man, however, possesses only in ideas and images; but these ideas and images are not the work of free creation; they are the products of divine-human encounters, of man's attempts to grasp the inexplicable as and when it happens to him. They are the traces of the mystery. . . . Images and ideas do emanate from it; what is revealed in it, however, is neither image nor idea, but God. Religious reality is called precisely that because it constitutes an undiminished relationship to God Himself. Man does not possess God Himself, but he encounters God Himself.[17]

Almost thirty years later, in 1951, Buber took up the same theme in a series of talks given at various American universities.[18] In some ages the God whom men believe to exist absolutely independent of themselves is the eternal Thou with whom they are in a "living relation," even though they can form only a most inadequate image of this reality. At other times the divine reality is replaced by various images that men possess and handle, or else it is replaced by a concept which bears only faint traces of the original image. At such times men fail to realize that this so-called religious relation no longer takes place between themselves and a reality independent of them, but has existence only within the mind.[19]

Need of encounters

At the same time there appear those who think that this is what religion really is, that religion has never been anything but an "intra-psychic process," a projection of the mind vested with reality by the soul. Finally, man clearly recognizes that "every alleged colloquy with the divine was only a soliloquy," it was only a conversation between the various strata of the self. Thereupon it becomes necessary to proclaim that God is dead. Actually this proclamation means that man is no longer capable of "apprehending a reality absolutely independent of himself" and of standing in direct relation with it; it means man is no longer capable of "imaginatively perceiving" divine reality and of representing it in images.

> For the great images of God fashioned by mankind are born not of imagination but of real encounters with real divine power and glory. Man's capacity to apprehend the divine in images is lamed in the same measure as his capacity to experience a reality absolutely independent of himself.[20]

Thus a given concept of God, "a conceptual apprehension of the divine," does not necessarily impair the concrete relation between man and God.

> Everything depends on the extent to which this concept of God can do justice to the reality which it denotes, do justice to it as a reality. The more abstract the concept, the more does it need to be balanced by the evidence of living experience, with which it is intimately bound up rather than linked in an intellectual system.

It is always the living encounter that gives substance to our concepts and images of the divine. The less anthropomorphic our concepts of God, the more the need for that "immediacy and, as it were, bodily nearness" which so overwhelms man in his encounters with the divine. For in the encounter we are confronted with something "compellingly anthropomorphic," something that demands a response, a "primary Thou." And this is true of those encounters of our daily life in which "we become aware of the reality that is absolutely independent of us," as well as of those "hours of great revelation" which are at the source of the religious of man. This encounter with the primary Thou cannot be replaced by any "self-encounter"; only here do our images and concepts of God derive their meaning. As Buber summed up his position: "Without the truth of the encounter, all images are illusion and self-deception."[21] In other words, our images and concepts of God are of value only insofar as they are forged in the existential encounter of man and God; they are true symbols only to the extent that they are based on this openness of man to God. One might say that they are true symbols only to the extent that they are rooted in a spirit of prayer.

A critical atheism

It is in that hour when our images of God are filled with illusion and self-deception that we need what Buber calls a "critical atheism," that is, a denial of the traditional gods. It is the hour or the philosopher who renders service to religion by pointing to the emptiness of our images of God. The actual encounter of man with God knows no image of Him, for the eternal Thou "shines through all forms and is Himself formless." The actual encounter knows only the "presence of the Present One." Symbols of God, whether they be images or ideas, come into being only "when and insofar as Thou becomes He, and that means It." Some symbols may be cast in earthly material to be seen by all, others tolerate no other sanctuary than that of man's soul. The problem arises when man confuses the symbol with the reality; when this happens, the symbol no longer leads man to God, but instead leads him far from the place of encounter.

Symbols supplement one another, they merge, they are set
before the community of believers in plastic or theological forms.
And God, so we may surmise, does not despise all these similarly
and necessarily untrue images, but rather suffers that one look
at Him through them. Yet they always quickly desire to be more
than they are, more than signs and pointers toward Him. It
finally happens ever again that they swell themselves up and
obstruct the way to Him, and He removes Himself from them.[22]

It is this critical point, when the images of God have become
a mere fiction, that the philosopher rejects both the image and
the God which it symbolizes. This rejection will earn for the
philosopher the enmity of the established religious powers. But
Buber sees in this critical atheism the prayer of the philosopher
to the again unknown God. "It is well suited to arouse religious
men and to impel them to set forth right across the God-
deprived reality to a new meeting. On their way they destroy
the images which manifestly no longer do justice to God. The
spirit moves them which moved the philosopher."[23]

For Buber, an honest atheism is far better than a "sanctioned
feigning" that God exists. Nothing could be worse than the man
who lives his life "play-acting," systematically proceeding as if
God existed; such a feigner "well deserves that God proceed as
if he, the feigner, did not exist."[24] It would be difficult to imagine a more severe condemnation coming from the pen of Martin Buber.

The death of God

This critical atheism, the role of the philosopher in destroying
empty images, is linked to philosophy's proclamation of the
death of God. "Men of all eras," Buber wrote in 1937, "have
heard the tidings of the death of gods. But it was reserved for
our era to have a philosopher [Nietzsche] feel called upon to
announce that God himself had died."[25] Ordinarily, to say that
a god is dead means that an image, which up to the present was
regarded and worshiped as God, can no longer be regarded and
worshiped as such. For what man calls the gods are nothing but
images of God and must suffer the fate of such images.

But Nietzsche's proclamation tries to say something different,
a difference that makes it "terribly wrong." Buber saw Nietzsche confusing an image of God, an image that *must* perish,
with the living God whose reality is always beyond any image.

Again and again the images must be destroyed, "the iconoclasts must have their way." For the iconoclast in man is simply that which rebels against images which can no longer be believed in or worshiped. Yet again and again, in their longing for a god men try to set up an image which is more genuine, more true, more glorious than the last, and hence only proves all the more unsatisfactory. The command to Israel not to make a graven image for itself meant also to Buber that "you cannot make such an image." This refers not only to painted and carved images, but to all the images of the mind and of the imagination. Man is compelled time and again to create such images and compelled time and again to destroy them.[26]

The living God remains always the eternal Thou, the Present One, whom man can only encounter, not possess. But in our human condition we are forced to create images of the divine, forms of Him who is ever formless. Whether produced by man's hand or created by man's mind, the images and ideas and concepts must ever again be destroyed in order to yield to new and more relevant symbols. Whatever its form, the symbol of the divine must be constantly renewed. And beyond every symbol is the living God. "The images topple, but the voice is never silenced." It is the Voice that speaks at every moment, in each event, in the guise of every happening. It is the Voice that speaks to every man; it makes demands on him; it summons him to accept his responsibility. For Buber, it makes no difference what name we give to the Voice. "All that matters is that you hear it."[27]

RELIGION AND LIFE

Genuine religion and genuine religious faith do not stand apart from man's concrete life situation. Religion embraces the whole of life. There are not two separate realms, that of faith and that of humanity, each with its own signs and its own special laws. Rather, as Buber pointed out just two years before his death, faith and humanity penetrate each other and are so centrally related to each other that we may say that "our faith has our humanity as its foundation, and our humanity has our faith as its foundation."[28]

A decade earlier, in 1951, Buber had addressed himself to this same topic, saying that the realer religion is, so much the more it means its own overcoming. It wills to cease to be the special domain "Religion" and wills to become life. It is concerned in the end not with specific religious acts, but with redemption from all that is specific. Historically and biographically, it strives toward the pure Everyday.

In Buber's view, the religious man should see "religion," that is, the system or structure of religion, as the *exile* of man; his homeland is the fullness of life lived "in the face of God." Religion must be described in such a way that its special characteristics are seen as grounded "in the fundamental relation of religion to the whole of life."[29]

Religion is everything

Buber's own life testifies again and again to this union of religion and humanity. The religious is open to man in every human experience. We have already cited Buber's conversation with a young student,[30] an experience which brought home to him so clearly that the "religious" can no longer be the exception but must embrace the totality of life. Life with its ordinary existence and affairs is not in one compartment, and religion with its "illumination and ecstasy and rapture" in another. Rather, religion is "just *everything*, simply all that is lived in its possibility of dialogue."

Buber recalls a meeting of political and religious leaders that took place in 1914. Its purpose was to discuss the possibilities of a supranational authority because of the fear of the catastrophe that was about to engulf the nations of Europe. For Buber, the conversations were marked by an unreserve "whose substance and fruitfulness I have scarcely ever experienced so strongly." It had such an effect on the participants that "the ficitious fell away and every word was an actuality." But when it came to the appointment of a certain committee of importance, one participant objected that too many Jews had been nominated and that several countries would be represented by an "unseemly proportion" of Jews. Buber described the objector, a clergyman, as a man of passionate justice and love, and he himself could understand the reasons for his objections, but, "obstinate Jew that I am, I protested against the protest." Somehow in his response, Buber came to speak of Jesus and how Jews know him from within, "in the impulses and stirrings of his Jewish being," in a way that non-Jews can never know him. He finished by telling the objector that Jews know Jesus "in a way that remains inaccessible to you." Then Buber describes the moving finale to this exchange:

> He stood up, I too stood, we looked into the heart of one another's eyes. "It is gone," he said, and before everyone we gave one another the kiss of brotherhood.
>
> The discussion of the situation between Jews and Christians had been transformed into a bond between the Christian and the Jew.[31]

Who would say that this was not a religious experience for Martin Buber? "In each *Thou* we address the eternal *Thou*."

Render to Caesar

In a 1953 commentary on a saying by Jesus, "Render therefore to Caesar the things that are Caesar's, and to God the things that are God's," Buber argues clearly against a division of religion from the rest of life. That one should render to Caesar, to the state, what the state legitimately demands of its citizens is clear enough from the nature of the limited reciprocal relation between the political authority and the citizen. But man's relationship with God cannot be put on the same level. Man has no claim on God; he knows this whenever "he prays in truth and reality." And the claim of God on man can in no way be limited.

Too often this saying of Jesus has been interpreted as meaning that one ought to comply with political authority as long as it does not conflict with the reverence and service due to God. One gives to Caesar what is his due, the remainder is given to God. But such a view clearly leads to a division between religion and life. As Buber pointed out, "thereby the sphere of the divine, the sphere in the life of man pledged to God, is inevitably reduced to cult and confession. In other words, instead of being the Lord of existence, God is made into the God of religion."[32]

Buber interprets this saying by first pointing out that the human person is a union of two spheres: the sphere of wholeness and the sphere of separation or division. These spheres closely parallel the twofold I of man in I-Thou and I-It. Insofar as a man becomes whole, he becomes God's, and he gives to God precisely this wholeness. The realization of wholeness in earthly affairs is ultimately connected with this relationship of wholeness to God. However, due to our human condition, our lives cannot be always caught up in wholeness; they are bound also to division or separation. But from the sphere of wholeness we should be able to elicit direction for the sphere of division.

Thus giving to the state what is due to it in the sphere of separation is authorized by the sphere of wholeness "in which we give to God what is due Him: ourselves." To put it in other terms, the man directed to God in his wholeness stands in direct relation to Him; all indirect relationship receives its direction from this. So what Jesus is telling us is to stand in direct relation to God, to give to God our immediacy, and from so doing we will learn ever anew what of our mediacy we shall give to Caesar.[33] Thus the saying of Jesus does not introduce a division of religion from the rest of life, but encourages man ever again to stand in direct relation to his eternal Thou; from this relationship, all others draw their ultimate meaning.

Meaning in the lived concrete

For Buber, the religious essence common to every religion is the certainty that the meaning of existence is open and accessible in the "actual lived concrete, not above the struggle with reality but in it." This meaning of existence is not to be had through any type of "synthetic investigation" or through any type of "reflection" upon the lived concrete. Meaning is to be experienced in living action and suffering, "in the unreduced immediacy of the moment." If a man aims at the experiencing of experience, he cannot be fully present and necessarily he will miss the meaning; he destroys the "spontaneity of the mystery." Only when a man stands firm, without holding back, before the whole might of reality and responds to it, does he reach the meaning. At this point man is ready "to confirm with his life the meaning which he has attained."[34]

Ever again, Buber roots man in the lived concrete: here is religion, here is meaning, here is truth. "There is no other means of obtaining truth than the lived hour"; truth exists wherever a person "really stands there where he stands." And the same can be said of meaning and of religion, of man's "holding fast to God." Religious doctrine and dogma are a "vain attempt" to do justice to the meaning and to the truth which has thus been attained. Every religious pronouncement can at best only hint at this attainment. "The meaning is found through the engagement of one's own person; it only reveals itself as one takes part in its revelation."[35]

This engagement of one's whole person in which meaning is given was covered in detail by Buber in *I and Thou*, as cited previously.[36] What is important to add here is not only his insistence on this *meeting* of the divine and human as the source of revelation, but his insistence on the character of that which proceeds from revelation: it is not something final and "once for all." That which is attributed either directly or indirectly to revelation, whether it be "word or custom or institution," cannot be understood simply to have been "spoken by God or established by God." Nor can we distinguish between what is divine and what is human in revelation. In other words, there is no refuge to which man may turn to avoid the responsibility of the lived moment. No religious institution or custom or law can relieve the man of faith of the responsibility of turning with the fullness of his being to his eternal Thou. Buber states quite clearly that

> there is no security against the necessity of living in fear and trembling; there is nothing else than the certainty that we share in the revelation. Nothing can relieve us of the task of opening ourselves as we are . . . to the continual revelation that can make all, all things and all events, in history and in our lives, into its signs.[37]

Man will find meaning only in the lived concrete.

The authority of revelation

Genuine religious authority is one "whose origin out of the real meeting of the divine and the human is certain to us in faith"; it exists only insofar as God's will is known. But God's will is known to us, as revelation is known to us, only in the fear and trembling of the lived moment. Certainly historical revelation can have a binding power on man because "the divine has a share in it." But this binding power can vary from person to person. One man of faith in God's revelation may "trustfully follow, without reservation," a traditional code that appeals to God's word as the source of its truth; certainly the share of what is of God and what is of man in this code cannot be objectively measured. But for the very same reason another believer in revelation may resist obeying "human prescriptions as divine commands," for he is tormented by the "all-too-human character of the human share in it." Such a believer frequently knows no other way than to hold his soul open to the whole traditional code and, "in the absence of objective criteria, to examine honestly in his own subjectivity"—that is, in fear and trembling— what he can accept as commanded and forbidden by God and what he cannot.[38]

There is no doubt that Buber placed himself in the latter class of believers, but he in no sense demeans those who adhere to a more traditional concept of religious authority. Looking back over the experience of his own life, he praises those who in their faith hold an exclusive claim for theology; he honors those who with all their strength can still bind theology and the philosophy of religion "to the strong bough of a revelation." But of himself he says simply:

> I have not been able to go their way. I pursue no theology as theology and no philosophy of religion as philosophy of religion. ... Is it still called philosophy of religion when I allow God's own relationship to the religions to address me in all its dreadful seriousness? Is it still called theology when I find it necessary to distinguish within my religion, familiar to me as no other, between that in it which I believe in the responsibility of faith and that which I just do not believe?[39]

Throughout his adult life Martin Buber sought no "protection" in a theological or religious system, or in a fixed moral code rooted in revelation; indeed, he possessed no security against the need to live in fear and trembling. But in the engagement of his whole person to the lived concrete, he found a meaning to life such as has been granted to very few men of this era.

GNOSIS AND MAGIC

In all historical religions there is a constant struggle between the religious element and the various nonreligious elements which attack it from all sides. Those powers which above all thwart the engagement of one's whole being to the present concrete situation, and which thus threaten man's religious situation more than any others, are termed by Buber gnosis and magic.[40]

Gnosis and magic, along with metaphysics and law and the like, seek to supplant the flow of faith which is renewed in each life situation. They find assistance in the myth and cult which originally served as an expression of the genuine religious relation, but which have now become rigid and meaningless. In order to preserve its purity, religion must root out these nonreligious elements which seek to become autonomous and to appear as the true essence of religion for the unaware believer. Religion must struggle to expose those nonreligious elements which seek to offer man security against the need to live in fear and trembling before the actual lived concrete.

> It is a struggle for the protection of lived concreteness as the meeting-place between the human and the divine. The actually lived concrete is the "moment" in its unforeseeableness and its irrecoverableness, in its undivertible character of happening but once, in its decisiveness, in secret dialogue between that which happens and that which is willed, between fate and action, address and answer.[41]

It is this lived concreteness which is threatened by gnosis and magic and the other nonreligious elements; they attack religion by seeking to turn man away from the lived concrete, the true meeting place between man and God.

The impulse to control

From the earliest times the reality of man's relation to God, the reality of his standing before the face of God, has been threatened by the impulse to "control" the power beyond. This, for Buber, is the essence of all magic. Religion understands God as turned toward us, descending toward us, revealing Himself to us, speaking to us; God comes of His own free will; man does not cause Him to come. This is what distinguishes religion from magic. In magic man imagines that he can summon God; God becomes for man "a bundle of powers" at the disposal of man's knowledge and might. But he who can be conjured by man cannot be believed in any longer as God. And he who thinks he conjures God is no longer a man who is addressed; no response is awakened in him; he may recite a prayer, but he is no longer praying.[42]

From ancient days man has divined that God has need of him, as man, as partner in dialogue, as comrade in work, as one who loves Him. "God needs His creature thus or wills to need him thus." On the other hand, just as God does not let Himself be conjured, so also He does not compel.

> He is of Himself, and He allows that which exists to be of itself. Both of these facts distinguish divine from demonic powers. It may not be, indeed, unimportant to God whether man gives himself or denies himself to Him. Through this giving or denying, man, the whole man with the decision of his whole being, may have an immeasureable part in the actual revelation or hiddenness of the divine.

God is revealed by man's being man. But he whose appearance can be effected by man clearly has only the name in common with Him "whom we men, basically in agreement despite all the differences in our religious teachings, address as God."[43]

The man who yields to the temptation of magic, instead of hearing in the events of his life the Voice which makes demands on him, prefers himself "to demand without having to hearken." He says with mistaken confidence: "I have power over the powers I conjure." This attitude is present, with various modifications, wherever one celebrates rites "without being turned to the Thou and without really meaning its Presence." It is present in any cult which misleads the faithful into feeling secure "in a merely 'objective' consummation without personal devotion, an *opus operatum*." It is present whenever man habitually worships without being seized and claimed in his whole being.[44]

Unveiling the mystery

The copartner of magic in undermining man's genuine religious spirit is gnosis. Buber defines gnosis as "a knowing relationship to the divine" in which man knows God as an object. Acting with "the mature power of the intellect," man unveils the mystery. Gnosis seeks to raise the veil which divides the revealed from the hidden and to lead forth the divine mysteries.[45]

The gnostic says simply: "I am acquainted with the unknown, and I make it known." For him there is no unknowable; there is no mystery, no meeting, no absolute other. Just as the magician supposedly manipulates the divine power, so the gnostic supposedly lays bare the "whole divine apparatus." All of this, quite naturally, involves no commitment. There stands over against the self "nothing with any higher right, nothing that can demand of it, visit it, redeem it." Traces of this gnostic attitude are found not only in the various "theosophies" and the like, but also in many theologies, for there, too, "unveiling gestures are to be discovered behind the interpreting ones."[46]

For Buber gnosis is a "universal" category, that is, it affects in some way every man's relation of faith. Religion must be constantly aware of this danger. Summing up his own lifelong opposition to gnosis, Buber wrote:

> I am against gnosis because and insofar as it alleges that it can report events and processes within the divinity. I am against it because and insofar as it makes God into an object in whose nature and history one knows one's way about. I am against it because in the place of the personal relation of the human person to God it sets a communion-rich wandering through an upper world, through a multiplicity of more or less divine spheres.[47]

And in his clearest condemnation, written in 1951, Buber says of gnosis: "It—and not atheism, which annihilates God because it must reject the hitherto existing images of God—is the real antagonist of the reality of faith."[48]

The decisive issue

Buber sharply contrasts gnosis with what he calls *"devotio."* This contrast is for Buber the "decisive issue" within Judaism, within Christianity, within every great religion of man; it is everywhere the "one thing essential." *Devotio* is life as "personal service of God"; it is an unreduced life of service to the divine present over against me and ever again as over against me. I can in no way presume to be on "intimate terms" with God, but wholly turned to Him in the lived concrete I can say Thou, and I can stand over against Him in freedom and service. In his freedom and service the man of *devotio* recognizes that "he holds in his hand his bodily death, his faithful mortality, as the most human of all presences and just thus, time after time, comes to meet the Eternal."[49] He seeks to serve with the gift of his life.

The man of gnosis cannot serve and does not want to serve; he is concerned with unveiling the mystery. The man of *devotio* is not concerned with the mysteries of his Lord who is his friend and who at one time or another shares with him what He wills to share with him; rather, the man of *devotio* seeks in his life to give the fullest expression to the relation of faith.

The great example of *devotio* cited by Buber is that of Jesus. What was most significant to Jesus was his "persevering in immediacy with God." Unlike the gnostics, Jesus did not seek to uncover the mysteries of the divine; rather, he points to the door that stands open here and now, and he calls it *emunah*, trust; man is to live his life in trust and service before the Lord. He who taught his followers to pray "Our Father" could not consider himself as the source and center of power. Rather, his is a readiness to serve and a readiness to suffer; his is a life lived before the face of God and rooted in the lived concrete. This is the man of *devotio*, the man of deepest faith, ready to offer the gift of his life in the service of God and to suffer for the many.[50]

OPPOSITION TO THEOLOGY

Closely allied to Buber's warnings on gnosis is his opposition to theology. We have already seen his assertion that "unveiling gestures" are to be found in some theologies. And to the very end of his life he saw theology as an adversary of the genuine conceptions of faith.[51] Theology is confronted constantly with the danger of becoming gnostic; it is constantly in danger of dealing solely with an It-God. The whole theological enterprise is caught up in the paradox of teaching *about* Him who can only be addressed, not expressed. It is a paradox which can never be resolved. It is a paradox which traditional Christian theology has admitted again and again. Nevertheless, Buber's criticism helps us to see anew, and perhaps more clearly, where the danger lies and how it may be avoided.

God known only in relation

What is always decisive for genuine religion is that "I relate myself to the divine as to Being which is over against me." Genuine religious faith is "living in relationship to Being 'believed in,' that is, unconditionally affirmed, absolute Being." From this point of view, then, theology is not needed for the genuineness of religion and of religious faith. Buber insists that it is not necessary to know something *about* God in order really to believe in Him: "Many true believers know how to talk *to*

God but not *about* Him." What is needed is that we dare to turn toward the unknown God, that we go to meet Him, that we call to Him; when we do this, "reality is present." Moreover, since God can be met only as Thou, man can acquire "no objective aspect" of Him. Buber insists that "God can never become an object for me"; the only possible relation with God is that of the I to its eternal Thou.[52]

Buber was very emphatic on this point, especially during the later years of his life. Theology must not be confused with that relation which is genuine religion and genuine faith. It is the failure to maintain this distinction that has so often set theology in opposition to religion. Religion does not understand knowledge as a "noetic relation" between subject and object, but rather as

> mutual contact, as the genuinely reciprocal meeting in the fullness of life between one active existence and another. Similarly, it understands faith as the entrance into this reciprocity, as binding oneself in relationship with an undemonstrable and unprovable, yet even so, in relationship, knowable Being from whom all meaning comes.[53]

God is known only in the actual relation, as Thou; outside this relation, any such knowledge is not knowledge of *God.*

Teaching about God

Writing in 1963 about the development of his life's work, Buber said he considered it to be rooted basically in an experience of faith; yet he refused to call the interpretation and communication of this faith-experience a theology. For by theology Buber understood "a teaching about God, even if it is only a 'negative' one"; and he goes on to explain:

> I am absolutely not capable nor even disposed to teach this or that about God. Certainly, when I seek to explain the fact of man, I cannot leave out of consideration that he, man, lives over against God. But I cannot include God himself at any point in my explanation, any more than I could detach from history the, to me indubitable, working of God in it, and make of it an object of my contemplation.[54]

Man's meeting with God, as discussed earlier,[55] does not take place in order that man may theologize about God, but that he may be concerned more deeply with the world and confirm that there is meaning in the world.

Continuing the explanation of his disavowal of theology, Buber points out again how a "He" spoken *of* God is a metaphor, while a "Thou" spoken *to* God is not. It is all part of his insistence that God is the eternal Thou, eternally Thou; speaking about God removes Him from the world of Thou; He is no longer eternally Thou, and hence it is not God of whom one speaks, except metaphorically.

> If one speaks *of* God, one makes Him into an existing being among other existing beings, into an existing being at hand and constituted so and not otherwise. But to speak *to* God means nothing other than to turn to Him Himself. How is that possible since He is not to be sought more in one direction than in another? Just nothing other is needed than the total turning. This says in general nothing more than that the one who has turned in no way limits his Thou to a being constituted so and not otherwise. The metaphor no longer has a place here.[56]

Buber never lets us forget that God can only be addressed, not expressed.

Need to express the Thou

Yet at the same time Buber realized the need to insert his own decisive experiences into the framework of human thought so that they might serve as a valid insight for others. Chief among these was his experience of faith. He admits that he "had to express what is by its nature incomprehensible in concepts that could be used and communicated." And he adds: "More precisely, I had to make an It out of that which was experienced in I-Thou and as I-Thou. I am convinced that it happened not otherwise with all the philosophers loved and honored by me." But this communication of his faith experience is philosophical rather than theological because it is not concerned with "teaching about God."[57]

Buber expressed a similar difficulty in his 1957 postscript to *I and Thou.* In order to answer difficulties that were raised about man's relation to God, Buber admits that he must speak *of* God.

> Of course, we speak only of what God is in his relation to a man. And even that is only to be expressed in paradox; more precisely, by the paradoxical use of a concept. . . . The content of the concept is revolutionized, transformed, and extended—but this

is indeed what we experience with every concept which we take out of immanence—compelled by the reality of faith—and use with reference to the working of transcendence.[58]

He goes on to say that the description of God as Person is indispensable if we mean by God the divinity with whom we enter into relation. "The concept of personal being is indeed completely incapable of declaring what God's essential being is, but it is both permitted and necessary to say that God is *also* a Person."

The paradox is evident when we consider the meaning of person. Person implies an independent self, but a self limited in the totality of its being because there are other independent selves; this cannot be true of God. Buber overcomes the problem by speaking of God paradoxically as the "absolute Person," that is, the Person who cannot be limited. "It is as the absolute Person that God enters into direct relation with us. The contradiction yields to deeper insight."[59]

Thus despite his reluctance Buber found it necessary to indulge in some form of speaking *about* God. He refused to call this a theology; rather, it was the use of a philosophy to serve and to make communicable "an experienced, a perceived attitude."[60] Some expression of man's encounter with God is needed for the sake of sharing this experience with others. This effort may be called theology or it may be given some other name. In any case, Buber's opposition to theology should be taken seriously. It helps us to see more clearly the risks and the abuses and the misunderstandings that are inherent in this most important undertaking of man.

RELIGION AS SYSTEM

From what has been said thus far it is evident that for Buber genuine religion is concerned with the lived moment, the actual presence of man here and now before the Present One. Genuine religion arises from man's encounter with the Thou, from man addressing his eternal Thou and God addressing his creature as Thou. It is in this meeting, and only in this meeting, that God reveals Himself to man.

This approach to religion necessarily means that genuine religion embraces the *whole* of life, just as genuine faith means living the *whole* of one's life in responsibility before the living

God. If religion does not embrace *everything* in life, then it becomes one compartment of life among many; God becomes, not the God of life, but the God of religion; man's relationship with God is confined to this one area called "religion"; religion becomes for man the bulwark in which he may find protection against the need to live in fear and trembling before the actual lived concrete. Buber's position is quite clear:

> Either religion is a reality, rather *the* reality, namely the *whole* existence of the real man in the real world of God, an existence that unites all that is partial; or it is a phantom of the covetous human soul, and then it would be right promptly and completely to replace its rituals by art, its commands by ethics, its revelations by science.[61]

Religion as system or structure is necessarily apart from the lived concrete; it is necessarily apart from the world of I-Thou, for with all other institutions it belongs to the world of It; it necessarily plays a limited role in man's "holding fast to God." If institutional religion poses as the only meeting ground between man and God, if it presumes to have the power to bring about the divine-human encounter simply by the exercise of certain rites, if it presumes to have a "once for all" understanding of God's will for mankind, if it encourages its members to prefer law and dogma to the encounter with the living God, then such an institutional religion comes under the full weight of Buber's condemnation of religion as system.

Hiding the face of God

Buber certainly had that type of institutional religion in mind when he wrote in 1937 that

> religious institutions and procedures which are supposed to be objective expressions of the reality of faith are so often and in so many different ways contrary to true faith and to the truth of faith. They have become stumbling blocks in the path of the true believer; they have placed themselves in opposition to his humble life, and on the side of whatever happens to be powerful and accepted as valid in this world.

It is this type of institutional religion that has "invalidated" the faith of whole generations; it has brought them to the point of rejecting not only a particular religion, but all religion and all religious faith.[62]

Whenever religion aims at being something other than the

fullness of life, it "misses its mark." Religion as risk, religion which is ready to die to itself, religion which seeks simply to become life, nourishes the development of religious faith in man. But religion as system, religion which is "possessing, assured and assuring," religion which believes in religion stifles genuine faith, it blocks the life-giving encounter of real faith. Buber condemned this type of religion in the harshest terms: *"Religion can hide from us as nothing else can the face of God."* He goes on to explain how structured religion destroys the dialogue between man and God:

> Principle there, dogma here, I appreciate the "objective" compactness of dogma, but behind both there lies in wait the—profane or holy—war against the situation's power of dialogue, there lies in wait the "once for all" which resists the unforeseeable moment. Dogma, even when its claim of origin remains uncontested, has become the most exalted form of invulnerability against revelation. Revelation will tolerate no perfect tense, but man with the arts of his craze for security props it up to perfectedness.[63]

Here is the real danger that organized religion presents to the religious striving of man: it can easily seek to displace God by religion and to substitute itself for the dialogical encounter which awaits man in the lived concrete. It is this type of religion that Buber spoke of in *Daniel*,[64] when he wrote that all religiousness degenerates into religion and church when it strives to provide man with what he must believe and what he must do; it is a religion which promises security and protection instead of the danger and risk of life lived in the present. Insofar as religion promises orientation, bringing the faithful to the point where they "know their way about," then such a religion is godless. For the living God is present as He is present; there are no rules and directions for His coming. Man cannot "know his way about" before God; he can only be present with the fullness of his being in trust and in holy fear. The warning that Buber gives in *I and Thou*[65] may well be paraphrased for a religion that seeks to provide orientation: "Woe to that religion so possessed that it thinks it possesses God!"

Religion more comfortable than God

To Buber's mind, when religion has appeared in history it has brought along with it a variety of forces that "diverted man

from God." The wide appeal of religion is due to the fact that
men much prefer to deal with religion than to deal with God:
"It is far more comfortable to have to do with religion than to
have to do with God." And this is so because for the most part
that which goes by the name of religion is perverted, "not
perhaps in the individual details of its contents, but in its whole
structure." Religion offers its adherents all kinds of security and
"aesthetic refreshments," while the living God sends man out
of home and fatherland into "restless wandering." God demands nothing less than our whole being offered in sacrifice by
a joyful but not necessarily by an enjoying heart.[66]

Prophetic voices through the ages have warned of the divert-
ing forces hidden in religion; and Buber himself, as mentioned,
has pointed to the craving for success as the most destructive
of these forces: "Always and everywhere in the history of religion the fact that God is identified with success is the greatest
obstacle to a steadfast religious life."[67] Man wants a tangible
security, he wants to have God at his disposal; it is this security,
this power, this success that religion all too often offers to man,
and in so doing religion itself becomes an obstacle to man's
religious life.

Furthermore, Buber sees much of organized religion as "fictitious," a façade which masks the real lack of faith of so many of
its adherents. Writing in 1928, he points out that

> all "religious" forms, institutions, and societies are real or ficti-
> tious according to whether they serve as expressions, as shape
> and bearer of real *religio*—a real self-binding of the human per-
> son to God—or merely exist alongside it, or even conceal the
> flight from actual *religio* which comprises the concrete response
> and responsibility of the human person in the here and now.
> . . . At present the prevailing religious forms, institutions and
> societies have entered into the realm of the fictitious.[68]

Once again the danger lies in permitting the forms and structures and doctrines of religion to replace the one thing necessary: man's personal turning to the Lord with all that he is.

Religion versus religiosity

One of Buber's clearest and sharpest criticisms of organized
religion is contained in an address published in 1916. Although
he is dealing directly with the opposition of religion and religi-

osity within Judaism, his remarks have a far wider implication. Religiosity stands for all that which binds man to God; religion implies a rigidity and a formalism that eventually destroys man's openness to God. Religiosity is "man's sense of wonder and adoration," his continual awe at the unconditioned mystery. Religiosity is man's longing to establish "a living communion with the unconditioned," his will to "realize the unconditioned" by his deeds, thus transposing it into the world of man.

On the other hand, religion is the sum total of customs and laws and doctrines formulated by a people's religiosity at a certain period in their history. These are handed on in the form of rigid prescriptions and dogmas unalterably binding upon all later generations, regardless of their own newly developed religious spirit which seeks its own forms. Religion is true as long as it remains creative; and it remains creative only as long as religiosity is able to imbue its laws and doctrines with new meaning that responds to the needs of today's generation, needs alien to earlier generations. But once the rites and dogmas of religion have become so rigid that religiosity can no longer shape them, then religion ceases to be creative and hence it ceases to be true.[69]

Religion must face up to the basic questions and problems of man ever anew. Once it assumes that it has answered every basic problem through its laws and dogmas, once it no longer searches for the truth, it loses touch with reality and with mankind; this type of religion soon becomes impermeable to the creative force of religiosity. Buber repeated this same theme seven years later in *I and Thou*, where, in a passage already cited,[70] he says that every culture (and we might say every religion) that ceases to be centered "in the living and continually renewed relational event" soon hardens into the world of It; such a culture, such a religion, soon becomes impermeable to the Thou. Religion without prayer is religion that is buried under "increasing objectification" where it becomes almost impossible for a man to say Thou.

Buber further contrasts religion and religiosity in his 1916 criticism:

> Religiosity starts anew with every young person, shaken to his very core by the mystery; religion wants to force him into a system stabilized for all time. Religiosity means activity—the

elemental entering-into-relation with the absolute; religion
means passivity—an acceptance of the handed-down command.
. . . Religiosity induces sons, who want to find their own God, to
rebel against their fathers; religion induces fathers to reject their
sons, who will not let their fathers' God be forced upon them.
Religion means preservation; religiosity, renewal.[71]

Without the creative force of religiosity, religion becomes simply a rigid system, an empty structure, a lifeless institution. It
becomes a fiction which could have little appeal to the man of
real faith.

Firm opposition

Thus Buber stands firmly opposed to the dangers inherent in
structured religion. By its structures religion is in danger of
hiding the face of God from man, it is in danger of simply
providing security and comfort for man, it is in danger of dis-
guising the real lack of faith within man. Religion must be made
to see that through its structures it contains the seeds for its own
downfall, that through its structures it has an inbred power to
divert man from God. Religion must be made to see the decisive importance of Buber's comment, recorded in *The Prophetic Faith*, that centralization and codification are a danger
to the very core of religion *"unless there is the strongest life of
faith"* within the community, a faith that never relaxes its
renewing activity.[72]

Throughout his life Martin Buber maintained a vigilant criticism of the dangers of structured religion. Writing shortly
before his death, he warns us that

the development of a religion, unfortunately, does not in fact
consist of a series of genuine conceptions of faith; ever again
there stand opposite each other a genuine conception of faith
and its adversary which likewise is represented "religiously,"
namely, in the development of cult and of creed; and, all too
often, the historical form, which belongs indeed to "religion" as
well, is determined by the adversary. Very soon it is joined by an
exegesis, a theology, an apologetic. . . . I see in this pseudo
security of "religious possession," of the intentionless sacrifice,
the intentionless fulfillment of command, in all *opus operatum*—
I see the arch enemy of religion that rises against it from within.[73]

For Martin Buber, God does not attach decisive importance to religion; He seeks ultimately something other than religion: He seeks the hallowing of the everyday, the hallowing of the whole of life, the hallowing of all creation.

Nevertheless, if religion can stand in opposition to this aim, it can also serve in its accomplishment. If religion has need of religiosity, one might also say that religiosity has need of religion. We will turn then to this final aspect of Buber's critique of religion: man's need of religion and the importance of religious community in the life of man.

THE NEED FOR RELIGION

Throughout his life, as we have seen, Martin Buber continually pointed out the dangers inherent in organized religion. But opposition to the dangers of organized religion does not necessarily imply opposition to organized religion itself. Through his own deep faith, Buber transcended religion in a narrow, sectarian sense of the word. But again, his transcendence of organized religion does not imply a denial of organized religion.

Buber's writings and teachings, especially his discourses on Judaism, very often had as their purpose the renewal of the dynamism within Judaism as he understood it and lived it. What Buber himself once said of his Hasidic writings might well be applied to all his works. It had been suggested to Buber that he "liberate" the Hasidic teachings from their "confessional limitations" and proclaim them as an "unfettered teaching of mankind." But he refused to do this, for such an attempt could not do justice to Hasidism: "Taking such a 'universal' path would have been for me pure arbitrariness. In order to speak to the world what I have heard, I am not bound to step into the street. I may remain standing in the door of my ancestral house: here too the word that is uttered does not go astray."[1] The more that one understands the thought of Martin Buber, the more it becomes evident that he was a man who constantly remained standing in the door of his ancestral house; he appreciated, as few others have, the values inherent in his own religious community.[2]

BUBER'S CHANGE OF ATTITUDE

Furthermore, one can notice a gradual change in Buber's attitude toward system and structure in religion. In *Daniel,* written in 1913, and in some of his earlier addresses on Judaism from this period, as already cited,[3] it is more church and religion as such that Buber is criticizing. In his later writings, especially from the time of his exodus from Germany to Palestine, Buber seems to speak more and more of the need of religious community and even of some type of organized religion. We are by no means speaking of a clear-cut division in Buber's thought, but rather of a gradual deepening and maturing of his thought in this area.

His experience of faith

What brought about this change of attitude? Three elements undoubtedly played a most important role. The first is Buber's own "experience of faith." He describes it simply: "What happened to me was that all the experiences of being that I had during the years 1912–1919 became present to me in growing measure as *one* great experience of faith."[4]

Buber does not analyze this experience of faith further, but it might be helpful to recall some of his ideas of faith. Faith is a living relation between God and man; it implies man's living before the face of God; it is the meeting of man and God. As he wrote in *I and Thou,* to say that one *believes* really means that one meets.[5] Or as he wrote some forty years after *I and Thou:* "The fundamental experience of faith itself may be regarded as the highest intensification of the reality of meeting."[6] Thus Buber's one great experience of faith was basically the experience of meeting or encounter.

Furthermore, Buber elsewhere described as central to his whole life's work the insight that the encounter between man and God is essentially related to the encounter between man and man. The Thou addressed to God and the Thou addressed to man are basically "related to each other."[7] Thus again this one great experience of faith, this encounter between man and God, would have led to a deeper understanding of the value of the encounter between man and man, and hence of the value of community among men. In any case, if we judge by his writings it would seem that the more Buber reflected on this one great experience of faith, the more value he saw in religion and in religious community. Certainly his writings after this period (1912–19) seem to reflect a more restrained criticism of church and of organized religion as a whole, while stressing more and more the dangers everywhere *inherent* in organized religion as such.

His translation of the Bible

The second element which influenced Buber's change of attitude was his work on the translation of the Hebrew Bible. It was in 1925 that he was asked by the Berlin publisher Lambert Schneider to work on a new translation of the Hebrew Bible into German. He agreed, but only on the condition that the work would be a joint collaboration with his gifted friend Franz Rosenzweig. Buber insisted on this condition despite the fact that Rosenzweig was already afflicted by a fatal illness that had left him almost completely paralyzed, unable to write or speak distinctly. For almost five years, until Rosenzweig's death late in 1929, the two friends produced together ten books of the Bible. Afterwards Buber continued alone and completed five more books (counting the twelve minor prophets as one book) until the rise of Nazism compelled him to put aside this work.[8]

In a poem written in 1945, entitled *Confession of the Author,* Buber hints at the transformation that came over him when he was summoned to translate the Hebrew Scripture:

> Once with a light keel
> I shipped out to the land of legends
> Through the storm of deeds and play,
> With my gaze fixed on the goal
> And in my blood the beguiling poison—
> Then one descended to me
> Who seized me by the hair
> And spoke: Now render the Scriptures!
> From that hour on the galley
> Keeps my brain and hands on course,
> The rudder writes characters,
> My life disdains its honor
> And the soul forgets that it sang.
> All storms must stand and bow
> When cruelly compelling in the silence
> The speech of the spirit resounds.
> Hammer your deeds in the rock, world!
> The Word is wrought in the flood.[9]

One might say that this period completed a transformation from a Hasidic to a biblical understanding of Judaism; or better, it was a period which enriched and complemented Buber's Hasidic Judaism.

There can be little doubt that this immersion into the biblical writings gave Buber an even deeper understanding of the meaning of Judaism and of the role of Israel among the community of nations. Israel was chosen by God *as a people*, and only as a people could it respond. God's dialogue with man in the Bible evokes, not the response of an individual, but the response of a whole people. Only a communal response can be adequate to the word which God has addressed to man. This aspect of Judaism, always prominent in Buber's thought, receives an even greater emphasis in his later writings.

His efforts for German Jewry

A third element that undoubtedly influenced Buber's attitude toward religious community and organized religion was his work among German Jewry during the rise of Nazism in 1933–38. Buber worked relentlessly for his people during these years, giving courses first at the Jewish Lehrhaus at Frankfurt, and later at another Lehrhaus opened at Stuttgart. Again and again his efforts were aimed at giving German Jews a basis which could weather all storms. For Buber, Jewish culture could have but one such foundation: the Hebrew Bible.

Ernst Simon, commenting on the efforts made in behalf of German Jews during this period 1933–38, writes: "Martin Buber stood at the center of all this work. He held Bible courses on the most varied themes. . . . For many people it was the first time they were brought face to face with the Bible. It was an experience that lived with them for decades."[10] This experience must have given Buber an even deeper appreciation of the role of community in safeguarding culture and in preserving and passing on tradition from one generation to the next. It was this period, perhaps more than any other, which brought out the practical applications of all the insights that Buber had into the role and meaning of Israel to the "nations."

Again it was Ernst Simon, speaking at the Buber Memorial Seminar on Arab-Jewish Understanding at Tel Aviv in 1966, who summed up the meaning of Buber's efforts in those years: "Anyone who did not see Buber then has not seen true civil courage."[11] A study of Buber's published talks during this period, especially those touching on Judaism and the responsibility of the man of faith, would easily bring out the meaning of this statement. It would be difficult to find in Nazi Germany a more radical challenge to false nationalism than that posed by Martin Buber. His was the courage of the prophets of old goading his people once again to see the meaning of their covenant with God and to realize the responsibility it imposed upon them, as well as the hope it bestowed upon them, in the face of unspeakable horror.

In his inaugural address at the Hebrew University in Jerusalem following his departure from Germany in 1938, Buber spoke of the role of the prophetic spirit in Judaism. His own efforts among his people must have been very much in his mind when he explained how the prophetic spirit is always directed toward the life men must live together.

> A people which seriously calls God Himself its King must become a true people, a community where all members are ruled by honesty without compulsion, kindness without hypocrisy, and the brotherliness of those who are passionately devoted to their divine leader. When social inequality, distinction between the free and the unfree, splits the community and creates chasms between its members, there can be no true people, there can be no 'God's people.'[12]

The prophet, Buber continued, fails in his own hour of history, but he instills in his people a vision that remains with them for all time to come. Directing his insights to *this* people, in *this* place, at *this* time, the prophet is compelled to speak his message. "That message will be misunderstood, misjudged, misused; it will strengthen and 'harden' the people still further in their untruth. But its sting will rankle within them for all time." The present crisis of the human race has made man only "more deaf to the spirit." But Buber never ceases to hope: this condition will surely change when men "despair of power and its autonomous decisions, when power for power's sake grows bewildered and longs for direction." And when the change comes, as it must come, the prophetic spirit must maintain its vigilance "so that the altered institutions may not fall into corruption and do violence to the life struggling upward."[13]

Buber concluded this address with an appeal to the faith and trust of his people:

There are situations in the lives of peoples in which the people become, as it were, plastic, and the impossible becomes possible. Perhaps such an hour is near. We think of this "perhaps" when we perform our service. We would also perform it, of course, if this possibility did not exist. For, resigned or unresigned, the spirit works.[14]

Certainly the experience of applying his biblical insights to the political and social problems of Judaism in the face of Nazism must have given Buber a much greater understanding of the importance and need of an organized religious community.

THE ECLIPSE OF GOD

One of the great problems which Buber confronted during the latter half of his life, accentuated no doubt by World War II, was the problem of evil, or in more particular terms, the problem of the "eclipse of God." If we can understand Buber's concern in this area, we may better appreciate the role he gives to religious community and to system and structure within religion.

Commenting on his Hasidic novel *For the Sake of Heaven* (its Hebrew title is *Gog and Magog*), Buber noted that its central theme is contained in the words of the Yehudi who explains the nature of Gog: "He can exist in the outer world only because he exists within us. The darkness out of which he was hewn needed to be taken from nowhere else than from our own slothful and malicious hearts. Our betrayal of God has made Gog to grow so great." Evil is rooted in the apathy and malice of man. Buber added the comment: "Fully to understand this passage the reader must recall the time at which the novel was written." *Gog and Magog* first appeared in serial form in Jerusalem in 1941 during the height of World War II.[15]

In this same novel a disciple asks the Yehudi why it is that God seems to let us sink deeper and deeper into the mud without pulling us out. The Yehudi replies that such periods of great trial represent the "eclipse of God":

It is as though the sun were to grow dark; if one did not know that it is there, one would believe there was no sun any longer. Thus it is in such periods. Something interposes between us and God's countenance, so that it seems as though the world must grow cold, lacking that light. But the truth is that precisely at such a time the great return and repentance which God expects of us becomes possible, in order that the redemption, which He desires for us, be a true self-redemption. We have no awareness of Him; it is dark and cold as though He were not; it seems senseless to turn to Him who, if He is here, will not trouble Himself about us; it seems hopeless to will to penetrate to Him who may, granted that He is, perhaps be the soul of the universe but not our Father. The unimaginable must take place in us to enable us to start on the return to Him. But when the unimaginable does happen, then the great return to God, which He awaits, is at hand. Despair shatters the prison which imprisons our latent energies. The sources of the primordial depths begin to flow.[16]

Certainly when we consider the time when Martin Buber wrote these words, we begin to fathom the great faith and hope which were always his.

The sickness of our age

It was not only the horror of Nazism which drove Buber to speak of the darkness which hides God from the eyes of men. In *I and Thou* he had warned that "the progressive augmentation of the world of *It*" could be clearly discerned in the study of history; and this growth of It in turn decreases man's ability to enter into relation. It was becoming increasingly difficult for man to say Thou. Buber put the problem in simple terms: "The sickness of our age is like that of no other age, and it belongs together with them all."[17]

Long after Nazism had been destroyed, Buber continued this same theme. The I-It relation has become "gigantically swollen"; it shuts off from us the light of heaven. The man of It, unable to say Thou, unable to encounter God, has become "lord of the hour."[18] Buber speaks further of this eclipse of God, this eclipse of the light of heaven: "Such indeed is the character of the historic hour through which the world is passing," he wrote in 1951. Just as an eclipse of the sun is something that occurs between the sun and ourselves, and not in the sun itself, so it is with the eclipse of God. One misses the whole point if he tries to discover within human thought the "power that unveils the mystery." What is needed is submission, the submission of man's whole being to the transcendent reality over against him. He who refuses this submission "contributes to the human responsibility for the eclipse"; he who is not present "perceives no Presence."[19]

Modern man has eliminated many of the concepts and images which traditionally have been closely allied with the divine. And during this process of elimination, that transcendent reality which no image can express may well be eclipsed for man; yet the eternal Thou lives intact "behind the wall of darkness." Man may even do away with the name "God," yet He who is denoted by the name continues to live in the light of His eternity. Rather, it is we, "the slayers," who remain "dwellers in darkness, consigned to death."[20]

The loss of trust

Another aspect of this problem of the eclipse of God which occupied Buber after World War II was the lack of trust between men: "Trust is increasingly lost to men of our time." And the lack of genuine dialogue among men is closely allied to men's loss of trust in one another: "I can only speak to someone in the true sense of the term if I expect him to accept my word as genuine." And the inability of men to address one another is reflected in man's inability to address God: "The fact that it is so difficult for present-day man to pray (note well: not to hold it to be true that there is a God, but to address him) and the fact that it is so difficult for him to carry on a genuine talk with his fellow-men are elements of a single set of facts." Because of this lack of trust, God becomes hidden from men's eyes. Thus the importance of Buber's appeal that we must not let this "contra-human in men," this lack of trust, prevent us from becoming a true humanity. "Let us release speech from its ban! Let us dare, despite all, to trust!"[21]

Some speak of the silence of God, meaning by this that God is dead. Buber would take literally this assertion that God "formerly spoke to us and is now silent"; and he would understand this in the biblical sense, namely, that "the living God is not only a self-revealing but also a self-concealing God." In this case we must learn what it means to live in an age of "such a concealment, such a divine silence." For Buber it is ultimately a reminder that God is absolute Other, the Absolute over against me.

> God can never become an object for me; I can attain no other relation to Him than that of the I to its eternal Thou, that of the Thou to its eternal I. But if man is no longer able to attain this relation, if God is silent toward him and he toward God, then

something has taken place, not in human subjectivity but in Being itself.

In other words, the reason for the divine silence is not to be found simply within man, as if all religion were a psychic projection of man. Rather, Buber seems to be saying that it is the "betweenness," the relation between man and God, which has been affected. Man is called upon to remain open, turned toward reality with the fullness of his being. The man of biblical faith is called upon to endure this silence as it is, and at the same time to move existentially "toward a new happening, toward that event in which the word between heaven and earth will again be heard."[22] And the beginning of this movement must take place here and now in men's trust and openness toward one another.

Turning always possible

Buber's attitude in the face of this "eclipse" or "hiding" of God was always one of great faith and hope. There is a Hasidic tale which perhaps explains the source of Buber's hope. A pupil complained to his rabbi that in times of adversity it was very difficult to maintain faith in God's goodness; it seems that during such hard times God is hiding His face; he asked what one can do to strengthen his faith. The rabbi replied: "It ceases to be a hiding, if you know it is hiding."[23]

At each point where he pointed out the sickness of man or the eclipse of the light of heaven, Buber also maintained a deep faith in its overcoming. In *I and Thou* he notes that despite the sickness of our age, wherever there is danger, "the rescuing force grows too." The greater man's perversion is, the more fundamental is his turning *(die Umkehr)*.[24] No matter how hopeless the situation may appear, no matter how far man may seem to have fallen, teshuvah, the turning, is always possible.

This turning for Buber is the greatest form of "beginning": "When God tells Israel: 'Turn to me, and I shall create you anew,' the meaning of human beginning becomes clear as never before. By turning, man arises anew as God's child." This turning implies a conversion of one's whole being which projects man into the way of God. "The man who turns finds himself standing in the traces of the living God." For Buber, this was the full meaning of the word with which Jesus began his preaching, echoing the cry of the prophets of old: "Turn ye!" The kingdom of God is at the hand of man; man is to grasp and realize it, not by any act of violence, but by the turning of his whole being.[25]

Turning overcomes the darkness

In Buber's Hasidic novel, referred to above, one of the teachers points out that the good that God has created is "man's utter turning to Him." When man turns away from evil with the fullness of his power, then "he has truly turned to God." The teshuvah is the light which breaks through the darkness; more precisely, "the darkness *is* in order that the light might be."[26] It is precisely this power of turning which gives the man of biblical faith an ever-present hope even in the midst of the seemingly hopeless.

In his writings and addresses following World War II, Buber continues to express the same deep-rooted faith, despite the darkness of the hour. "The eclipse of the light of God is no extinction; even to-morrow that which has stepped in between may give way."[27] The future is not fixed; the prophetic spirit continues to confront man with the alternatives of decision. God wants man to come to Him in full freedom, to return to Him "even out of a plight of extreme hopelessness and then to be really with Him." Man is always the center of surprise in creation. "Because and so long as man exists, factual changes of direction can take place towards salvation as well as towards disaster, starting from the world in each hour, no matter how late." Turning is always possible for man here and now; this is the prophetic message proclaimed to all generations, and to each one in its own language.[28] We can well understand the force of Buber's reply when he was asked at this time if he did not despair of Israel: the Israel of his vision was so far from the Israel of reality. Buber leaned forward eagerly: "Despair! Despair! In the darkest days of our history I did not despair and I certainly do not despair now!"[29]

DECISION AND DIRECTION

Closely associated with the idea of turning is Buber's emphasis on decision and direction. The future is dependent on man's "real decision," that is, the decision which man makes here and now in *this* hour.[30] Buber's teaching on decision is given its fullest expression in his *Good and Evil*, published in 1953. When Buber speaks of decision he is speaking of an act of "the whole soul"; it is again the turning of the whole man to a specific goal. This wholehearted decision gives man "direction"; it sets him on the path which is ultimately the path or direction toward God. The failure to come to a decision leaves a man without direction; and this indecision, this lack of decision, is the basis of evil. Hence evil can never be done with the whole soul. It should be pointed out that Buber is concerned here with an "anthropological definition" of good and evil, one that is revealed to man in retrospect, with his "cognizance of himself in the course of the life he has lived." Buber is not trying to set down norms or criteria for what is good or evil.[31]

Obstacles to decision

As a human being matures he is often overcome by the full range of possibilities opened to him. This plenitude of possibility "floods over his small reality and overwhelms it." Fantasy, the vast imagery of possibilities, distracts man from his proper reality; it clouds man's vision; the potential submerges the actual. Man is caught in a swirling chaos and strives to escape.

There are two options or two paths open to him . One is really a setting out upon no path, where man clutches at any object and sets his passion upon it. But this is pseudodecision, it is indecision, it is the "flight into delusion and ultimately into mania." The other option is *the* path, for there is only one; here the soul sets upon the daring work of "self-unification"; it gives up the undirected plenitude of possibility in favor of "the one taut string, the one stretched beam of direction." Even where this work is unsuccessful, the soul has nevertheless gained an inkling of what direction is. Insofar as the soul is successful in achieving unification, it becomes aware of direction, of *the* direction, for there is only one direction; and it becomes aware that it is sent in quest of this direction.[32]

The situation occurs again and again in our lives: we are confronted with the responsibility of decision, of decision which must be taken by the whole person. The whole person must enter into it, otherwise we have nothing but "a stammer, a pseudo-answer, a substitute for an answer." Everything in the nature of inclinations, of laziness, of habits, of daydreaming and the like, must be overcome—not by elimination or suppression, but rather by plunging all these forces into the "mightiness of decision" so that they "dissolve within it." The "soul as form" must overcome the immense resistance of the "soul as matter." But so frequently the effort terminates in a "persistent state of indecision." And man knows this state of indecision as evil, as well as "all other indecisions, all the moments in which we did no more than leave undone that which we knew to be good."[33]

Evil as indecision

Evil, then, stems "primarily from indecision," provided that by decision is understood, not a partial decision, but that of the whole soul. There is no such thing as a decision for *evil;* there is only the partial decision, one which leaves "the forces opposing it untouched," and to Buber's mind this is not really decision.

> Evil cannot be done with the whole soul; good can only be done with the whole soul. It is done when the soul's rapture, proceeding from its highest forces, seizes upon all the forces and plunges them into the purging . . . fire, as into the mightiness of decision. Evil is lack of direction and that which is done in it. . . . Good is direction and what is done in it; that which is done in it is done with the whole soul, so that in fact all the vigour and passion with which evil might have been done is included in it.[34]

Thus we can understand why Buber so often criticizes this lack of decision in man. He points out elsewhere the dangers of that "massive decisionlessness whose true name is the decision for nothing." Inertia, he says, is "the root of all evil."[35] But it was in *I and Thou* that he issued his strongest warning. Here too Buber speaks of the necessity of directing our whole strength toward the decision we have made, so that even that in us which opposes the decision enters into the reality of what is chosen: "He alone who 'serves God with the evil impulse' makes decision, decides the event." If this is understood, then that which is decided, that toward which direction is set, "is to be given the name of upright." And then Buber adds: "If there were a devil it would not be one who decided against God, but one who, in eternity, came to no decision."[36]

Decision implies direction

In his *Good and Evil,* Buber points out that man's repeated experiences of evil as indecision do not remain a series of isolated moments; rather, they merge into a "course of indecision," a fixation with indecision.[37] Such experiences leave man wayless, without direction. But when true human decision is had, a decision taken by the unified soul, then "there is only One direction." All true decisions, no matter how diverse, are merely variations of a single decision, which is continually made anew in a "single direction." This direction may be understood either as the "direction towards the person purposed for me," that is, the direction toward the fulfillment of that uniqueness to which I perceive that I am called; or else the single direction is understood as "the direction toward God." These are two ways of viewing the one direction. For by "God" is meant my creator, the author of my uniqueness; and my uniqueness, this unrepeatable form of being, is experienced as a "designed or pre-formed" uniqueness which is "entrusted to me for execution." Man exists not merely for the sake of existence but for the fulfillment of his uniqueness.[38]

Creation has a goal; that which is humanly right serves to put man in the one direction; the humanly right is ever the service of the person who realizes the "uniqueness purposed for him in his creation." Thus by my decision, by the turning of my whole being, I am put on the path; this means that I am taking the direction toward that point of being at which "I encounter the divine mystery of my created uniqueness, the mystery waiting for me."[39]

Need of relation

Man's failure to turn, his failure to come to decision with the fullness of his being, is akin to his failure to enter into relation, his failure to say Thou; man's indecision and his lack of relation both indicate that man is directionless; they manifest his inability to be present and his inability to be free. Evil is both absence of decision and absence of relation; it is ultimately absence of the Thou. Once again we are brought back to the dialogical relation, to what is central in Buber's thought. Turning and decision and direction are closely allied with the relation of I-Thou; turning and decision involve man's whole being; good can only be done with one's whole being; Thou can only be spoken with one's whole being. Evil can never be done with the whole being, just as It can never be spoken with the whole being. The individual entrapped in the world of It cannot come to decision; he is not free. Buber pointed this out in *I and Thou* when he wrote: "Only he who knows relation and knows about the presence of the *Thou* is capable of decision. He who decides is free, for he has approached the Face." Only the man who makes "decision out of the depths" is really a free man.[40]

If man is to turn, if he is to come to decision, if he is to be free, ultimately if light is to come into the darkness of God's eclipse, then man must enter into relation. The world of It in its various forms, which can eclipse the light of heaven, must be penetrated by the world of Thou. It can give order to the world and order to our lives, but it cannot give them meaning. An ordered world is not necessarily a meaningful world. Meaning comes only when man has direction, when he enters into relation. Meaning comes only from those "moments of silent depth," the moments of pure relation. "These moments are immortal, and most transitory of all; no content may be secured from them, but their power invades creation and the knowledge of man, beams of their power stream into the ordered world and dissolve it again and again."[41] This is what Buber calls "the great privilege of pure relation" which overcomes the power and privileges of the world of It. By virtue of this privilege "formative power" belongs to the world of Thou, that is, "spirit can penetrate and transform the world of *It.*" By virtue of this privilege man is not given up to alienation from the world and to directionlessness; by his turning, by entering into relation, light pierces the darkness. "Turning is the recognition of the Centre and the act of turning again to it. In this act of the being the buried relational power of man rises again, the wave that carries all the spheres of relation swells in the living streams to give new life to our world."[42] What matters most is that the "spirit which says Thou," the spirit in man which responds to the address of the everyday, "remains by life and reality." And this same spirit which abides in man's personal life must also be assimilated into communal life. Only in this way can the spirit confront and permeate and transform the world. The world of It, no matter how important certain aspects of it are in the life of man, does not weigh heavily on him "who is not limited to the world of *It*, but can continually leave it for the world of relation." For here man is assured of freedom and meaning and direction.[43]

Primacy of Thou

Writing shortly before his death, Buber said that it is to the primacy of the Thou that he had dedicated his efforts in the various spheres of his work. His primary goal was to make man aware of the need and importance of relation in his life.[44] Man cannot always persevere in relation; in this sense there is discontinuity in his life, the discontinuity of I-Thou and I-It. For Buber, "religious thought"—or perhaps we might say religious faith—means the acceptance of human existence in the face of this discontinuity. But what is important for man is that he remain open to the I-Thou relation and grant it the leadership in his life. There is no security and there are no once-for-all precepts that can be drawn from this "grace that appears ever anew" in our lives. And yet it can lead, even after it has been replaced by the I-It relation, if only "we do not shun its influence," if only "we remain open to it." This "remaining open" is the basic presupposition of the religious life, and it is the mark of him who in his life has realized the "primacy of the dialogical."[45]

Buber admits that it is quite easy to label him a "romantic optimist" because of his insistence on the power of relation to give men meaning and direction. But he replies that the charge is quite false: "For I have never and nowhere asserted that man can overcome his disharmony . . . through his own 'good will.' I am a realistic meliorist; for I mean and say that human life approaches its fulfillment, its redemption in the measure that the I-Thou relation becomes strong in it."[46]

Man approaches fulfillment and redemption insofar as the I-Thou relation assumes the primacy in his life. It is interesting to note that Buber here joins fulfillment and redemption as he elsewhere joins "turning" and "salvation." What he says of the latter may well be applied to the former: "Both belong together, the 'turning' and the 'salvation,' both belong together, God knows how, I do not need to know it. That I call hope."[47] They both belong together because of Buber's deep faith in God as Creator and Redeemer; it is not for man to know the role of man and the role of God in the fulfillment and redemption of mankind. Buber can only point to what he has called his basic insight: "The same Thou that goes from man to man is the Thou that descends from the divine to us and ascends from us to the divine." The biblical command of love of God and love of man "directs our gaze to the transparence of the finite Thou" as well as to "the grace of the infinite Thou, which appears when and as it will."[48]

We have already seen how, in Buber's thought, organized religion can hinder man from achieving the relation with the eternal Thou, so important for his personal fulfillment and redemption; organized religion can prevent the Thou from assuming the primacy in man's life. We will now turn our attention to the final two aspects of this study: the role of community and the need for system and structure in man's life of faith.

THE ROLE OF COMMUNITY

Martin Buber was a man with a deep sense of community, not only in the community of Israel, but also in the community of man; perhaps it would be more accurate to say that he had a deep *belief* in the community of man. God gives each historical hour its own sign, and the sign for this hour is community. "Thus it is clear today," Buber wrote in 1957, "that community shall be something real and genuine."[49] Man will no longer be satisfied with a merely fictitious realization of community. Two years before his death Buber wrote that his faith was rooted in the present hour, in the life of individuals and in the life of the human race. "I believe in this hour because I know it. I know that it opens men to each other and establishes community between them."[50] And this hour is always God's hour; it is God's address to men here and now.

Some forty years earlier Buber had said that community can only happen "out of breakthrough, out of turning."[51] And to the very end of his life he continued to express his hope in the growth of community and in the "growing capacity of society to contain community"; but such a growth is inconceivable without a "transformation of men in their relations to one another." In other words, growth of community is impossible without the turning. And then he adds:

> That this hope is deeply connected with trust in God—however one may call him—is clear. But I by no means identify this trust with a "trust in the exclusive activity of God"; I do not

believe in *such* an activity, I contest it. . . . I believe that man is created as a partner of God; which means that I believe in a co-working of the deed of mortal man and the grace of eternity incomprehensible to the human mind.[52]

Buber never lost this hope: community is to be realized by man working as the co-partner of God.

Responsibility in community

Much can be said, and much has been said, concerning the danger to personal responsibility that exists in community life. Buber insisted on this danger time and again, especially as the growing threat of Nazism loomed in the distance. The more a human group lets itself be represented in the determination of its common affairs, "so much the less community life exists in it, so much the poorer in community does it become." Community cannot endure without "the common active handling of the common." Centralization, the tendency toward "letting oneself be represented," must be allowed only insofar as it is necessary. One must constantly be alert to what must be centralized and what must not, alert to "the law of unity and the claim of community."[53]

But Buber was also quick to point out that genuine community need not be an escape; rather, it should deepen man's "consciousness of responsibility." In a 1937 talk, delivered during the height of Nazi power in Germany, Buber spoke of the "disastrously unjust reluctance to recognize the insight that true community among men cannot come into being until each individual accepts full responsibility for the other." Crises within a community can only be overcome when the individual takes upon himself a "share in the situation, and discharges it as a personal responsibility." But contemporary man seeks to evade that demand for steadfastness imposed by true community, and instead he tries to escape into a collective for which he decides but once; thereafter, the collective "relieves him of all further worry about responsibility." He no longer must concern himself, so he thinks, about the means used to achieve the common end; he no longer must be alert to see whether the end presently pursued by the group is compatible with the original hopes of the group.[54]

However, Buber added, this attitude so often found among contemporary men is not a condemnation of communal or group life; rather, it is a condemnation of man's lack of responsibility. Buber clearly indicates the responsibility conferred on each true member of a community:

> Membership in a group need not constitute escape from more and more new and different responsibilities; it can be the place for the *truest and most serious responsibility,* and its constant test. When the membership is of such a nature, the responsible human being can prove himself more wholly and profoundly there than anywhere else.

Nowhere can personal responsibility be so well tested as it is in community. At the same time the individual must not let the group prevent him from standing up for what is right:

> He must have the courage to stand up for true realization and against mere empty accomplishment, and to pledge his entire existence not only to fight the world without in behalf of the just demand of his group, but to fight within the group against false interpretations and applications of that demand, with the whole of his personal responsibility.[55]

Thus personal responsibility in communal life is a "two-edged sword": each member must give himself entirely to the accomplishment of the just ends and demands of his group, and at the same time he must vigorously oppose within the group any unjust demands or false interpretations of the purposes of the group. Indeed, here in community life is the testing ground for "the truest and most serious responsibility."

Religion and community

Much has already been said in the earlier chapters concerning the need for joining religion and community, on the need for a religious community.[56] Israel's existence was rooted in its awareness of a divine mission which cannot be realized by individuals in their private lives, but "only by a nation in the establishment of its society." And if Israel is passing through a crisis of faith, as Buber wrote in 1939, it is but a reflection of mankind's crisis of faith. The solution to this crisis will not be found in the lives of isolated individuals, but rather in the "life of a community which begins to carry out the will of God, often without being aware of doing so, without believing that God exists and that this is his will."[57]

Buber's clearest statement on this wedding of religion and

community was expressed in a short essay written in 1928 and entitled "Three Theses of a Religious Socialism." (Since Buber defines socialism in this context as "mankind's becoming a fellowship, man's becoming a fellow to man," we may here take the liberty of interchanging the words "socialism" and "community.") Religious socialism means that religion and community are essentially directed to each other, that each of them "needs the covenant with the other for the fulfillment of its own essence." Religion, man's binding of himself to God, can attain its *full* reality only "in the will for a community of the human race"; from this alone can God prepare his kingdom. Community, on the other hand, can only develop by means of a common relation to the divine center, even if this center be again and again nameless.

Unity with God and community among men belong together. Religion without community is "disembodied spirit," and therefore it is not genuine spirit; community without religion is "body emptied of spirit," and therefore not genuine body. Community without religion "does not hear the divine address, it does not aim at a response," even though it happens to make a response. Religion without community "hears the call but does not respond."[58]

In these remarks on religion and community we can see once again the influence of Buber's central insight that the Thou spoken to God and the Thou spoken to man are essentially related to one another. If one severs the two Thou's, he does violence to their meaning; and if one severs religion and community, he does violence to their meaning. Religion and community are as much bound together as are the Thou between man and God and the Thou between man and man.

Community as helper

Two of Buber's strongest commentaries on the role of community in assisting the religious quest of man appear in talks directed toward Jewish youth. Perhaps this reflects Buber's own experience as a youth, already described,[59] in which he saw his return to Judaism as giving him the one thing he so desperately needed: "the renewed taking root in community." It is above all youth who are searching for a meaningful faith who need this "saving connection with a people," and this is especially true of

Jewish youth; on such youth as these, community confers "the holy insignia of humanity—rootedness, binding, wholeness."[60] Thus from his own life-experience Buber understood quite clearly the stabilizing role of the community for the young who are torn in their search for religious truth.

However, it is in one of Buber's earliest addresses on Judaism, delivered in 1909, that we find the germ of his insights which are developed more fully in the later two discourses.[61] This talk provides us with some of Buber's basic ideas on the need for community, in a direct sense for the Jews, but indirectly for every man. Buber speaks here of a "community of blood," that is, of the community that is rooted in one's blood. As a person begins to mature he grows aware that "blood is a deep-rooted nurturing force within individual man; that the deepest layers of our being are determined by blood; that our innermost thinking and our will are colored by it."[62]

The forces that shape a man's life, Buber adds, are "his inwardness and his environment." Then, in terms at once richly Jewish and richly human, he continues:

> But the innermost stratum of man's disposition . . . is that which I have called blood: that something which is implanted within us by the chain of fathers and mothers, by their nature and by their fate, by their deeds and by their sufferings; it is time's great heritage that we bring with us into the world. We Jews need to know that our being and our character have been formed not solely by the nature of our fathers but also by their fate, and by their pain, their misery and their humiliation. We must feel this as well as know it, just as we must feel and know that within us dwells the element of the prophets, the psalmists, and the kings of Judah.[63]

Community is thus rooted in one's flesh and blood. With this in mind we can perhaps better appreciate Buber's stress on the need for community in his talks to Jewish youth.

A bond with one's people

In the first of these two addresses, delivered in 1919,[64] Buber pointed out one of the great dangers facing youth in its attitude toward the divine. It is not so much a negation or evasion of the confrontation with the "unconditional," but rather the individual's "illusion" that he has surrendered himself to the divine, whereas in reality he has done no such thing. He has given only a "quasi-acceptance" to the unconditional; he becomes a collector of religious "experiences" *(Erlebnis);* he boasts of his religious "moods" *(Stimmung);* but there is no genuine surrender.

How can youth be saved from this error? For Buber, the answer lies in the community. Youth has "a great helper by its side: the living community of the people." Only the one who lacks roots in community, who is "incapable of drawing upon any source deeper than that of his private existence," only such a man will degrade the confrontation of man and God to religious "experiences" and "moods." The man who is "truly bound to his people" cannot make this error. It is not simply because he has at his disposal the symbols formed by the religious tradition of his people through the ages, but because "the faculty to create images and forms flows into him from this bond to his people."[65]

And when he is truly bound to his people, a man realizes that the "living community" of this people is composed of three elements: preceding him there is the sacred literature and history of his people, which expresses their relation to God; around him there is the present body of his people in which the divine Presence continues to dwell; finally, within him there is the "silent, age-old memory" from which springs a truer knowledge than from the shallowness of one's own private experiences. But the richness of this tradition comes only to him who has made a "wholehearted decision" for this bond of solidarity with his people.[66]

An individual can make no adequate response to the divine, he can conceive of no appropriate symbol to express the divine-human encounter, unless he is a part of the continuity of mankind's spiritual process. Response and symbol are given to man in the religiously creative life of his people. Without this rootedness, man can do no more than "stammer and falter." For Buber, even the founders of new religions, however new their words and deeds may appear, stand within the continuity of their people's creation of symbolic images. All religious founding, as well as all genuine personal religion, is merely "the discovery and raising of an ancient treasure." Without a bond to his people, man remains "amorphous and adrift" when God calls him. It is only from his rootedness in community that man derives the depth and substance needed so that he can dare confront Him who calls.[67]

Reverent and unbiased attitude

Buber sees in the Jewish youth of this era (1919) two "painful failings," failings which are by no means limited to Jewish youth: a lack of reverence and a lack of freedom from bias. These failings are not found only in those who have turned their back on religion. There are many who consider themselves as religious and yet treat the great historical religious systems as either "obsolete or irrelevant to their own religious emotions." Such youth do not recognize that their religious emotions lack substance and that they will remain sterile unless they derive nurture "from the records and forms in which the effect of the unconditional upon the spirit of the people has become manifest during the four millennia of its path." And there are other youth who easily fall prey to the bias that looks on these records and forms, as long as they are sanctioned by "official tradition," as an undivided whole, making no distinction "between living and dead forces, or between symbols of vital or of negligible import."[68]

To counteract these failings Buber calls for a "reverent and unbiased knowledge" of Jewish religious literature, and above all of the Bible; and he asks for a "reverent and unbiased understanding" of the Jewish people and of all their beliefs and customs. Only in this way can a Jewish youth approach the inner life and ardor of his people and realize that they "have not been diminished, and indeed cannot be diminished, by any misery." Only in this way can he see that there still burns within Judaism the desire "to hallow the earthly and to affirm the covenant with God in everyday life."[69] Only with this reverent and unbiased attitude can youth fully appreciate the role of community in their search for religious meaning.

Need for tradition

The second of Buber's addresses to youth dealing with this subject was delivered in 1937 on "The Prejudices of Youth."[70] He speaks here, among other matters, of a prejudice against history which can easily lead to divorce from community. It is a prejudice which prevents "the living stream of tradition from entering their souls." When this occurs, youth are diverted from contact with those eternal values which they are called upon "to represent and incarnate in this era in their own particular way." Their urge to realization, which is so needed in the world, is "severed from the primal reality of being itself."

> True, every new generation is a link in the great chain, and every new ring must be white-hot in the passion of its new existence before it can be welded to the chain as a new link. But both: the passion for a new beginning and the ability to join as a link in the chain, must go together. Youth must have the essential knowledge that the generations which produced them are within them, and that whatever new thing they accomplish draws its real significance from that fact.[71]

For Buber, man must be bound to his tradition if he is to be a genuine innovator.

A second prejudice which involves community is the prejudice against faith. The prejudice is often well founded because of the way faith is presented in many religious groups; furthermore, faith itself, the ability to endure life in the face of unconditional mystery, presents numerous difficulties to man. For at times it is very difficult to live with mystery; it is very difficult to be constant in the face of ever new and overpowering experiences. Here again the community can help man overcome the prejudice and the difficulties: "There is something which can help us and there are helpers. There is the living transmission of those who have really lived with the mystery, and above all, those who are of our kind and who had our tidings. They help us through the pure strength with which they experienced the mystery, faced it, and engaged their lives to it."

It is the believing community, the community of faith, which assists man in his efforts to believe, to live before the face of the mystery. Buber admits that this religious tradition often reaches us "in the rigid and often conventional form of mechanical religion." But the rigid forms can be broken, so that once again we can reach the vital force of "that which has been lived and transmitted to us, back to the life in our Bible. We too can hear the voice ring forth from the black letters."[72] But without the aid of the living tradition of the community, the Voice will so often be silenced or distorted. And even those who hear the Voice will lack the base from which to respond; they can indeed do nothing but stammer and falter.

Community and law

Most of Buber's thoughts on the relation of structure and law to community are found in his biblical writings. Here the Decalogue becomes the primary example of the role of law in community. Israel comes into being and remains in being only as the people of Yahweh; and the Decalogue plays a vital role in making of Israel a people, a community. The Decalogue is Israel's constitution, but it is not a law which possesses objective value in itself. Its value comes from the fact that it has been spoken by Yahweh; apart from the living relationship between Israel and Yahweh, the Decalogue loses its meaning.[73]

Certainly one of the clearest treatments by Buber of the role of law and structure in community occurs in *Moses*, where he treats of the revolt of "Korah and his band."[74] Buber puts Korah's argument in simple terms: "The people are holy, for YHVH is in their midst; the whole people is holy, and because it is holy all the individuals in it are holy." With this as his base, Korah then argues against any human formulation of the law and against any human lawgiver; he thus attacks Moses: "If all are holy, you have no priority over the others. If all are holy, there is no need for any mediation. If all are holy, there is no need for human beings to exercise any power over other human beings. Everybody is given instruction directly by YHVH as to what he is to do."[75]

For the band of rebels, Yahweh's presence in their midst was a guarantee of their holiness; and this common holiness was reason enough for throwing off the yoke of the law, the yoke of "what should be done and what must not be done," the yoke that Moses imposed upon them "hour by hour, and day by day, in the name of God." As if God dwelt with Moses alone! As if Moses alone had access to God! Thus the rebels rise up against the fact that *"one* man leads the people in the name of God," and that this man "decides in the name of God what is right and what is wrong." Since the whole people are holy, nobody can issue orders or prohibitions to anybody else out of respect for what the latter's own holiness suggests to him. "Since the people are holy, commandments from without are no longer necessary."[76]

In Buber's analysis the rebels are in all seriousness seeking power over the divine, or more precisely, of actualizing the "god-might" which a person has in himself. It is a question of the "free" man as opposed to the man "bound" by a leader whose power is thought to be superhuman, with all the taboos used to shackle his freedom. But the rebels can succeed only by placing those who are not members of their group into a state of "non-freedom and exposure," which is in many cases "far worse than any previous abuse ever was." But for the rebels this is only a secondary effect which is regarded as being "unworthy" of consideration.[77]

Freedom and law

Ultimately the issue between Korah and Moses is one of "divine freedom" against "divine law." The true argument of the rebellion is that the law continually becomes emptied of the spirit, yet in this state it continues to maintain its full force over men. And the true conclusion is that the law "must again and again immerse itself in the consuming and purifying fire of the spirit."

The false argument of the rebels is that "the law as such displaces the spirit and freedom"; the false conclusion is that the law should therefore be replaced by spirit and freedom. But this conclusion will not be seen as false as long as the expectation of an immanent *eschaton* is maintained, that is, the expectation of the "direct and complete rule of God over all creatures," or better, the expectation of "His presence in all creatures that no longer requires law and representation." In fact Korah's false argument would become true once "the presence of God comes to be fulfilled in all creatures." It is at this point that Buber finds the "greatness and the questionability" in every genuine eschatology: "Its greatness in belief and its questionability *vis-à-vis* the realities of history." In the face of this, the attitude of Moses, and undoubtedly the attitude of Buber, is to believe in the future of a "holy people" and at the same time "to prepare for it within history."[78]

The importance of Korah's rebellion is appreciated only when viewed in large enough terms. This elementary need for independence and for freedom from others in a life of faith can develop into two opposite directions. It can grow into "an unconditional submission to the will of God and His will alone," or it can become "empty stubbornness" wherein a man "submits to his own willfulness" and feels that this very willfulness is something which is holy, which is religiously correct, which brings salvation.[79]

Both Moses and Korah wanted the people to be the people of God, the holy people. But for Moses this was the *goal*. In order to reach it, generation after generation had to choose again and again between the two directions: "between the way of God and the wrong paths of their own hearts." For Korah, the people were already holy. They had been chosen by God and he dwelt in their midst; what further need was there of ways and of choice? The people were holy just as they were. It is precisely this attitude which for Moses was the death of the people. Buber finishes his comments on this episode by speaking of the zealous response of Moses:

> He was zealous for his God as the one who sets a goal and shows a path and writes a guide to that path on tablets and orders men to choose again and again, to choose that which is right; and he was zealous against the great and popular mystical Baal which, instead of demanding that the people should hallow themselves in order to be holy, treats them as already holy.
>
> Korah calls that Baal by the name of YHVH; but that does not change anything in his essence.[80]

The false god advocated by Korah remains an eternal attraction for man in his life of faith. The tension between law and freedom remains always with us. To choose one and reject the other is indeed "death" for man as man. There is no once-for-all solution to this problem; there is no universal solution. Each man must choose, and choose again and again. But in his searching and in his choosing, as Buber has pointed out, he has assistance. It is the assistance of those who have heard and who have responded; it is through his rootedness in community that man is enabled to make his own response; it is through his rootedness in community that man comes to value his own unique responsibility here and now; it is through his rootedness in community that man is enabled to live ever before the face of the mystery.

ROLE OF RELIGION AS SYSTEM

We have already noted Buber's warnings on the dangers of codification and centralization undertaken in the interests of religion; we have already noted his insistence that religion is *everything,* that it must embrace the whole of life; we have noted his emphasis that the God of Israel is not the God of "religion" but the God of people who desires men living in community with one another, a genuinely human people. We have noted in particular his criticism of the Christian Church[81] for distorting the teaching of Jesus who sought a genuine spirit of realization in the world and not a community apart from the world. For Buber, religion as system, as an institution apart from life, must ultimately yield to religion as life, as something which embraces the totality of life. Nevertheless, we also find in Buber's thought a certain emphasis on the need and importance here and now of religion as system. It is to this final aspect of Buber's thought that we now turn.

Need for structure

Certainly the stand taken by Buber in his analysis of the rebellion of Korah and his band indicates the need for some codification of God's revelation to man. This in turn implies the need for authority and for law; the people of God are *not yet* holy; a way must be pointed out to them, and they must choose. In other words, some sort of structure or institution is needed for man in his life of faith. Buber himself, in a work published in 1963, noted that if men are really to form a genuine community of God's people, there is need of institutions: *"True institutions belong to true relations as the skeleton to the flesh."*[82] The problem is always with "true institutions": for Buber these would be institutions which are continually open to the spirit and which recognize the primacy of the dialogical.[83]

Some fifty years earlier, in a discourse already cited,[84] Buber pointed out that religiosity needs some type of form or structure if it is to manifest itself in a community of men and to endure as a religion. Unless there is a common way of life formed by structure and authority there can be no "continuous religious community, perpetuated from generation to generation." Buber calls for a continuity of religious structure and tradition that is also in a constant process of renewal; structure must give form and shape to man's religious life, not enslave or stifle it. Structure and institution are needed if religiosity is to be manifested in the world of men, and if religious traditions are to be preserved from one generation to the next. In institutional religion* law and doctrine should free men, not bind them; they should give men a base on which to build freedom and not exclude freedom.

Religion is not of its nature a sum of dogmas and rules, or a dispenser of norms and prescribed rituals; in reality it should convey the impact of the meeting of God and man, a meeting which is expressed through the life and law and worship of the community. Religion as system should help man live what Buber calls the truth of religion, namely, the "standing and withstanding in the abyss of the real reciprocal relation with the mystery of God." And it should help man understand and take seriously what Buber calls the fundamentals of this life: "the fact that God is, that the world is, and that he, this human person, stands before God and in the world."[85]

Man needs a religion

Perhaps Buber's clearest and final statement on the need of structure and tradition in religion, as well as on its danger, was published in 1964, just a year before his death.[86] He points out again that every religion is rooted in a revelation and that no religion possesses "absolute truth." No religion is a "piece of heaven that has come down to earth." Rather, each religion is a "human truth"; each religion is the effort of a particular human community to represent its relation to the Absolute. Buber then describes in picturesque terms both the vital importance of religion for man and the limitations it imposes on man:

> Each religion is a house of the human soul longing for God, a house with windows and without a door; I need only open a window and God's light penetrates; but if I make a hole in the wall and break out, then I have not only become houseless but a cold light surrounds me that is not the light of the living God. Each religion is an exile into which man is driven; here he is an exile more clearly than elsewhere because in his relationship to God he is separated from the men of other communities; and not sooner than in the redemption of the world can we be liberated from the exiles and brought into the common world of God.[87]

*By institutional religion, or religion as system, I mean that complexus of structure and authority, of law and tradition, always in a state of renewal, that would be essential to the type of religious community of which Buber so often speaks.

God's light reaches man within a religion, not outside it. This will not be the fullness of God's light, for man cannot find the fullness of light within a particular house; but it is the most that man can achieve in this life. Man is fated to remain in a particular house, and hence exiled from other communities, but in his fidelity he shares with them the common light of God.

The religions that realize this need and this limitation are bound together "in common expectation"; they can greet one another, from one exile to another, "through the open windows." And such religions, furthermore, can enter into association and work with one another in order to clarify "what can be done from the side of mankind to bring redemption nearer." Even though each religion is limited to working within "its own house," nevertheless common action by the religions is conceivable. But all this is possible only to the extent that each religion is faithful to its origins, that is, "to the revelation in which it has its origin"; this in turn demands that each religion take note and attempt to correct that divergence from its origin which has taken place in the "historical process of development."[88]

Not a substitute for God

Buber continues by emphasizing what we might consider the major defect of the great religions of man: the tendency to substitute themselves for God.

> The historical religions have the tendency to become ends in themselves and, as it were, to put themselves in God's place, and, in fact, there is nothing that is so apt to obscure the face of God as a religion. The religions must become submissive to God and his will; each must recognize that it is only one of the shapes in which the human elaboration of the divine message is presented, that it has no monopoly on God; each must renounce being God's house on earth and content itself with being a house of the men who are turned toward the same purpose of God, a house with windows; each must give up its false exclusive attitude and accept the true one.[89]

The religions of man too often forget that they are but means to an end; in adapting an attitude of exclusivity they are closed to one another, and they are closed to God. They no longer then hear the Voice that continually addresses them; they no longer possess the spirit of their origins, a spirit so eloquently expressed by him who called himself the Son of man and who came "not to be served but to serve, and to give his life as a ransom for many."[90] This is the spirit needed by all religions if they are to remain submissive to God's will and if they are not to obscure man's vision of God.

Finally, something else is needed: the religions of man must be attentive with all their force "to what God's will for this hour is"; and they must strive to realize this will in the present historical hour. If this is done, then the religions will be united "not only in the common expectation of redemption but also in the concern for the still unredeemed world."[91] Each religion must remain faithful to the truth, as much as it can, and strive toward its goal. If each succeeds in doing this, then what Buber once said of individuals can be applied to the religions: "The goals are different, very different, but if each way has been trod in truth, the lines leading to these goals intersect . . . in the truth of God." At this point those who stand at the crossroads, those who know nothing of one another, "have to do with one another."[92] Each religion shares in God's truth, each shares in His light; in fidelity to the truth which is theirs, each religion follows a unique path to the one truth and to the one light, to the one redemption of man and the world.

A CONCLUDING WORD

We have seen Buber's views on man's need of religious community and on man's need of law, structure, and tradition in religion; we have seen the dangers inherent in any system of religion as well as in any group or community to which man may belong. It is left for man to choose. Each must choose for himself; no one can make this choice for another. Clearly, Martin Buber will make no choice for us. Time and again, especially in the last years of his life, he expressed his view on this point: a reverent refusal to choose for another, a reverent refusal to offer proofs or arguments or guarantees.

No guarantee

Buber offers us no "book of principles" to tell us how to decide in a given situation; he offers us no "system of ethics." He offers only a hint or a direction hidden in his "indication of the two primary words and of their true relation to each

other."[93] He offers us too the example of his own life and of the
choices he often had to make. When confronted with the traditional "laws" that have come from man's interpretation of
God's revelation, Buber often found himself in conflict: "My
faith compels me at times to prostrate myself and ask for illumination as to what I must do in a given situation, and what I must
not do." As a result, Buber often refused to follow the traditional
interpretations because "my faith prevents me from acknowledging that God wants this of me."[94] Each man must choose for
himself from the depths of his own faith.

Buber expressed himself quite forcefully on this matter in his
1953 foreword to *For the Sake of Heaven:*

> I, myself, have no "doctrine." My function is to point out reali-
> ties of this order. He who expects of me a teaching other than
> a pointing out of this character, will always be disillusioned. And
> it would seem to me, indeed, that in this hour of history the
> crucial thing is not to possess a fixed doctrine, but rather to
> recognize eternal reality and out of its depth to be able to face
> the reality of the present.[95]

Buber's writings, his life, his faith, had as their purpose to help
man stand fast and to face the reality of the present; he reverently but persistently refused to give proofs and guarantees.

The appeal to faith

Writing late in life in response to questions about his thought,
Buber insists:

> I know no cogent proof of God's existence. If one were to exist,
> there would no longer be any difference between faith and un-
> belief; the risk of faith would no longer exist. I have dared to
> believe—not on the basis of arguments, and I cannot bolster my
> faith with arguments. I have no metaphysics on which to estab-
> lish my faith, I have created none for myself, I do not desire any,
> I need none, I am not capable of one. . . . I give my faith-
> experience the conceptual expression necessary for its being un-
> derstood, but I posit no metaphysical thesis.[96]

Later in this same work Buber resumes this theme:

> I repeat once more that I know no "objective criteria" and no
> "methods" in the relation to God. He who asks me concerning
> such misunderstands my intention. The question "How do you
> know?" is answered of itself in the personal experience of the

believing man and in the genuine living-together of men who have analogous experiences; rather, there it is not asked.

It is the lived faith of the individual and of the community which should give man the direction for which he is searching. The personal faith of the individual should be complemented by the communal faith of the community. Buber continues:

> I give no guarantees, I have no security to offer. But I also demand of no one that he believe. I communicate my own experience of faith . . . and I appeal to the experience of faith of those whom I address. To those who have none, or imagine they have none, I recommend only that they do not armor their souls with preconceived opinions. I turn to those readers who either know from their own experience that of which I speak or are ready to learn it from their own experience. The others I must leave unsatisfied, and content myself with that.[97]

Once again we have come full circle to the starting point of this study: Martin Buber's life of faith. One cannot separate his thought from his faith. His basic life experience was the experience of faith; his faith penetrated the very fiber of his being; even if he willed, he could not divorce any aspect of his life from his faith. Buber's life reflects so well his description of faith with which we began this work: "The relationship of faith is a relationship of my entire being."[98]

An apologia

Perhaps the most eloquent apologia from the pen of Martin Buber appeared in his 1963 "Replies to My Critics." It must be quoted in full:

> No system was suitable for what I had to say. Structure was suitable for it, a compact structure but not one that joined everything together. I was not permitted to reach out beyond my experience, and I never wished to do so. I witnessed for experience and appealed to experience. The experience for which I witnessed is, naturally, a limited one. But it is not to be understood as a "subjective" one. I have tested it through my appeal and test it ever anew. I say to him who listens to me: "It is your experience. Recollect it, and what you cannot recollect, dare to attain it as experience." But he who seriously declines to do it, I take him seriously. His declining is my problem.
>
> I must say it once again: I have no teaching. I only point to

something. I point to reality, I point to something in reality that had not or had too little been seen. I take him who listens to me by the hand and lead him to the window. I open the window and point to what is outside.

I have no teaching, but I carry on a conversation.[99]

For some this will not be enough; for others too much has already been presumed. But I do not believe we can ask more of Martin Buber. He takes us by the hand and leads us to the window and opens it and points to what is outside. It is now for us to listen and to respond.

"I have no teaching, but I carry on a conversation." The conversation generated by Martin Buber has by no means ceased with his death. It is carried on wherever men are present to one another, open to one another, turned to one another. It is carried on wherever men are guided by the spirit, wherever true meeting takes place, wherever man seeks to be truly man. Indeed, it is carried on wherever man truly says Thou.

8

SOME PERSONAL REFLECTIONS

The preceding chapters have been devoted almost exclusively to an exposition of Buber's own thought. I have refrained for the most part from giving any personal comments or criticisms. Yet at the same time I realize that in the very selection and structure of this work, I have already in a sense expressed my own opinion and judgment of Martin Buber's thought. To attempt now a résumé of Buber's views incurs the risk of being at once repetitive and superfluous.

Nevertheless it might be helpful at this point to emphasize some of the more important aspects of Buber's religious thought so that we might see more clearly the significance of his contribution. We will then take up some of the more common objections to Buber's thought; afterwards we will explore the relevance of Buber's critique to man's religious situation today. We might also come to see that Buber's own religious experience and his criticism of religion have striking parallels in what is commonly called traditional Christian theology.

HUMAN RELIGIOUSNESS

Perhaps the term which best summarizes Buber's religious attitude is one which he himself used in describing the impact of his initial call to Hasidism; this experience, he writes, was basically one of "human religiousness" *(menschlichster Religiosität).*[1] Genuine religious faith embraces the full humanity of man. Religion for Buber can never be something apart from human life; the man who seeks to be genuinely human is at the same time a man who seeks to be genuinely religious. Man's quest for true humanity is at once his quest for true religion. Human religiousness expresses the heart of Buber's message, not only for Jews and Christians and other "believers," but for all mankind.

Much depends on our understanding of Buber's basic insight: that the Thou spoken to God and the Thou spoken to man are basically related to each other. It is in our everyday efforts to live truly human lives, it is in our efforts to live in the present and to fulfill that peculiar uniqueness which belongs to each man, it is in our efforts to humanize and to hallow this world: it is here above all that we find our religious task.

The truly human life

How does man live a truly human life? How does he become a genuine person? For Buber, the answer is quite clear. The fundamental fact of human existence is "man with man"; that which is truly human takes place *"between* man and man, *between* I and Thou."[2] By turning to another and saying Thou with the fullness of his being, by his life of relation and of openness toward others, man becomes truly man. This encounter with the other is the cradle of genuine humanity: "All real living is meeting." Only when I truly meet another, only when I am present to him with the fullness of my being, only when I say Thou, do I really become I. Man becomes a genuine person only through his saying Thou. The more that a man tries to use and experience and possess the persons and things around him, the more that he becomes immersed in the world of It, so much the less human he becomes and the deeper does his I "sink into unreality." In contrast, the more that man tries to meet the other, the more that he tries to share reality rather than to use reality, the more that he says Thou rather than It, so much the more does he become truly human.[3]

This openness to the Thou, this relation of dialogue to the other, so central to Buber's thought, is central also to his human religiousness. For every Thou points to the eternal Thou; every particular Thou is a glimpse of the eternal Thou; by means of every particular Thou I address the eternal Thou. Thus in man's very effort to become human, by his taking his stand in relation to the world and to his fellowman, he is at the same time turning toward God and addressing his eternal Thou. The true human being cannot remain godless; the man who gives himself fully to the other in meeting is also in some way giving himself to the Other who is eternally Thou.[4]

This is what Buber means when he points to the inner relatedness of the Thou spoken between man and man, and the Thou spoken between man and God. Man cannot divide his life into a relation of Thou to God and a relation of It to the world and to his fellowmen. The man who makes an It out of the world makes an It out of God too. Such a man is incapable of faith, for he is incapable of meeting. Buber describes this man of It as being "without sacrifice and without grace, without meeting and without presentness"; he is wholly entangled in the unreal; he is not a man.[5] This, in Buber's view, is the truly godless man: the man who seeks to profit by the world and to profit by God, and not the so-called atheist or unbeliever who in his openness to the world and to man "addresses the Nameless out of the night and yearning of his garret window." The man who truly goes out to meet the world goes out also to God.[6]

Need for presence

Closely allied to this striving for a truly human life is Buber's emphasis on presentness and on the fulfillment of that uniqueness to which each man is called. It is an aspect of Hasidic thought which pervades much of Buber's writings. The realization of my uniqueness demands my full presence to the lived situation here and now. Finding my way to the particular task for which I have been destined implies an awareness of that address which comes to me here and now in the events of everyday life. There is no escape from this responsibility to be myself; I am not called upon to repeat the achievements of another, but to fulfill my own unique potential; this can be done only in my own unique way and by my own efforts. Hence the Hasidic rabbi who had no desire to change with Abraham: "Rather than have this happen, I think I shall try to become a little more myself." To become more myself demands that I bring as much presence as possible to bear on what I am doing here and now. Again, Buber has given us the response of the Hasid who was asked what was most important to his master; the disciple replied: "Whatever he happened to be doing at the moment."[7]

This idea of presence is vital to Buber's thoughts on meeting, on dialogue, on relation. In his account of the student who came to him in an hour of despair, seeking help in a decision, Buber tells us what this young man had a right to expect from him:

"Surely a presence by means of which we are told that never-theless there is meaning." Meaningful presence is essential to man's life of dialogue.[8] True meeting, true dialogue, take place only in the present moment when two persons are fully present to one another. The life of relation can be lived only in the present. Thou can only be spoken in the present moment; there is no present unless the Thou becomes present to me. The world of Thou knows only the present. The world of It has no present; it knows only the past.[9] The failure to be present to the lived concrete is a sign that man is living in the world of It. On the other hand, the effort to be wholly present is a sign of man's effort to be open in dialogue, to enter into relation, to hear the address of the present moment.

This emphasis on presence is also vital to Buber's human religiousness. Man encounters God only in the present; God is eternally Thou; the only relation that man can attain with God is that of the I to its eternal Thou. It is in the world of Thou that man encounters God, and Thou can only be spoken in the present moment. Thus he who dwells in the world of It dwells in the past where there can be no meeting with the divine. The man of It does not live in the present, and he who is not present "perceives no Presence." The eternal Thou is eternally present; He is the Present One whom man can only address, not possess.[10]

Thus the dialogue between man and God is always of the present moment. The essential teaching of Judaism becomes the essential truth of Buber's humanism: human life is a dialogue between man and God. The Bible witnesses to this dialogue; it gives vivid expression to a happening that recurs again and again in the life of man: God speaks to man, and man responds to God. God can be addressed because He is the One who addresses. This dialogue takes place always in the present hour. Revelation is always a *present* experience. God addresses man in each historical hour. It can never be a question of listening and responding once-for-all. In every hour man must go his way and listen all over again to the God who addresses each man as He addressed Moses, revealing himself as the Present One: "I will be there as I will be there."[11]

For the man who is present, who listens, who is aware, all reality becomes a bearer of the word. "Nothing can refuse to be a vessel for the Word." The signs of this address are simply the events of each day, the things that happen again and again in our lives. For Buber, living means "being addressed"; this assumes that man is present and attentive. However, too often we prefer to live in the past; presence and awareness imply too much of a risk, and so we encase ourselves in armor and ward off the signs.[12] The world of It is far more comfortable and secure than the world of Thou, just as it is far easier and more comfortable for man to deal with religion than to risk the encounter with the living God.

Hallowed worldliness

The man who lives in the present and who is aware of the signs that address him at each hour, the man who is brought to that point of "pure" or "absolute" relation with the eternal Thou, this man is also the one who understands anew his responsibility in the world. Revelation is a meeting, and this meeting takes place, not so much that man may concern himself about God, but that he may concern himself about the world. The heart of all revelation is "summons and sending"—a summoning to the encounter and a sending forth into the world to confirm that there is meaning in the world. Revelation concerns man's task in the world. There is no "life in the world" that separates man from God, nor is there any approach to God other than through the world. The world is not an obstacle on man's road to God; rather, it *is* the road to God. Man will find God not by denying the world, but rather by hallowing the world, by entering into relation with the world.[13]

This, then, is the task of the man who is genuinely human: to hallow the world. God needs man because He has willed to need him. He needs man for the task of completing creation, for the task of sanctifying all things. Man fulfills this task when he lives each day to the full, when he considers each action here and now as the most important and enters into it fully and genuinely. There is no division of sacred and profane; rather, it is a division of the hallowed and the not-yet-hallowed. Man hallows the world by an authentic relation which is open to the transcendent; the world is hallowed when man says Thou, thus opening it to the transcendent. Every Thou is a glimpse of the eternal Thou.[14]

Man's task ultimately is to realize God in the world: "God

does not want to be believed in, to be debated and defended by us, but simply to be realized through us."[15] In Hasidic terms, man is ultimately responsible for God's presence in the world; man is to let God into the world by living a truly human life. It is through man, through man's actions, that God's presence will be manifested in creation.[16] Here again is Buber's human religiousness: man's religious task, the hallowing of this world, is accomplished by his living a truly human life. All real living is meeting. Thus man hallows the world by meeting the world, by his presence to the world. When man really lives, he meets, he says Thou; in his meeting, in his openness, in his saying of Thou, man fulfills his religious task of sanctifying and redeeming the world.

Hence we can understand why Buber insisted that his primary goal in all his writings was to make man aware of the need and importance of relation, of meeting. The primary word "I-Thou" is essential for man as man; it is essential for human religiousness; it is essential for hallowing the world. We cannot always persevere in the I-Thou relation, but we can strive to give this relation primacy in our lives. Even when immersed in the world of It, as often as we must be, we can remain open to the influence of the Thou, to this "grace that appears ever anew" in our lives. This effort to remain open to the influence and leadership of relation is the basic presupposition of Buber's human religiousness; indeed, this openness is the mark of the man who has realized in his life the "primacy of the dialogical."[17]

Religion is inseparable from life

Buber's religious ideal is a full human life lived before the face of God. He constantly strives to show the relation of religion to the whole of life. He insists that religion is *everything* in its possibility of dialogue; there is nothing that we encounter in this life which is excluded from the possibility of relation. Thus everything, insofar as it may become Thou for me, provides a possible "glimpse" of the eternal Thou; everything, insofar as it may be addressed as Thou, is capable of bearing my address to the eternal Thou. This implies that I must strive to live in the present moment and to develop real relationships with everything that I encounter in the course of my life.[18]

Thus genuine religion can never be separated from my concrete life situation; for at each moment, in each situation, the possibility of dialogue is open to me. To set aside a separate domain and call this religion is, in Buber's mind, to do violence to the meaning of religion and to the meaning of life. Genuine religion and genuine life are rooted in the lived concrete situation; or better, life is religious insofar as the possibility of dialogue is realized in the lived concrete here and now. To enter into dialogue, to speak the primary word "I-Thou," is to fulfill that opportunity given to me here and now to hallow the world. Here we see the importance of Buber's Hasidic insight for his human religiousness: "One must serve God with one's whole life, with the whole of the everyday, with the whole of reality."[19]

Buber's insistence that religion is everything parallels his insistence that faith claims one's whole life, that it embraces the totality of one's life. Genuine faith means a personal relationship to the existing Lord. Of its very nature this relationship can be nothing less than all-embracing. Thus real faith imposes an awesome responsibility on the believer: I must assume before God personal responsibility for the whole of my life. I must answer before God for *this* hour; nothing can relieve me of this responsibility; no one can provide the response I must give to the present situation which confronts me. No individual, no institution, no authority, no law can answer for me; *I must not let them.* For the man of faith there can be no substitute for personal responsibility: I stand before God at each hour responsible for the whole of my life. Buber's human religiousness, then, implies that I recognize that religion is the whole of my life, that every hour and every situation is an occasion for hallowing the world, and that I alone must assume responsibility before God for my response here and now in this hour.[20]

The problem of institutional religion

If religion is *everything,* if it is rooted in the lived concrete and in the world of Thou, if man can encounter God only in the relation of the I to its eternal Thou, of what value is institutional religion? Any type of institutional or organized religion must pose serious problems to the achievement of Buber's human religiousness. Insofar as it is institutionalized, religion is not the whole of life; it is apart from the lived concrete and from the world of Thou. As institution, religion is often supported by a cult which tends to manipulate God, a creed which tends to define God, a theology which tends to unveil the mystery of God, a law which tends to be the unique path to God. As institution, religion is inclined to possess God and to substitute itself for God. God becomes the God of religion and not the God of the whole of life. Thus by means of institutional religion man is often led further and further away from the place of the encounter, from the lived concrete, from the world of Thou. Through institutional religion man too often learns to address God as "He, He," and not as "Thou, Thou." Indeed, when looked at from this point of view, nothing can hide the face of God from man so effectively as religion; religion of this sort is a stumbling block in the path of the true believer.

Institutional religion often tends to emphasize security and success, thus aggravating what Buber has called "the greatest danger" to religious life: the identification of God with success. Institutional religion often forgets the biblical warning, expressed anew by Buber, that centralization and codification threaten the whole religious undertaking of man unless they are accompanied by the strongest life of faith on the part of all those who pertain to the religious community. Institutional religion all too often permits man to substitute its creed and cult and laws for the one thing necessary: his personal turning to the Lord here and now with the fullness of his being.[21]

This is why Buber calls religion the great temptation of man; it is man's "primal danger." For institutional religion is inclined to withdraw man from the world where real communion with God takes place; in turn, religion offers itself as the privileged place where man encounters God; it becomes a substitute for the real encounter between God and man in the world. In isolating man from the world, religion becomes in reality irreligious. God wants to be realized in the world by man, and so often this genuine realization is thwarted by religion.[22] Insofar as institutional religion becomes an obstacle to man's encounter with God in the world, insofar as it hinders human religiousness, to this extent institutional religion will be rejected by the man of genuine faith.

Role of the religions

Human religiousness does not imply individual religiousness. Genuine religion cannot be separated from genuine community. The task of every real believer is to work for the community of man as it ought to be. The adequate response to the word that comes to man in each life situation here and now can never be a response of isolated individuals. Buber's biblical and Hasidic roots are evident in his insistence that only a *communal* response can be adequate to the word which God has addressed to man. What mankind needs above all is a community which in its life carries out the will of God. Religion, then, can achieve its full reality only by striving for a true community of mankind; and community can be achieved only by a common relation to the divine center. Religion and community are thus essentially related to each other; they complement one another. Religion and community are as essentially related as the Thou between man and man and the Thou between man and God.[23]

Furthermore, structure and law are needed in order that the great religious encounters of mankind may be passed from one generation to another. Here one can see the influence of Buber's Judaic roots. Individual man cannot adequately respond to the divine unless he is in some way part of mankind's spiritual tradition. He cannot give expression to this encounter unless he stands within the religious tradition of his people. The man of real faith, the man of human religiousness, will have a reverent and unbiased attitude toward the great religious traditions of mankind. Yet without some type of structure and law there can be no religious tradition; and without this tradition man has no basis from which to respond when God calls him. Without institutional religion there can be no enduring religious community.

How can institutional religion, with its cult and law, its dogma and theology, avoid becoming an obstacle to the man of genuine faith? How can it avoid stifling or enslaving man's religious spirit? How can it be made to serve human religiousness? Buber points to one way above all: cult and law and dogma and theology can be brought into the "living relation" between man and God by means of a true spirit of prayer. The structures of religion are open to the influence of the spirit when real prayer abides in the religion. Institutional religion can thus serve human religiousness as long as true prayer lives within it. Without prayer institutional religion becomes entombed in the world of It, empty and lifeless; it becomes incapable of leading man to the encounter with the eternal Thou; and without the truth of this living encounter, all religion is basically meaningless. Every man of faith should take to heart Buber's warning: "Degeneration of the religions means degeneration of prayer in them."[24] Without this spirit of prayer, without the turning of man's whole being to his eternal Thou, there can be no survival of institutional religion; nor, in fact, can there be any survival of human religiousness.

OBJECTIONS AGAINST BUBER

The possible questions and objections that can be raised against the thought of Martin Buber are enormous. I have no intention of examining them exhaustively. Much of this work has already been done elsewhere.[25] Furthermore, I am in strong general agreement with Buber's thought. Objections can be raised, but if we understand the whole of what Buber is trying to convey to us, I think these objections for the most part can be answered satisfactorily.

However, there are three general criticisms that we might examine briefly. It is said, in the first place, that Buber adopts a position which is anti-intellectual; second, that he is vague and imprecise in his language; and third, that his ideals are beyond the reach of the average person. To each of these criticisms I can respond with a qualified "Yes, I agree"; but the qualifications are such that it would be preferable to say that I seek to defend Buber against each of these objections.

His anti-intellectualism

Buber refuses to call his central insight, the I-Thou relation, a philosophy of existence, for philosophy removes man from the realm of the Thou. He does not want to be called an existentialist, and only reluctantly accepts that label. He *must* philosophize, as he admits, but his goal cannot be grasped philosophically. He communicates to us his faith experience, but he refuses to call this communication a theology; he considers himself absolutely incapable of teaching anything *about* God. He refuses to give arguments or proofs for many areas of his thought, especially that dealing with the I-Thou relation; he offers simply the philosophical communication of an experience to those who are ready to make that experience their own. He offers no objective criteria for understanding that which is experienced in the I-Thou relation; no such criteria are even conceivable for Buber. To establish objective criteria would mean being untrue to his basic experience, which is an experience of faith; he offers no arguments for his faith. Finally, Buber rejects any kind of metaphysics as a basis of his faith: "I have created none for myself, I do not desire any, I need none, I am not capable of one." He insists on the ontological character of his faith relation, that is, "that it happens between my body-soul person and God." He wants to express this faith experience conceptually so that it may be understood by others, but he posits no metaphysical basis for the support of his conceptual expression.[26]

In these and in many other ways, Buber has taken a stand which is decidedly anti-intellectual. However, he insists that we must also understand what he is trying to do. His goal cannot be grasped philosophically, it cannot be grasped intellectually. He seeks rather to lead us to the lived concrete, to be present and open to the full dimension of the existing situation in which we find ourselves. Buber can be understood only by those who live, or endeavor to live, fully in the present. His appeal is to no intellectual argument; it is to experience, to the full breadth and meaning of experience. Yet it is not an appeal to "subjectivism"; Buber himself witnesses to the experience and tests it ever anew. In his anti-intellectual stand Buber says to those who listen to him: "It is your experience. Recollect it, and what you cannot recollect, dare to attain it as experience."[27]

His lack of precision

The charge that Buber is not clear and precise in the expression of his thought is closely allied to his anti-intellectualism. He is often engaged in a paradoxical undertaking: the expression of that which has been made present to him in the I-Thou relation. This can only be done by making an It out of that which was experienced in I-Thou. He is seeking to express in concepts what he realizes is by its nature incomprehensible.[28] Thus some difficulties in precision and clarity must be expected.

Furthermore there is a certain tendency in Buber toward overstatement or exaggeration. To cite but one example, Buber speaks of early Christianity as a renewal of Judaism, but his judgment of Christianity is harsh and polemical: "Whatever was creative in the beginnings of Christianity was nothing but Judaism. . . . Whatever in Christianity is creative is not Christianity but Judaism. . . . But whatever in Christianity is not Judaism is uncreative, a mixture of a thousand rites and dogmas."[29] Given the early date of this address (published in 1911), we can presume that it is not typical of his later thought. Certainly Buber overstates his case for Judaism here, and he gives a gross caricature of real Christianity. In an address given some twenty years later Buber pointed out how Jew and Christian must show "a religious respect for the true faith of the other," that they must each acknowledge "the real relationship in which both stand to the truth." And in 1950 he wrote that Israel and Christianity, each striving for a renewal of its faith, "have something as yet unsaid to say to each other and a help to give one another— hardly to be conceived at the present time."[30] Buber's later writings clearly indicate the lack of precision present in his earlier accusation against Christianity.

It must also be recalled that Buber's style is often highly poetic. The language he employs lacks the sharp clarity that one might find in a more intellectually disciplined thinker. His insights are often conveyed in a style that is vividly descriptive and imaginative. This is especially true of two of his most important works: *Daniel*, published in 1913, and *I and Thou*, published in 1923. Thus the literary character of Buber's writing often permits a freedom of expression which might hinder clarity and preciseness, but which makes him far easier to read than most thinkers of his stature.

Finally, it would be helpful to recall the wide variety of areas touched by Buber's writings. He is a translator and interpreter of the Bible; he is perhaps the foremost exponent of Judaism and Hasidism in this century; he is an existential philosopher deeply rooted in the lived concrete; he displays a great interest in social and political philosophy; his writings carry him into the fields of psychotherapy, mysticism, and education; and through all of his works there is reflected his intense faith. Thus Buber's thought fits no single category. This, combined with his poetic style and his constant appeal to experience, makes it extremely difficult to apply any norms of criticism to Buber, and this in turn deepens the impression of a lack of precision in his thought. Buber himself uses experience as his primary criterion; perhaps it would be wise for his critics to apply the same norm.

Too idealistic

Perhaps the criticism of Buber that is most frequently made is that he is unrealistic and too idealistic for the ordinary person. Buber himself anticipated the objection in several of his works.[31] He pointed out that the life of dialogue "begins no higher than where humanity begins." It is not a question of being gifted or ungifted; rather, it is a question of "those who give themselves and those who withhold themselves." It is open to every man, no matter how pressed with work or business he may be. Dialogue is not a matter of spiritual luxury. It is meant for those in the factory, in the shop, in the office, on the farm, in the classroom. No place is so abandoned that "a creative glance" could not fly from one person to another, guaranteeing presence and openness and unreserve. Furthermore, dialogue is possible for the business executive and corporation director. He practices it when he makes present to him, as far as this is possible, the business that he directs; he practices it when inwardly he is so aware of the multitude of nameless employees that when one of them steps forward, he is present to him "not as a number with a human mask but as a person." He practices it, finally, when he is aware of his workers as persons and treats them as persons. For Buber, everyone and everything can be caught up in the life of dialogue.[32]

Yet again and again toward the end of his life Buber had to insist on this same point. In his "Responsa," published in 1964, he insists that the life of relation does not belong "to an upper story of human nature." It is open to the small child as well as to "primitive" man. Buber continues: "As for the so-called idiots, I have many times perceived how the soul of such a man extends its arms—and thrusts into emptiness. On the other hand, I have . . . learned to know persons of a high spiritual grade whose basic nature was to withhold themselves from others." Buber addresses no "spiritual elite" but simply man as man. Obstacles will occur both from without and within; it is our own desire and grace together "that help us mature and awake men to overcome them and grant us meeting."[33]

Buber is not interested in perfection; he is concerned that the I-Thou relation be realized wherever it can, and that the life of man be determined and formed by it: "For I believe that it can transform the world, not into something perfect, but perhaps into something very much more human." There is no such thing as an "ideal dialogic relationship" in our world as we know it. Buber writes: "I am a meliorist and not an idealist, and so I want only as much dialogic element as can be realized in human life here and now."[34]

Thus despite various interpretations given to his thought, Buber insists that his ideals are not meant for any type of elite. They are meant for man as man; they are meant for each one of us, here and now where we stand. The one thing needed is that we begin.

RELEVANCE OF BUBER'S CRITIQUE OF RELIGION

For anyone who understands what Buber is trying to say or who shares the experience toward which he is trying to lead us, the relevance of Buber's thought for man today should be evident. We have already seen how Dag Hammarskjøld was particularly interested in Buber's social and political philosophy. Of Buber's thought in this area, Hammarskjold remarked in a 1959 press conference: "I think that he has made a major contribution and I would like to make that more broadly known." In a similar way we could cite his influence in education, psychiatry, philosophy.[35]

However, we wish to restrict ourselves to the relevance of his critique of institutional religion; and since my own religious experience is that of a Christian, and more precisely a Roman Catholic, I will limit myself primarily to Buber's relevance for the Christian Church. Here again we can by no means be comprehensive; rather, we will discuss briefly Buber's relevance for the present controversy within the church, for the widespread phenomenon of unbelief, and for the growing trend toward religious secularism.

The turmoil within the church

There can be no doubt that much of the present turmoil within the church is in reality a revolt against the institutional church. For countless believers the church as institution is empty, unappealing, even repelling. The institutional church speaks in a language which has so little to do with the lived concrete situation of its adherents. Perhaps this is precisely the problem: in its institutional aspects the church has become a world apart; it has become the great mecca of the sacred sealed off from the profane. Insofar as it has adopted this attitude, the church has immersed itself in the world of It; it provides orientation rather than direction; it seeks to possess God rather than to address God; it provides the security of dogma and creed rather than the risk and responsibility of giving oneself to the lived moment. Religious structure has so often imprisoned genuine religious faith; it has imposed its system of laws and doctrines on those who are seeking to give new expression to the meaning of their faith; it has aimed primarily at conserving religious tradition rather than renewing religious tradition. In so doing the Christian Church is following today the same negative path of which Buber spoke in one of his earliest addresses on Judaism.[36]

If the institutional church is looked on by many as a relic of the past, if its spokesmen are so often irrelevant, is this not due in large measure to its failure to recognize that religion *is* everything, that the world, not the church, is the privileged place of encounter between man and God? Is it not due in large measure to the fact that the great relational events which are at its source, the revelation of God through Israel and through Jesus Christ, have been surrounded by a creed, a law, a theology, and have thus been hardened into the world of It? Is it not due in large measure to the fact that the church has so often substituted itself for God, and to this extent has become incapable of leading man to the real relational event with the eternal Thou? Would not the church be more meaningful to man if it heeded Buber's plea that "God does not want to be believed in, to be debated and defended by us, but simply to be realized through us?" Would not the church be more meaningful if it were more willing to point beyond itself in order to lead man to that fullness of religion which is life? Would not the church be more meaningful if it more clearly recognized that it has "no monopoly on God," that it is not God's sole house on earth but one of the many houses where men are turned toward the same purpose of serving God in the world?[37]

Many Christians, especially among the young, identify the

institutional church with certain middle-class values for which they have only contempt. Many of them claim that they reject the church and that they reject God. Very often they are rejecting that which they ought to reject; they are rejecting a concept of God which is distorted and parochial, not the one true God but an idol made by man.[38] So many of the young are forced into the position Buber calls a "critical atheism," a position which, by pointing to the emptiness of our images and concepts of God, prepares the way for a new and vital encounter. They reject man-made idols in their search for authenticity, for that encounter which knows no image but only the "presence of the Present One."[39]

Buber reminds us again and again of God's continual presence. If we understand his insight, we could never assume a pessimistic attitude toward the current trend away from belief. Buber would have been in wholehearted agreement with the opinion of sociologist Robert Bellah, given several years ago at a conference in Rome on "The Culture of Unbelief": "The modern world is as alive with religious possibility as any epoch in human history."[40] God is ever present to His people; He is eternally Thou; it is only man who at times has turned away.

The phenomenon of unbelief

Much has been written and much has been discussed on the widespread phenomenon of unbelief, especially among the young. However, when one examines the problem closely, is it really a question of unbelief or is it more a question of the meaning of belief and of the restlessness of believers? At the conference on "The Culture of Unbelief" mentioned above, Harvey Cox expressed sentiments that strongly echoed the insights of Buber in this area. He charged that hypocrisy, not unbelief, is the major religious problem today. Any perusal of the writings of the Catholic Left would confirm this opinion. Cox suggests that, instead of a secretariat on unbelief, the church would do better to establish a secretariat on hypocrisy to deal with the churchgoers who know all the correct answers, but who in reality have no living belief which forms and motivates their life. Where does one look today to find a faith that is being truly and genuinely lived? Is it really correct to label as unbelievers those whose search for the transcendent is so much more serious and ardent than that of many so-called believers? Such young people may call themselves Marxists or scientific humanists or the like, but in their heart they do not know themselves as unbelievers. This analysis by Cox recalls Buber's insistence in *I and Thou* that it is the man who seeks to profit by God and by the world who is really godless, "not the 'atheist,' who addresses the Nameless out of the night and yearning of his garret window."

Harvey Cox concluded his remarks by blaming the church for much of the widespread unbelief. "It may be that the major reason for unbelief is not that people find the Gospel incredible but that they find the Church incredible."[41] In a similar way, Buber claimed that the teaching of Jesus on a genuine spirit of realization in the world was distorted by the church. If it is true that many young people are saying in their own way "Jesus—yes, the church—no," may not the cause be that the church has removed the teaching of Jesus away from realization in the world and limited it to realization in "religion"? Is it possible that many young people see in the gospel the genuine relation of Jesus to the Father and to the world, and that they see in the church an elaborate structure immersed in the world of It? Is it possible that the church has emphasized law and dogma and creed to the neglect of that genuine relation to the world and to God? To the extent that this is true, then to that extent the church is to blame for much of the unbelief in the world.

Finally, the common Christian notion of faith equates belief with an intellectual assent to specific doctrinal truths; this tends to remove the believer from that relation of the whole being to the living God which is Buber's understanding of faith. Thus the Christian act of faith is, more often than not, rooted in the world of It; it is not a turning of one's whole being to Him who is eternally Thou, but rather an act of the intellect in assenting to the truth of certain doctrines. Thus the Christian believer begins with a relation very close to that of I-It, a relation far removed from that total commitment which is the biblical demand made of man. Unless faith involves this total commitment, religion is destined to become only a part of life, something removed from the totality of life. Too often the church presents to the young not the God of life but only the God of religion. To many young people today such a commitment is simply not enough; they are not satisfied with a religious commitment to the church because this is not a commitment embracing the whole of life. The church has so often divorced religion from life. We might well recall Buber's comments in a 1937 address to youth:

> Real faith does not mean professing what we hold true in a ready-made formula. On the contrary: it means holding ourselves open to the unconditional mystery which we encounter in every sphere of our life and which cannot be comprised in any formula. It means that from the very roots of our being, we should always be prepared to live with this mystery as one being lives with another. Real faith means the ability to endure life in the face of this mystery.[42]

It is unfortunate that for many this total commitment "from the very roots of our being" can only be found outside the church and outside religion.

Religious secularism

This general disenchantment with the church and with traditional religious belief are two of the principal reasons for the rise of religious secularism in our midst. Many young people feel that they encounter within the church few authentic believers in the gospel, few who seek something other than their own security and comfort; they tend to identify the church with a fear and mistrust of the world. On the other hand, they encounter outside the church the dedication of those who might be called the secular saints, those who work in the secular city with total devotion and apparently with no religion. Not surprisingly, many have concluded that only when they leave the false security of the church can they recover the ability to embrace with their whole undivided being both God and the world. Thus they seek to prove their faith, not by acts of belief, but by their service and concern for the after the manner of Jesus, who was the "man for others."[43]

In their commitment to the needs of the world instead of to the needs of the churches are not these men and women in their own way searching for Him who is Lord of the world and not just the God of religion? We have seen Buber's insistence again and again that it is always here and now, at this present moment, in this situation, that God is addressing me and that I am called upon to make my response. Meeting with God takes place in order that man may concern himself with the world, not with God and not with religion. This attitude has been taken up by many theologians today who suggest that the rise of this so-called secular response to life must be interpreted positively as the fruit of the gospel; they feel that institutional religion must not be regarded as the cause we are called upon to defend, but rather as something that we are called upon to transcend if we are to be free for true faith in the living God who reveals himself to us in each concrete life situation.[44] It is not a question of considering the world to be already redeemed, but of looking upon the world, the "secular," as both full of God-given promise and yet also as a potential source of dehumanization.

Once again there is a parallel with Buber's thought. Man is indeed capable of a twofold relationship toward the world, but it is through authentic meeting with the world that he both hallows the world and stands in the presence of the eternal Thou. Institutional religion must realize its own role here: it is never an end in itself but must bring man to that proper understanding of the church and of the world so that there will be no division between religion and life, between the God of religion and the God of life. If the institutional church adopts this stance, then not only will man have come of age, but the church also will have done so.

For Buber, as well as for many present-day theologians, secularization is by no means an enemy of religion, but comes about as a result of genuine biblical faith; it is a change from a static institutional view of religion to a dynamic temporal view of religion. Secularization will not save the world; but it points to that world where God is at work, and where we are called to meet Him in the lived concrete situation. Buber's message is clear: for the church and for all men of genuine faith the world of time, the world of our everyday living, the "secular" is of central importance, for the God we worship is not just the God of religion but the Lord of life, the Lord of the world.

TRADITIONAL ASPECTS OF BUBER'S CRITIQUE

Martin Buber's critique of religion is not only relevant to actual problems within the churches today, but also it deals with these problems from a point of view which is deeply traditional, traditional in the sense of being rooted in the Judeo-Christian approach to faith. Here again we must limit ourselves in discussing this aspect of Buber's thought. We have cited several times his emphasis on the need for community and for genuine religious tradition; we have discussed his ideas on the need for law and structure in religion; we have pointed out the basic necessity of prayer in man's life of faith. Furthermore, Buber's basic insight, that the Thou spoken between man and God and the Thou spoken between man and man are fundamentally related to each other, strongly echoes what one finds in the New Testament. There is a remarkable similarity between Buber's insistence on the inner relatedness of love of God and love of man and the New Testament teaching on this point, especially as found in the first epistle of John. We will treat at length, then, just one aspect of Buber's critique: his opposition to theology.

No objective knowledge of God

Buber insists that we can achieve no "objective aspect" of God. Speaking for himself he says: "God can never become an object for me." This is the basis of his opposition to theology, which he looked on as a teaching *about* God; he himself was absolutely incapable of any kind of teaching about God. Furthermore, theology tends to misinterpret the purpose of the divine-human encounter which takes place, not that man might concern himself about God, but that he might be more deeply concerned with realizing God in the world. Moreover, God is eternally Thou, and speaking *about* God removes Him from the realm of Thou so that it is no longer God about whom one speaks. God cannot be expressed or possessed by man, only addressed.[45] Theology is thus classified by Buber among those elements which are opposed to a genuine conception of faith; it is one of the elements that comprise the "arch-enemy of religion that rises against it from within."[46]

Yet Buber also admits that a given concept of God does not necessarily impair "the concrete religious relationship." Everything depends on the extent to which this concept can do justice to the reality of God, "do justice to it as a reality."[47] More importantly, Buber found it necessary to speak about God in the communication of his own faith experience; he found it necessary to speak about God in His relation to man. This can only be done, however, in a paradoxical manner by which the content of the concept about God is "revolutionized, transformed, and extended." Buber explains, as mentioned above, how he applies this paradoxical manner of speaking about God in referring to God as the absolute Person, that is, the Person who cannot be limited.[48]

I would submit that Buber has overstated his opposition to theology. Theology need not be classified as an enemy of the genuine conception of and communication of faith experience; the real theologian in Christian tradition is, like Buber, interested in communicating the experience of this divine-human encounter; the abuses which Buber sees in theology should be discerned from the authentic theological tradition. It is not possible to cover all of these aspects in detail, but I think much can be gained by comparing Buber's remarks on theology with the negative theology, or Christian agnosticism, of the early fathers of the church. Here the insights and attitudes of traditional Christian theology are strikingly similar to the insights and attitudes of Martin Buber.

Christian agnosticism

Christian agnosticism reached its major development around the latter half of the fourth century under the impetus of the claim of Eunomius to know God as God knows himself: "God does not know His own being any better than we do; His essence is no more manifest to Himself than it is to us."[49] This is ultimately a denial of the transcendence and majesty of God. The reply of Christian theology at that epoch and down through the centuries is emphatic: if man understands, then what he understands is not God.[50]

The fathers of the church were quick to take up the argument against Eunomius. Basil wrote that an understanding of God is simply "beyond the comprehension of men"; faith leads us to an understanding *that* God is, not *what* God is; man's knowledge of God consists in recognizing "that He cannot be comprehended."[51] Gregory of Nyssa wrote in his *Contra Eunomium* that God cannot be comprehended by any name or concept because he is beyond any name, ineffable and unspeakable.[52] With John Chrysostom comes the formal profession of Christian agnosticism: "We know God is, but we are ignorant about what God is"; God remains always "ineffable, unintelligible, invisible, incomprehensible, beyond the power of human language."[53] This insight is echoed again and again in Christian theology; Thomas Aquinas restates a firm theological truth when he writes: "One thing about God remains completely unknown in this life, namely what God is."[54]

Thus Christian theology insists that we can affirm *that* God is, but we cannot understand *what* God is. I can affirm that God is wise and good and just and loving, but I cannot understand what divine wisdom and goodness and justice and love are. Yet these names tell me *something* about God; I am not caught in complete agnosticism.[55] Buber himself considered the names of God as hallowed because in them God is not only spoken *about* but also spoken *to.*[56]

Theology's "narrow ridge"

Here we approach what Buber has called the moment of paradox, that which for Christian theology is its own "narrow ridge." We speak of the delicate balance between gnosticism and agnosticism. As one theologian writes: "In the things of God it is perilous to misplace either one's agnosticism or one's gnosticism. The risk is the loss of one's God, who is lost both when he ceases to be God, because no longer unknown, and when he ceases to be our God, because not known at all."[57]

The patristic period confronted the paradox of speaking about God by positing what would later be elaborated by Thomas Aquinas as the analogy of being.[58] We can find in the early fathers the essential structure of the famous *triplex via.*[59] For example, I affirm that God is good. I deny that God is good in the way that creatures are good. Then with a sense of divine transcendence, I am conscious, as I affirm and deny, that God is good in a mode of being that is infinite—and ultimately incomprehensible. Christian theology brings us to the point of admitting that we are united to God as to one who is unknown. I do not think that Martin Buber would contest this conclusion. Moreover, I think he would be in basic agreement with the remarks of the eminent theologian John Courtney Murray, commenting on the *triplex via:*

> The way of man to the knowledge of God is to follow all the scattered scintillae that the Logos has strewn throughout history and across the face of the heavens and the earth until they all

fuse in the darkness that is the unapproachable Light. Along this way of affirmation and negation all the resources of language, as of thought, must be exploited until they are exhausted. Only then may man confess his ignorance and have recourse to silence. But this ignorance is knowledge, as this silence is itself a language—the language of adoration.[60]

I confess to seeing very little difference between this traditional Christian doctrine of the *triplex via* and Buber's insistence, as seen above, that the content of a concept applied to God must be "revolutionized, transformed and extended," or his admission "that no concept can be applied to God without a transformation taking place in it, and that it is the task of him who thus applies the concept to characterize and explain this transformation so far as possible."[61]

Some expression of man's encounter with God is necessary, as Buber himself realized. This endeavor is naturally open to abuse, to risk, to misunderstanding, to all the weaknesses inherent in our human condition. If Martin Buber had been more aware of the full dimensions of the theological tradition in Christianity, I doubt that he would have been so categorically opposed to all theology. On the other hand, if theologians were more aware that God can never become an object for man, that every "He" uttered of God is a metaphor, that God can only be addressed, not expressed, then I doubt that Martin Buber would have found so much to criticize in theology. Theology must always be renewed and made relevant to man here and now. Buber's critique has provided a great impetus to this needed renewal. He has reminded theologians of the one thing necessary: the turning of our whole being to Him who is eternally Thou. He has reintroduced the awe, the wonder, the reverence that is part of every man's relation with God. He has pointed to the dangers of a religion encrusted in law, in dogma, in theology. He has pointed to the task of the religions: to assist man toward the saving dialogue with the living God, so that in turn he may better understand his task in the world. Religion, after all, is a question of "holding fast to God."

I cannot speak for other religions, nor can I speak for other Christians, and I certainly cannot "baptize" Martin Buber, but I believe that in many areas his attitude and his thought are essentially one with Christianity. Or it might be better to say that we can see more clearly, because of the writings of Martin

Buber, that in many areas genuine Christianity is in basic agreement with genuine Judaism. At least it must be said that we who call ourselves Christian would be much more faithful to our task and to our vocation if we could follow, each in his own way, the spirit of Buber. Perhaps Martin Buber should be called a man of universal religion, for he was indeed a man of God.

CONCLUSION: THE WITNESS OF THE MAN

Little remains to be said. If the thought of Martin Buber remains confusing or unsatisfying to some, it will have to remain so. I can only hope that it is not due to my presentation of his thought. Buber has fulfilled his own task, which of its very nature he considered to be a selective one. He has handed on to us those truths in Hasidism and Judaism, and undoubtedly in other areas as well, which in his view are decisive for the past and future history of the human spirit. In fulfilling this task Buber had to act as a filter. "I have not made use of a filter," he tells us, "I became a filter. . . . I have chosen what I have chosen; rather I have let it go through my heart as through a filter."[62]

He offers us no arguments, no guarantees, no security. He communicates his experience of faith and he appeals to our experience of faith. He speaks to those who are ready to learn from their own experience that of which he speaks.

The ultimate "proof" for Buber was life itself. The manner in which he lived his life rests always as the greatest witness to his teachings. As is evident in the preceding pages, Buber appears to have combined an extraordinary sensitivity toward others with an extraordinary sensitivity toward God. These are the twin foci of his life which he again and again pointed out as being basically related. Both of these aspects appear in an expression of thanks he wrote in 1958 for all those who had sent greetings on his eightieth birthday:

> The older one becomes, so much the more grows in one the inclination to thank.
> Before all, to what is above. Now, indeed, so strongly as could never have been possible before, life is felt as an unearned gift, and especially each hour that is entirely good one receives, like a surprising present, with outstretched, thankful hands.
> But after that it is necessary time and again to thank one's fellow man, even when he has not done anything especially for one. For what, then? For the fact that when he met me, he had

really met me, that he opened his eyes and did not confuse me
with anyone else, that he opened his ears and reliably heard what
I had to say to him, yes, that he opened what I really addressed,
his well-closed heart.[63]

It would be difficult to imagine a more sensitive expression of
man's Yes to his God and to his fellows. For Buber, the encounter with God and the encounter with man are the gifts which
form the genuine foundation of human life.

Buber's sensitivity for others is brought out so beautifully in
a poem written just a year before his death, entitled "The Fid-
dler":

> Here on the world's edge at this hour I have
> Wondrously settled my life.
> Behind me in a boundless circle
> The All is silent, only that fiddler fiddles.
> Dark one, already I stand in covenant with you,
> Ready to learn from your tones
> Wherein I became guilty without knowing it.
> Let me feel, let there be revealed
> To this hale soul each wound
> That I have incorrigibly inflicted and remained in illusion.
> Do not stop, holy player, before then![64]

Here Buber seeks to know all the hidden guilt and insen-
sitivity through which he has caused harm to others. He expresses in poetic fashion a sensitivity which he revealed so often
in his life. It indicates that Buber possesses what might be called
an extremely delicate conscience; another example of this appears in a 1951 address where he speaks directly of man's conscience:

> Each one who knows himself . . . as called to a work which he
> has not done, each one who has not fulfilled a task which he
> knows to be his own, each who did not remain faithful to his
> vocation which he had become certain of—each such person
> knows what it means to say that "his conscience smites him."[65]

Buber's sensitivity for God, so evident to anyone who reads
his works, was emphasized again in what was perhaps the final
act of his literary career. Just several months before his death,
he published his *Nachlese*, his gleanings,[66] which he called a
witness to "an experience, a feeling, a decision, yes even of a
dream." As the final entry to this witness of his life, he chose a

very brief essay, written in 1928, on "After Death." It deserves to be cited in full:

> We know nothing of death, nothing other than the one fact that we shall die—but what is that, dying? We do not know. So it behooves us to accept that it is the end of everything conceivable by us. To wish to extend our conception beyond death, to wish to anticipate in the soul what death alone can reveal to us in existence, seems to me to be a lack of faith clothed as faith. The genuine faith speaks: I know nothing of death, but I know that God is eternity, and I know this, too, that he is my God. Whether what we call time remains to us beyond our death becomes quite unimportant to us next to this knowing, that we are God's—who is not immortal, but eternal. Instead of imagining ourselves living instead of dead, we shall prepare ourselves for a real death which is perhaps the final limit of time but which, if that is the case, is surely the threshold of eternity.[67]

This is indeed the testimony of a man who has lived his life in the presence of the divine. This was the essence of Martin Buber's life and work: to make us aware of this divine Presence in the lived concrete of our everyday lives. A final anecdote from Buber's life illustrates his own understanding of this awareness, an awareness which he would share with each one of us:

> When I was a child I read an old Jewish tale I could not understand. It said no more than this: "Outside the gates of Rome there sits a leprous beggar, waiting. He is the Messiah." Then I came upon an old man whom I asked: "What is he waiting for?" And the old man gave me an answer that I did not understand at the time, an answer I learned to understand only much later. He said: "He waits for you."[68]

The witness of his life reflects Martin Buber's own understanding of these words; his was the responsibility of life, and the joy of life, lived in the presence of God and in relation to his fellowman. "He waits for you." This is the challenge issued to us here and now. It is now for us to respond. The responsibility must be borne by every man.

In the notes, the following works by Buber are cited only by their titles: details of publication are given in the bibliography.

"Autobiographical Fragments" (in *The Philosophy of Martin Buber*)
A Believing Humanism
Between Man and Man
Daniel
Eclipse of God
For the Sake of Heaven
Good and Evil
Hasidism and Modern Man
I and Thou
Israel and the World
Kingship of God
The Knowledge of Man
Moses
On Judaism
The Origin and Meaning of Hasidism
Paths in Utopia
Pointing the Way
The Prophetic Faith
"Replies to My Critics" (in *The Philosophy of Martin Buber*)
"Responsa" (in *Philosophical Interrogations*)
Tales of the Hasidim I (The Early Masters)
Tales of the Hasidim II (The Later Masters)
Tales of Rabbi Nachman
Ten Rungs
Two Types of Faith

NOTES

PREFACE

1. Quoted by Seymour Siegel in *Martin Buber: An Appreciation of His Life and Thought* (New York: American Friends of the Hebrew University, 1965), p. 6.
2. *I and Thou*, p. 128.
3. "Gaudium et Spes" in *The Documents of Vatican II*, ed. Walter Abbott (New York: Guild Press, 1966), pp. 199–200.
4. In *Martin Buber: An Appreciation of His Life and Thought*, p. 1.

BUBER BIOGRAPHY

1. Maurice Friedman, *Martin Buber: The Life of Dialogue* (New York: Harper Torchbooks, 1960), p. 16.
2. Ephraim Fischoff, introduction to *Paths in Utopia*, pp. xi–xii.
3. Friedman, *Martin Buber*, p. 8.
4. Paul Schilpp and Maurice Friedman, eds., *The Philosophy of Martin Buber* (La Salle, Ill.: Open Court Press, 1967), pp. 3–39.
5. *Between Man and Man*, pp. 13–14; Schilpp and Friedman, *Philosophy of Martin Buber*, pp. 25–26.
6. *Between Man and Man*, pp. 13–14.
7. Ibid., p. 13.
8. Ibid., p. 14.
9. *Eclipse of God*, pp. 3–9; Schilpp and Friedman, *Philosophy of Martin Buber*, pp. 26–31.
10. *Eclipse of God*, p. 4.
11. Ibid., p. 5.
12. Ibid., pp. 5–6.
13. Ibid., p. 7.
14. Ibid., pp. 7–8.
15. Ibid., p. 9.
16. Friedman, *Martin Buber*, p. 8.
17. *Pointing the Way*, pp. 3–4; Schilpp and Friedman, *Philosophy of Martin Buber*, pp. 37–39.
18. *Pointing the Way*, p. 3.
19. Ibid., p. 4.

20. Ibid., p. 4.
21. Ibid., p. 146.
22. Seymour Siegel, in *Martin Buber: An Appreciation of His Life and Thought* (New York: American Friends of the Hebrew University, 1965), pp. 6–7.
23. Ibid., p. 10.
24. *Ten Rungs*, p. 69.
25. *Israel and the World*, pp. 231, 233. Various parts of this letter appear both in *Pointing the Way* as "A Letter to Gandhi" and in *Israel and the World* as "The Land and Its Possessors"; hence the two different references to the same letter. The entire letter is published in *The Bond* (Jerusalem: Rubin Mass, April 1939), pp. 1–22.
26. *Israel and the World*, p. 257.
27. Ibid., pp. 261, 263.
28. *Two Types of Faith*, pp. 12–13.
29. *Pointing the Way*, pp. 238, 239.
30. Karl Wilker, "Martin Buber," *Neue Wege* (Zurich) 17 (April, 1923): 183 ff. Cited in Friedman, *Martin Buber*, p 5.
31. Paul Tillich, in *Martin Buber: An Appreciation of His Life and Thought*, p. 11.

CHAPTER 1: BIBLICAL THOUGHT

1. *Two Types of Faith*, p. 40.
2. Ibid., p. 38.
3. *Israel and the World*, p. 29.
4. Cf. the remarks of Maurice Friedman in *Martin Buber: The Life of Dialogue* (New York: Harper Torchbooks, 1960), pp. vi, 33; also idem, "Martin Buber's Challenge to Jewish Philosophy," *Judaism* 14 (1965): 267–76.
5. *Two Types of Faith*, pp. 7–9.
6. Ibid., pp. 38–39.
7. Ibid., p. 40.
8. Ibid., p. 29. Cf. also *Good and Evil*, pp. 16–17.
9. *Israel and the World*, pp. 235–36.
10. Ibid., pp. 140–42.
11. Ibid., pp. 16–19, 37.
12. Ibid., p. 33.
13. Ibid., p. 21.
14. *Moses*, p. 88.
15. Ibid., p. 128.
16. Ibid., p. 127.
17. Ibid.

18. Ibid., p. 132.
19. *The Prophetic Faith*, pp. 49, 61–62.
20. Ibid., pp. 94–95.
21. *On Judaism*, pp. 88–89.
22. *The Prophetic Faith*, p. 85.
23. *Moses*, p. 129; *On Judaism*, p. 89.
24. *The Prophetic Faith*, pp. 171–72, 175.
25. *Two Types of Faith*, p. 42.
26. Ibid., pp. 56–57.
27. Ibid., pp. 57–58; "Replies to My Critics," p. 727.
28. *Two Types of Faith*, pp. 58–59.
29. Ibid., pp. 63–64.
30. *Moses*, pp. 130–31.
31. Ibid., pp. 187–88.
32. *The Prophetic Faith*, p. 170 (emphasis added).
33. Cf. *The Prophetic Faith*, pp. 19–30; *Moses*, pp. 39–55; *Israel and the World*, pp. 23, 30, 64; *The Kingship of God*, pp. 104 ff.
34. *The Prophetic Faith*, pp. 28–29; cf. *Moses*, pp. 51–52.
35. *Israel and the World*, p. 23; cf. *Moses*, pp. 52–53.
36. *Israel and the World*, p. 30.
37. *The Prophetic Faith*, p. 52.
38. *Moses*, pp. 53–54.
39. *Two Types of Faith*, p. 130.
40. *Good and Evil*, pp. 12, 49; *The Prophetic Faith*, p. 200.
41. *Good and Evil*, p. 55.
42. Ibid., pp. 39–40, 46, 59.
43. Ibid., pp. 34–41; *The Prophetic Faith*, p. 199.
44. *The Prophetic Faith*, p. 201.
45. *Good and Evil*, p. 43.
46. Ibid., pp. 44–47.
47. *The Prophetic Faith*, p. 202.
48. *Israel and the World*, pp. 22, 209.
49. *Good and Evil*, p. 21.
50. *The Prophetic Faith*, p. 88.
51. *Moses*, p. 66; cf. *The Prophetic Faith*, pp. 43 ff.
52. *Moses*, p. 137.
53. Ibid., pp. 106–7.
54. *The Prophetic Faith*, p. 78; *Moses*, p. 131.
55. *Israel and the World*, p. 251.
56. Ibid., pp. 223–24; *The Prophetic Faith*, pp. 99, 233.
57. *Israel and the World*, pp. 250–51.
58. *The Prophetic Faith*, p. 150.
59. Ibid., pp. 233–34.

CHAPTER 2: HASIDIC WRITINGS

1. *Hasidism and Modern Man*, pp. 52–53.
2. Ibid., pp. 56–60.
3. *For the Sake of Heaven*, p. xii.
4. "Responsa," pp. 88, 90, 91.
5. *The Origin and Meaning of Hasidism*, p. 22.
6. *Hasidism and Modern Man*, p. 180; *The Tales of Rabbi Nachman*, pp. 12, 13.
7. *Tales of the Hasidim I*, pp. 2–3.
8. *Hasidism and Modern Man*, pp. 49–50 (emphasis added).
9. *The Origin and Meaning of Hasidism*, pp. 116–17.
10. *The Tales of Rabbi Nachman*, pp. 15–17.
11. *On Judaism*, p. 48.
12. *The Origin and Meaning of Hasidism*, p. 127.
13. Maurice Friedman, in introduction to ibid., pp. 13–14; pp. 178–81.
14. *Hasidism and Modern Man*, p. 110.
15. Rabbi Pinhas of Koretz, d. 1791.
16. *Hasidism and Modern Man*, pp. 250–51.
17. Ibid., p. 164.
18. Ibid., pp. 134–35.
19. *Tales of the Hasidim I*, p. 4.
20. Rabbi Yaakov Yitzhak of Lublin, d. 1815.
21. *Tales of the Hasidim I*, p. 313; *Hasidism and Modern Man*, p. 138.
22. *Hasidism and Modern Man*, pp. 138–39 (emphasis added).
23. Rabbi Menehem Mendel of Kotzk, d. 1859.
24. *Tales of the Hasidim II*, p. 284.
25. Rabbi Simha Bunham of Pzhysha, d. 1827.
26. Rabbi Meshullam Susya of Hanipol, d. 1800.
27. *Hasidism and Modern Man*, p. 140. Cf. also *Tales of the Hasidim I*, p. 251; *Tales of the Hasidim II*, p. 256.
28. *Hasidism and Modern Man*, pp. 139–41.
29. Rabbi Baruch of Mezbizh, d. 1811.
30. *Hasidism and Modern Man*, pp. 140–42; *The Origin and Meaning of Hasidism*, p. 141.
31. *Hasidism and Modern Man*, pp. 163, 166.
32. Ibid., pp. 126–27.
33. *The Origin and Meaning of Hasidism*, pp. 139–40, 181.
34. *Ten Rungs*, p. 15.
35. *Hasidism and Modern Man*, pp. 172–73.
36. Ibid., pp. 173–74. Cf. also *The Origin and Meaning of Hasidism*, p. 86: "Only on the path of true intercourse with the things and beings does man attain to true life . . . only on this path can he take an active part in the redemption of the world."
37. Rabbi Hanokh of Alexander, d. 1870.

38. *Tales of the Hasidim II*, p. 317; *Ten Rungs*, p. 137; *Hasidism and Modern Man*, p. 174.
39. *Hasidism and Modern Man*, pp. 175–76; *Tales of the Hasidim II*, p. 277.
40. *The Origin and Meaning of Hasidism*, pp. 69, 70.
41. Ibid., p. 50 (emphasis added).
42. *Hasidism and Modern Man*, p. 235.
43. *The Origin and Meaning of Hasidism*, p. 94.
44. Ibid., pp. 94–95.
45. Ibid., pp. 96–97.
46. Ibid., pp. 98–99.
47. Ibid., p. 99.
48. *Hasidism and Modern Man*, pp. 143–44.
49. Ibid., pp. 28–30.
50. *The Origin and Meaning of Hasidism*, pp. 55–56.
51. *Hasidism and Modern Man*, p. 40.
52. Ibid., pp. 130–34.
53. *The Origin and Meaning of Hasidism*, pp. 86–88.
54. Ibid., p. 171.
55. *Hasidism and Modern Man*, pp. 31, 43.
56. *The Origin and Meaning of Hasidism*, p. 152.
57. Rabbi Moshe of Kobryn, d. 1858.
58. *Tales of the Hasidim II*, p. 173.
59. See note 15.
60. *Tales of the Hasidim I*, p. 122.
61. *On Judaism*, p. 48.
62. *The Origin and Meaning of Hasidism*, pp. 107, 111–12.
63. *Hasidism and Modern Man*, p. 233.
64. *Tales of the Hasidim I*, p. 130.
65. Rabbi Rafael of Bershad, d. 1816.
66. *Tales of the Hasidim I*, p. 130.
67. *Hasidism and Modern Man*, pp. 247–48.
68. *The Origin and Meaning of Hasidism*, p. 141.
69. *Hasidism and Modern Man*, p. 118.
70. Ibid., p. 117.
71. *Ten Rungs*, p. 82. The similarity to 1 John 4:20 is obvious; the rapport between Hasidism and Christianity is especially evident in this whole section on Hasidic love.
72. *Hasidism and Modern Man*, pp. 237–38.
73. *Ten Rungs*, p. 79.
74. *Hasidism and Modern Man*, p. 249.
75. Rabbi Yehiel of Mikhal of Zlotchov, d. circa 1786.
76. *Tales of the Hasidim I*, p. 156; *Ten Rungs*, p. 82; *Hasidism and Modern Man*, p. 254.

77. Rabbi Shmelke of Nikolsburg, d. 1778.
78. *Tales of the Hasidim I*, pp. 189–90.
79. Rabbi Moshe Leib of Sasov, d. 1807.
80. *Tales of the Hasidim II*, p. 86.
81. *Tales of the Hasidim I*, p. 25.
82. *The Origin and Meaning of Hasidism*, p. 198.
83. *Hasidism and Modern Man*, pp. 52–53.
84. *The Origin and Meaning of Hasidism*, p. 24.
85. *For the Sake of Heaven*, p. 265.
86. *Ten Rungs*, p. 31.
87. *The Origin and Meaning of Hasidism*, pp. 25–27.
88. Rabbi Israel of Koznitz, d. 1814.
89. *For the Sake of Heaven*, p. 201.
90. *The Origin and Meaning of Hasidism*, pp. 202–6.
91. *Hasidism and Modern Man*, p. 69.
92. *For the Sake of Heaven*, p. 125.
93. *The Origin and Meaning of Hasidism*, pp. 130–36.
94. Ibid., p. 174.
95. *Tales of Rabbi Nachman*, p. 14 (emphasis added).
96. *On Judaism*, pp. 212–13.
97. "Replies to My Critics," p. 744.

CHAPTER 3: ADDRESSES ON JUDAISM

1. *On Judaism*, p. 119.
2. *Hasidism and Modern Man*, pp. 57–58.
3. *On Judaism*, pp. 23, 31.
4. Ibid., p. 158.
5. Ibid., pp. 215–16.
6. *The Origin and Meaning of Hasidism*, pp. 91–92. Buber adds here what is for him one of Judaism's basic objections to Christianity: that it allows God to be addressed only through Jesus, as the Christ; "the 'way' to the Father now only goes through him. In this modified form the peoples received Israel's teaching that God can be addressed. It came to pass that they learned to address Christ in His place."
7. *A Believing Humanism*, p. 177.
8. *Israel and the World*, p. 16.
9. Ibid., pp. 131–32.
10. Ibid., p. 132; *Pointing the Way*, p. 206.
11. *On Judaism*, pp. 224–25.
12. *Israel and the World*, pp. 81–82; cf. also *For the Sake of Heaven*, p. 239; *Tales of the Hasidim I*, pp. 212–13.
13. *Pointing the Way*, p. 197; *Israel and the World*, p. 14.
14. *On Judaism*, pp. 161–64.

15. *Israel and the World*, pp. 114, 209.
16. Ibid., p. 131.
17. Ibid., pp. 15, 30.
18. Ibid., pp. 30–31.
19. *On Judaism*, pp. 210–11. Cf. Simone Weil, *La Pesanteur et la grace* (Paris, 1948).
20. *Israel and the World*, p. 31.
21. *Two Types of Faith*, p. 40.
22. *Israel and the World*, p. 19.
23. Ibid., p. 91.
24. Ibid., p. 92.
25. Ibid., pp. 236–37.
26. Ibid., pp. 237–38.
27. Ibid., pp. 251–52.
28. Ibid., pp. 245–46.
29. Ibid., pp. 246–47.
30. *On Judaism*, pp. 217–18.
31. Ibid., pp. 12–13.
32. Ibid., pp. 200–201.
33. Ibid., pp. 203, 207.
34. Ibid., pp. 8–10.
35. *A Believing Humanism*, pp. 174–79.
36. *Israel and the World*, p. 22; *On Judaism*, p. 220.
37. *Israel and the World*, pp. 93–96.
38. Ibid., p. 98.
39. Ibid., p. 209.
40. Ibid., pp. 177, 180–81.
41. Ibid., pp. 32–33.
42. *On Judaism*, pp. 38–49, passim.
43. Ibid., pp. 93–94 (emphasis added). In the preface to the 1923 edition of his *Reden über das Judentum*, Buber clarifies any misunderstanding that might arise from his speaking of the "realization" of God. He states specifically that "only a primal certainty of divine *being* enables us to sense the awesome meaning of divine becoming, whereas without this primal certainty there can be only a blatant misuse of God's name" (ibid., pp. 8–9).
44. Ibid., pp. 91–92.
45. Ibid, pp. 92–93. Buber delivered this address prior to World War I; it is probably his clearest and most direct warning against the dangers inherent in religion, and yet an insistence on the need for religion. We will refer later to this same address; its ideas appear again and again in the writings of Buber to the very end of his life.
46. Ibid, pp. 109–10. Published in 1919, four years before *I and Thou*,

this address obviously reflects clearly the ideas of Buber's personalism expressed in this later writing.

47. Ibid, pp. 110–11, 113.
48. Ibid, pp. 122–23.
49. Ibid, pp. 124–26.
50. Ibid, pp. 66–67.
51. *Israel and the World*, p. 18.
52. *On Judaism*, pp. 81–83.
53. Ibid, pp. 86–87.
54. Ibid., pp. 65–67, 82; cf. *Israel and the World*, p. 18.
55. *On Judaism*, p. 174.
56. *Israel and the World*, p. 163.
57. Ibid., pp. 41–42, 51.
58. *On Judaism*, pp. 149–51.
59. Ibid., p. 152.
60. Ibid., pp. 134–36.
61. Ibid., pp. 136–39.
62. *Israel and the World*, pp. 39–40.
63. *Two Types of Faith*, pp. 173–74.
64. *On Judaism*, pp. 110–11.
65. Ibid., p. 113.
66. *Israel and the World*, pp. 157–59.
67. Ibid., pp. 170, 185.
68. Ibid., pp. 185–86.
69. *On Judaism*, pp. 141, 145.
70. Ibid., p. 114.
71. *Israel and the World*, pp. 169, 186–87.
72. Ibid., p. 210.
73. Ibid., pp. 229–30.
74. Ibid., pp. 193–94.
75. Ibid., pp. 143–45.
76. Ibid., pp. 248, 172.

CHAPTER 4: THE DIALOGUE BETWEEN MAN AND MAN

1. "Responsa," pp. 99–100.
2. *Pointing the Way*, p. 109.
3. Ibid., p. 110.
4. Foreword to *Between Man and Man*, p. xi.
5. *Between Man and Man*, pp. 203–4.
6. *The Knowledge of Man*, p. 151.
7. *Between Man and Man*, p. 160.
8. Ibid., pp. 180–81.
9. *A Believing Humanism*, p. 94 (emphasis added); *Between Man and Man*, p. 203.

10. *Between Man and Man*, p. 205.
11. *The Knowledge of Man*, pp. 67–69.
12. *Good and Evil*, pp. 135–36.
13. *The Knowledge of Man*, p. 71.
14. Ibid., pp. 75–77.
15. Ibid., pp. 78–81.
16. *Pointing the Way*, pp. 228–29; *The Knowledge of Man*, pp. 80–81.
17. *Between Man and Man*, p. 209.
18. *The Knowledge of Man*, p. 86.
19. *Pointing the Way*, pp. 234–38.
20. Ibid., pp. 237–38.
21. *A Believing Humanism*, pp. 57–58.
22. *Between Man and Man*, pp. 3–4.
23. Ibid., pp. 10–11.
24. Ibid., pp. 16–17.
25. Ibid., pp. 22–24.
26. *The Knowledge of Man*, pp. 86, 79–80.
27. Ibid., pp. 85–87.
28. Maurice Friedman, introduction to *Between Man and Man*, p. xvii.
29. *Between Man and Man*, p. 92.
30. Ibid., pp. 34–35.
31. Ibid., p. 36.
32. Ibid., pp. 36–39.
33. Ibid., p. 39; *The Knowledge of Man*, p. 79.
34. *A Believing Humanism*, pp. 58–59.
35. Quoted by Maurice Friedman in preface to *Daniel*.
36. *Daniel*, pp. 74–75.
37. Ibid., pp. 94–96.
38. *I and Thou*, pp. 3–5.
39. Ibid., pp. 3–8.
40. "Responsa," p. 21; cf. "Replies to My Critics," p. 691.
41. *I and Thou*, pp. 9, 11; *Eclipse of God*, pp. 127–28.
42. *I and Thou*, pp. 12–13.
43. *Eclipse of God*, pp. 88–89.
44. *I and Thou*, pp. 9, 31–32; "Replies to My Critics," p. 691.
45. *I and Thou*, pp. 32–33.
46. Ibid., pp. 16–17, 33.
47. Ibid., pp. 39–40.
48. Ibid., pp. 33–34.
49. Ibid., pp. 3, 4, 62; cf. "Responsa," p. 63.
50. "Responsa," p. 34.
51. *I and Thou*, pp. 9, 11, 64 (emphasis added).
52. Ibid., p. 63.

53. Ibid., p. 65.
54. *Eclipse of God,* p. 128.
55. *I and Thou,* pp. 65–67.
56. Ibid., pp. 59–60, 76–78.
57. Ibid., pp. 60–61.
58. *Between Man and Man,* pp. 192–93.
59. Ibid., pp. 20–21.
60. *I and Thou,* pp. 14–15.
61. *Israel and the World,* p. 48; *A Believing Humanism,* p. 121.
62. *Eclipse of God,* p.129.
63. *I and Thou,* pp. 39, 43; "Replies to My Critics," p. 704; "Responsa," p. 39.
64. *Eclipse of God,* p. 129.
65. *I and Thou,* p. 48.
66. Ibid., pp. 43–44.
67. Ibid., pp. 44–45.
68. Ibid., pp. 47–48.
69. Ibid., pp. 46, 48–51.
70. *Between Man and Man,* pp. 175–76.
71. *Pointing the Way,* p. 155; *Paths in Utopia,* p. 65.
72. *Between Man and Man,* pp. 176–77.
73. *The Knowledge of Man,* p. 106.
74. Ibid., p. 108.
75. *Paths in Utopia,* p. 132.
76. *The Knowledge of Man,* p. 108.
77. Ibid., pp. 108–9.
78. *Paths in Utopia,* p. 133; *A Believing Humanism,* p. 87.
79. *Paths in Utopia,* pp. 134–35; *A Believing Humanism,* pp. 88–89.
80. *A Believing Humanism,* pp. 89–90; *Paths in Utopia,* p. 135.
81. *Paths in Utopia,* p. 145; *Pointing the Way,* p. 102.
82. *Between Man and Man,* p. 184.
83. "Responsa," pp. 54, 58.
84. Ibid., p. 63.
85. *Between Man and Man,* pp. 14, 98.
86. *A Believing Humanism,* pp. 100–101.
87. "Responsa," pp. 28–29.
88. Ibid., p. 51.

CHAPTER 5: THE DIALOGUE BETWEEN MAN AND GOD

1. *I and Thou,* p. 99.
2. Ibid., p. 100..
3. Ibid., pp. 6, 75, 101.
4. *Between Man and Man,* p. 30; *On Judaism,* p. 151.
5. *I and Thou,* pp. 102–3.

6. Ibid., pp. 78–79.
7. Ibid., pp. 75, 80.
8. Ibid., p. 112.
9. Ibid., pp. 79–81; *Eclipse of God*, p. 128 (emphasis added).
10. *I and Thou*, pp. 75–76.
11. Ibid., pp. 112–13.
12. "Replies to My Critics," p. 705; *I and Thou*, pp. 113–14.
13. *I and Thou*, p. 114.
14. Ibid., p. 83.
15. Ibid., p. 106.
16. *Between Man and Man*, p. 17; *I and Thou*, pp. 136–37.
17. *Between Man and Man*, pp. 14–15; *Israel and the World*, pp. 31–32.
18. *Between Man and Man*, p. 15.
19. *A Believing Humanism*, pp. 113–14, 135.
20. *I and Thou*, pp. 109–10; *A Believing Humanism*, p. 114.
21. *A Believing Humanism*, p. 113; *I and Thou*, pp. 110–11.
22. *I and Thou*, pp. 111–12.
23. Ibid., pp. 116–17.
24. *Between Man and Man*, p. 15.
25. Ibid., p. 65; *I and Thou*, pp. 94–95.
26. *Between Man and Man*, pp. 51–52; *Origin and Meaning of Hasidism*, pp. 51–52; *Origin and Meaning of Hasidism*, p. 198.
27. *I and Thou*, p. 79.
28. Ibid., p. 80.
29. Ibid., p. 107.
30. Ibid., pp. 82, 108–9.
31. Ibid., pp. 114–15.
32. Ibid., pp. 115–16; cf. *Israel and the World*, p. 209.
33. *Israel and the World*, p. 242.
34. *I and Thou*, p. 95.
35. Maurice Friedman directed such a question to Buber: see "Responsa," pp. 85–86.
36. "Responsa," p. 86.
37. *Eclipse of God*, p. 126.
38. *I and Thou*, pp. 103–4.
39. *Between Man and Man*, p. 12; *A Believing Humanism*, p. 126.
40. *A Believing Humanism*, p. 132–33.
41. *Between Man and Man*, p. 12; *A Believing Humanism*, p. 126.
42. *Israel and the World*, p. 49.
43. *Between Man and Man*, pp. 67–68; *A Believing Humanism*, pp. 205–6. It is interesting to note that these two articles, "On the Ethics of Political Decision" (*A Believing Humanism*, pp. 205–10) and "The Question to the Single One" (*Between Man and Man*,

pp. 40–82) were published in 1933 and 1936 respectively, during the early years of the Nazi regime in Germany.

44. *Between Man and Man*, p. 68; *A Believing Humanism*, pp. 206–7.
45. *A Believing Humanism*, p. 207; *Between Man and Man*, pp. 68–69.
46. *A Believing Humanism*, p. 207–9; *Between Man and Man*, p. 69.
47. *Between Man and Man*, pp. 70–71; *A Believing Humanism*, pp. 208–10.
48. *Between Man and Man*, p. 91.
49. Ibid., pp. 91–92.
50. Ibid., p. 76.
51. M. Friedman in introduction to *Daniel*, pp. 26 ff.
52. *Daniel*, pp. 88–90; cf. *A Believing Humanism*, p. 133.
53. *Daniel*, pp. 90–91.
54. Ibid., p. 91.
55. Ibid., p. 92.
56. *Between Man and Man*, p. 115; *Daniel*, pp. 92–93.
57. See the discussion on this subject by Friedman in introduction to *Daniel*, pp. 27 ff.
58. *Daniel*, pp. 95–98.
59. Ibid., p. 98.
60. Ibid., pp. 98–99; *A Believing Humanism*, p. 133.
61. *Between Man and Man*, pp. 80–82, 176.
62. *Pointing the Way*, pp. 110–11.
63. Ibid., p. 111.
64. *Between Man and Man*, p. 202.
65. *A Believing Humanism*, p. 152.
66. *I and Thou*, p. 115.
67. Ibid., p. 54.
68. Ibid., p. 118.
69. Ibid., p. 118–19.
70. Ibid., pp. 119–20.

CHAPTER 6: THE DANGERS OF RELIGION

1. *Eclipse of God*, p. 123.
2. *A Believing Humanism*, p. 127.
3. *Eclipse of God*, pp. 123–25.
4. Ibid., p. 49; *Between Man and Man*, p. 57.
5. *Eclipse of God*, pp. 49–50.
6. Ibid., pp. 44–45.
7. Ibid., pp. 31–32.
8. *A Believing Humanism*, p. 132; *Eclipse of God*, p. 128.
9. *A Believing Humanism*, p. 130.
10. *Eclipse of God*, p. 32.

11. *A Believing Humanism,* p. 130; *Eclipse of God,* pp. 38, 40.
12. *Eclipse of God,* pp. 42–43; *A Believing Humanism,* p. 130.
13. *Eclipse of God,* p. 43; *A Believing Humanism,* p. 133.
14. *Eclipse of God,* pp. 43–44; *A Believing Humanism,* pp. 131, 134.
15. *On Judaism,* pp. 150–51; *A Believing Humanism,* p. 72.
16. *On Judaism,* p. 4.
17. Ibid., pp. 4–5.
18. These lectures are found in *Eclipse of God.*
19. Ibid., p. 13.
20. Ibid., pp. 13–14.
21. Ibid., pp. 14–18; 23.
22. Ibid., pp. 45–46.
23. Ibid., p. 46.
24. *On Judaism,* p. 5.
25. Buber is referring to the proclamation of the Madman in Friedrich Nietzsche's *Die fröhliche Wissenschaft.*
26. *Israel and the World,* pp. 50–51.
27. Ibid., p. 51.
28. *A Believing Humanism,* p. 117.
29. *Eclipse of God,* p. 34.
30. *Between Man and Man,* pp. 13–14; see biography of Buber above, pp. xix ff.
31. *Between Man and Man,* pp. 5–6.
32. *Pointing the Way,* pp. 209–10.
33. Ibid., pp. 211–12.
34. *Eclipse of God,* p. 35.
35. *Pointing the Way,* p. 92; *Eclipse of God,* pp. 35–36.
36. See above, p. 126.
37. *A Believing Humanism,* p. 114; "Replies to My Critics," pp. 698–99.
38. *A Believing Humanism,* pp. 113–14; "Replies to My Critics," pp. 699–700.
39. "Replies to My Critics," p. 703.
40. See above, p. 6.
41. *Eclipse of God,* pp. 34–35.
42. Ibid., pp. 74–75, 125.
43. Ibid., pp. 75–76.
44. Ibid., p. 125; *The Origin and Meaning of Hasidism,* p. 168.
45. *Eclipse of God,* p. 125; *The Origin and Meaning of Hasidism,* p. 243.
46. *Eclipse of God,* p. 125; *The Origin and Meaning of Hasidism,* pp. 243–44.
47. "Replies to My Critics," p. 716.
48. *Eclipse of God,* p. 136.

49. "Replies to My Critics," p. 716; *The Origin and Meaning of Hasidism*, p. 244.
50. *The Origin and Meaning of Hasidism*, pp. 245, 247–48.
51. "Responsa," p. 97.
52. *Eclipse of God*, pp. 28, 31, 68, 128.
53. Ibid., pp. 32–33.
54. "Replies to My Critics," p. 690.
55. See above, p. 131.
56. "Replies to My Critics," pp. 713–14 (emphasis added).
57. Ibid., pp. 689–90.
58. *I and Thou*, pp. 134–35.
59. Ibid., pp. 135–36.
60. "Replies to My Critics," p. 691.
61. *A Believing Humanism*, p. 111.
62. *Israel and the World*, p. 49.
63. *Between Man and Man*, p. 18 (emphasis added); *A Believing Humanism*, p. 57.
64. See above, pp. 141 ff.
65. *I and Thou*, p. 106.
66. *A Believing Humanism*, p. 110.
67. *Moses*, p. 88; see above, p. 7.
68. *Pointing the Way*, p. 113.
69. *On Judaism*, p. 80.
70. See above, p. 146.
71. *On Judaism*, pp. 80–81.
72. *The Prophetic Faith*, p. 170 (emphasis added).
73. "Responsa," p. 97.

CHAPTER 7: THE NEED FOR RELIGION

1. *Hasidism and Modern Man*, p. 42.
2. Roy Oliver, *The Wanderer and the Way: The Hebrew Tradition in the Writings of Martin Buber* (Ithaca, N.Y.: Cornell University Press, 1968), pp. 1–3.
3. See above, pp. 70, 141, 176–77.
4. "Replies to My Critics," p. 689.
5. *I and Thou*, p. 60.
6. *A Believing Humanism*, p. 121.
7. "Responsa," p. 99.
8. Oliver, *The Wanderer and the Way*, pp. 5–7.
9. *A Believing Humanism*, p. 33.
10. Ernst Simon, "Jewish Adult Education in Nazi Germany as Spiritual Resistance," in *Leo Baeck Institute Year Book* (London: East and West Library, 1956), pp. 87–88. Ernst Simon is professor of education at the Hebrew University in Jerusalem. A long-

time friend and colleague of Buber's, he is Buber's literary executor.

11. Quoted in Oliver, *The Wanderer and the Way*, p. 8.
12. *Pointing the Way*, p. 188.
13. Ibid., pp. 190–91.
14. Ibid., p. 191.
15. *Good and Evil*, p. 65; *For the Sake of Heaven*, p. 54. The Hebrew title, *Gog and Magog*, comes from the reference in Ezekiel 38 and 39, cf. also Revelation 20:7.
16. *For the Sake of Heaven*, p. 116.
17. *I and Thou*, pp. 37–39, 55.
18. *Eclipse of God*, p. 129.
19. Ibid., pp. 23–24, 126–27.
20. Ibid., p. 24.
21. *Pointing the Way*, pp. 237–39.
22. *Eclipse of God*, pp. 66–68.
23. *Tales of the Hasidim I*, p. 122.
24. *I and Thou*, pp. 56, 120.
25. *Israel and the World*, pp. 20–21.
26. *For the Sake of Heaven*, p. 44.
27. *Eclipse of God*, p. 129.
28. *Pointing the Way*, p. 198.
29. Malcolm Diamond, *Martin Buber: Jewish Existentialist* (New York: Oxford University Press, 1960), p. 211.
30. *The Prophetic Faith*, pp. 2–3.
31. *Good and Evil*, pp. 130–31.
32. Ibid., pp. 125–28.
33. Ibid., pp. 128–30.
34. Ibid., pp. 130–31.
35. *Hasidism and Modern Man*, p. 39; *Israel and the World*, p. 18.
36. *I and Thou*, p. 52.
37. *Good and Evil*, p. 134.
38. Ibid., pp. 140–42.
39. Ibid., p. 142; cf. "Replies to My Critics," pp. 720–21.
40. *I and Thou*, pp. 51, 53; cf. Maurice Friedman, *Martin Buber: The Life of Dialogue* (New York: Harper Torchbooks, 1960), pp. 101–3.
41. *I and Thou*, pp. 31, 53.
42. Ibid., p. 100.
43. Ibid., pp. 50–51.
44. "Replies to My Critics," p. 744.
45. Ibid., pp. 743–44.
46. "Responsa," p. 117.
47. "Replies to My Critics," p. 715.
48. *Between Man and Man*, p. 219.

49. *A Believing Humanism*, p. 178.
50. "Responsa," p. 35.
51. *A Believing Humanism*, p. 151.
52. "Responsa," pp. 73–74.
53. *A Believing Humanism*, pp. 87–88; *Paths in Utopia*, pp. 137 ff.
54. *A Believing Humanism*, p. 151; *Israel and the World*, p. 47.
55. *Israel and the World*, pp. 47–48 (emphasis added).
56. See above, pp. 77 ff.
57. *Israel and the World*, pp. 229–30.
58. *Pointing the Way*, p. 112.
59. See above, pp. 24–25, 52.
60. *Hasidism and Modern Man*, pp. 57–58.
61. "Judaism and the Jews," in *On Judaism*, pp. 11–21.
62. Ibid., p. 15.
63. Ibid., p. 17.
64. "Herut: On Youth and Religion," in *On Judaism*, pp. 149–74.
65. Ibid., pp. 153–54.
66. Ibid., pp. 154–55.
67. Ibid., pp. 155–56.
68. Ibid., pp. 171–72.
69. Ibid., pp. 172–73.
70. *Israel and the World*, pp. 41–52.
71. Ibid., pp. 42–43.
72. Ibid., pp. 49–50.
73. *Moses*, pp. 130–31.
74. Ibid., pp. 182–90; Numbers, 16.
75. *Moses*, p. 184.
76. Ibid., pp. 185–86.
77. Ibid., p. 187.
78. Ibid., pp. 187–88.
79. Ibid., pp. 188–89.
80. Ibid., pp. 189–90.
81. See above, p. 70.
82. "Replies to My Critics," p. 715 (emphasis added).
83. See above, pp. 109 ff. Lowell Streiker agrees that in Buber's view, religious institutions are at once the greatest obstacle to, and yet a necessary condition for, the realization of true humanity. Cf. *The Promise of Buber* (Philadelphia: J. P. Lippincott Co., 1969), pp. 62 ff.
84. See above, p. 68.
85. *Pointing the Way*, pp. 113–14.
86. *A Believing Humanism*, pp. 113–16.
87. Ibid., p. 115.
88. Ibid.

89. Ibid., pp. 115–16.
90. Mark 10:45.
91. *A Believing Humanism*, p. 116.
92. *Pointing the Way*, pp. 218–19.
93. "Replies to My Critics," p. 718.
94. "Responsa," p. 87. On Buber's attitude toward the law, cf. his correspondence with Franz Rosenzweig in Nahum Glatzer, ed., *On Jewish Learning* (New York: Schocken Books, 1955), pp. 109 ff. In the letter of 24 June 1924 Buber writes: "I do not believe that *revelation* is ever a formulation of law." Again, on 5 July 1924 he insists: "I cannot accept the laws and the statutes blindly, but I must ask myself again and again: Is this particular law addressed to me and rightly so?" In these letters Buber argues that revelation becomes law only through man; he cannot accept both the law and an openness to the unmediated word of God.
95. *For the Sake of Heaven*, p. xiii.
96. "Responsa," p. 84.
97. Ibid., p. 96.
98. See above, pp. 3–4.
99. "Replies to My Critics," p. 693.

CHAPTER 8: SOME PERSONAL REFLECTIONS

1. *Hasidism and Modern Man*, p. 59.
2. See above, p. 88; *A Believing Humanism*, p. 94; *Between Man and Man*, p. 203.
3. See above, pp. 104 ff.
4. See chapter 5, passim.
5. See above, p. 107.
6. *I and Thou*, pp. 95, 107.
7. See above, pp. 32, 41.
8. See above, p. xx.
9. See above, p. 102.
10. See above, pp. 161, 187.
11. See above, pp. 15 ff., 53 ff.
12. See above, pp. 94 ff.
13. See above, pp. 127 ff.
14. See above, pp. 39, 64.
15. *On Judaism*, p. 94.
16. See above, pp. 35–36.
17. See above, p. 194.
18. See above, pp. 161–62.
19. *Hasidism and Modern Man*, p. 50.
20. See above, pp. 64, 135.
21. See above, pp. 174 ff.

22. See above, pp. 37, 70.
23. See above, pp. 197 ff.
24. *I and Thou*, p. 118.
25. Cf. *The Philosophy of Martin Buber*, especially Buber's own "Replies to My Critics," pp. 689–744: "Responsa," pp. 13–117.
26. Cf. "Responsa" and "Replies to My Critics," passim, especially "Responsa," pp. 28–29, 84.
27. "Replies to My Critics," p. 693.
28. Ibid., p. 689.
29. *On Judaism*, pp. 45, 47.
30. *Israel and the World*, p. 40: *Two Types of Faith*, p. 174.
31. *I and Thou*, pp. 47–51; *Between Man and Man*, pp. 34–39.
32. *Between Man and Man*, pp. 35–39.
33. "Responsa," p. 36.
34. Ibid., pp. 39, 79.
35. See above, pp. 93, 99; Maurice Friedman in introduction to *Pointing the Way*, pp. vii–viii. Cf. also *The Knowledge of Man*, passim; Maurice Friedman, "Martin Buber and Psychotherapy," *Cross Currents* 5 (1955):297–310.
36. *On Judaism*, pp. 80 ff.
37. See above, pp. 68, 205 ff.
38. Editorial, *Commonweal* 87 (1967): 5–6.
39. See above, p. 159.
40. Quoted in *Time* (Atlantic Edition), 4 April 1969, p. 38.
41. Quoted in *Time* (Atlantic Edition), 4 April 1969, pp. 38–39.
42. *Israel and the World*, p. 49.
43. Cf. Thomas Merton, *Faith and Violence* (South Bend, Ind.: University of Notre Dame Press, 1968), pp. 268 ff.
44. Cf. the analysis of theologians Cornelius van Peursen, Harvey Cox, and Arend Th. van Leeuwen in Colin Williams, *Faith in a Secular Age* (New York: Harper and Row, 1966), pp. 19–33.
45. See above, pp. 170–72.
46. "Responsa," p. 97.
47. *Eclipse of God*, p. 14.
48. See above, pp. 172–73.
49. Cited in J. N. D. Kelly, *Early Christian Doctrines*, 2d ed. (London: Adam and Charles Black, 1960), pp. 249 ff.
50. For an excellent brief explanation of Christian agnosticism, see John Courtney Murray, *The Problem of God* (New Haven: Yale University Press, 1964), pp. 60–73.
51. Rouet de Journel, *Euchiridion Patristicum*, 931, 923; (hereafter referred to as *RJ*).
52. *RJ*, 1041.
53. *RJ*, 1121, 1125.

54. *In Epistula ad Romanos,* 1, 6.
55. Thomas Aquinas, *Summa Theologiae,* I, q. 13.
56. *I and Thou,* p. 75.
57. Murray, *The Problem of God,* p. 65.
58. Aquinas, *Summa Theologiae,* I, q. 13, a. 5.
59. For example, John Damascene, *De Fide Orthodoxa, RJ,* 2347; Thomas Aquinas, *Commentary on the First Book of Sentences,* d. 8, q. 1, ad 4; *In Epistula ad Romanos,* 1, 6.
60. Murray, *The Problem of God,* p. 73; cf. also Guy de Maulde, "Analyse linguistique et langage religieux," *La nouvelle revue théologique* 91 (1969): 169–202.
61. "Responsa," p. 88.
62. "Replies to My Critics," pp. 731, 737.
63. *A Believing Humanism,* p. 225.
64. Ibid., pp. 228–29:

> Hier, am Weltrand, habe ich zur Stunde
> Wunderlich mein Leben angesiedelt.
> Hinter mir im grenzenlosen Runde
> Schweigt das All, nur jener Fiedler fiedelt,
> Dunkler, schon steh ich mit dir im Bunde,
> Willig, aus den Tönen zu erfahren,
> Wes ich schuld ward ohne eigne Kunde.
> Spüren lass michs, lass sich offenbaren
> Dieser heilen Seele jede Wunde,
> Die ich heillos schlug und blieb im Schein.
> Nicht eher, heil'ger Spielmann, halte ein!

65. *Eclipse of God,* p. 87.
66. In English, *A Believing Humanism.*
67. *A Believing Humanism,* pp. 27, 231.
68. *On Judaism,* p. 21.

SELECTED BIBLIOGRAPHY

The following bibliography includes only those works by Buber and about Buber that were directly employed in this study. A chronological listing of Buber's works, in German, Hebrew, and English, has been compiled by Maurice Friedman in *The Philosophy of Martin Buber*, edited by Paul Schilpp and Maurice Friedman (La Salle, Illinois: Open Court Press, 1967). Extensive bibliographies of works about Buber appear in Maurice Friedman, *Martin Buber: The Life of Dialogue* (New York: Harper Torchbooks, 1960) and in Hans Kohn, *Martin Buber: sein Werk und seine Zeit* (Cologne: Joseph Melzer Verlag, 1961).

WORKS BY BUBER

"Autobiographical Fragments." Translated by Maurice Friedman. In *The Philosophy of Martin Buber*, edited by Paul Schilpp and Maurice Friedman, pp. 3–39. La Salle, Illinois: Open Court Press, 1967.

A Believing Humanism. Translated by Maurice Friedman. New York: Simon and Schuster, 1967.

Between Man and Man. New ed. Translated by Ronald Gregor Smith; afterword translated by Maurice Friedman. New York: Macmillan, 1965 (first English edition appeared in 1947).

Daniel: Dialogues on Realization. Translated by Maurice Friedman. New York: McGraw-Hill, 1965.

Eclipse of God. Translated by Maurice Friedman et al. New York: Harper Torchbooks, 1957 (first English edition appeared in 1952).

"Elijah: A Mystery Play." Translated by Maurice Friedman. In *Martin Buber and the Theater*, edited by Maurice Friedman, pp. 114–64. New York; Funk and Wagnalls, 1969.

For the Sake of Heaven. New ed. Translated by Ludwig Lewisohn. New York: Harper Torchbooks, 1966 (first English edition appeared in 1945).

Good and Evil. Two Interpretations. Translated by Ronald Gregor Smith and Michael Bullock. New York: Charles Scribner's Sons, 1961 (first English edition appeared in 1953).

Hasidism and Modern Man. Edited and translated by Maurice Friedman. New York: Harper Torchbooks, 1966 (first English edition appeared in 1958).

I and Thou. 2d ed. Translated by Ronald Gregor Smith. New York: Charles Scribner's Sons, 1958 (first English edition appeared in 1937).

Israel and the World: Essays in a Time of Crisis. 2d ed. Translated by Olga Marx et al. New York: Schocken Books, 1963. (first English edition appeared in 1948).

Kingship of God. 3d ed. Translated by Richard Scheimann. New York: Harper and Row, 1967.

The Knowledge of Man. Edited by Maurice Friedman. Translated by Maurice Friedman and Ronald Gregor Smith. New York: Harper Torchbooks, 1965.

Moses: The Revelation and the Covenant. New York: Harper Torchbooks, 1958 (first English edition appeared in 1946).

On Judaism. Edited by Nahum N. Glatzer. Translated by Eva Jospe et al. New York: Schocken Books, 1967. (Includes the addresses which appeared in *At the Turning*, published in 1952 by Farrar, Straus and Young.)

The Origin and Meaning of Hasidism. Edited and translated by Maurice Friedman. New York: Harper Torchbooks, 1966 (first English edition appeared in 1960).

Paths in Utopia. Translated by R.F. Hull. Boston: Beacon Press, 1958 (first English edition appeared in 1949).

Pointing the Way. Edited and translated by Maurice Friedman. New York: Harper Torchbooks, 1963 (first English edition appeared in 1957).

The Prophetic Faith. Translated by Carlyle Witton-Davies. New York: Harper Torchbooks, 1960 (first English edition appeared in 1949).

"Replies to My Critics." Translated by Maurice Friedman. In *The Philosophy of Martin Buber*, edited by Paul Schilpp and Maurice Friedman, pp. 689–744. La Salle, Illinois: Open Court Press, 1967.

"Responsa." Edited and translated by Maurice Friedman. In *Philosophical Interrogations*, edited by Sydney and Beatrice Rome, pp. 13–117. New York: Holt, Rinehart and Winston, 1964.

Tales of the Hasidim: Early Masters. Translated by Olga Marx. New

*I did not use the most recent and more scholarly translation of *I and Thou* (Charles Scribner's Sons, 1970) by Walter Kaufmann. Professor Kaufmann translates the German *du* by You instead of Thou, and this would conflict with all other English translations of Buber used in this study. This is by no means a judgment on the merits of this new translation.

York: Schocken Books, 1961 (first English edition appeared in 1947).

Tales of the Hasidism: Later Masters. Translated by Olga Marx. New York: Schocken Books, 1961 (first English edition appeared in 1948).

Tales of Rabbi Nachman. Translated by Maurice Friedman. Bloomington, Indiana: Indiana University Press, 1962 (first English edition appeared in 1956).

Ten Rungs: Hasidic Sayings. Translated by Olga Marx. New York: Schocken Books, 1962 (first English edition appeared in 1947).

Two Types of Faith. Translated by Norman P. Goldhawk. New York: Harper Torchbooks, 1961 (first English edition appeared in 1951).

WORKS ABOUT BUBER

Books

Balthasar, Hans Urs von. *Martin Buber and Christianity.* Translated by Alexander Dru. London: Harvill Press, 1961.

Cohen, Arthur A. *Martin Buber.* London: Bowes and Bowes, 1957.

Diamond, Malcolm L. *Martin Buber: Jewish Existentialist.* New York: Oxford University Press, 1960.

Friedman, Maurice S. *Martin Buber: The Life of Dialogue.* New ed. New York: Harper Torchbooks, 1960.

———, ed. *Martin Buber and the Theater.* New York: Funk and Wagnalls, 1969.

Hodes, Aubrey. *Martin Buber: An Intimate Portrait.* New York: The Viking Press, 1971.

Kohn, Hans. *Martin Buber: sein Werk und seine Zeit.* 2d ed. Nachwort von Robert Weltsch. Cologne: Joseph Melzer Verlag, 1961.

Martin Buber: An Appreciation of His Life and Thought. New York: American Friends of the Hebrew University, 1965. (Contributors: Judah Nadich, Maurice Friedman, Seymour Siegel, Paul Tillich, Henry Sonneborn.

Martin Buber: L'homme et le philosophe. Centre National des hautes études juives. Bruxelles: Editions de l'Institut de Sociologie de l'Université Libre de Bruxelles, 1968. (Contributors: Robert Weltsch, Gabriel Marcel, Emmanuel Levinas, André Lacocque.)

Oliver, Roy. *The Wanderer and the Way: The Hebrew Tradition in the Writings of Martin Buber.* Ithaca, New York: Cornell University Press, 1968.

Pfeutze, Paul. *Self, Society, Existence.* New York: Harper and Row, 1961.

Schaeder, Grete. *The Hebrew Humanism of Martin Buber.* Translated by Noah J. Jacobs. Detroit: Wayne State University Press, 1973.

Schilpp, Paul A., and Maurice Friedman, eds. *The Philosophy of Martin Buber.* LaSalle, Illinois: Open Court Press, 1967.

Streiker, Lowell D. *The Promise of Buber.* Philadelphia: J.P. Lippincott Co., 1969.

Articles

Cohen, Arthur A. "Revelation and Law: Reflections on Martin Buber's Views on Halakah." *Judaism* 1 (1952): 250–56.

Frankenstein, Carl. "Buber's Theory of Dialogue: a Critical Re-examination." *Cross Currents* 18 (1968): 229–41.

Friedman, Maurice S. "Martin Buber and Christian Thought." *The Review of Religion* 18 (1953): 31–43.

————. "Revelation and Law in the Thought of Martin Buber." *Judaism* 3 (1954): 9–19.

————. "Martin Buber's View of Biblical Faith." *The Journal of Bible and Religion* 22 (1954): 3–13.

————. "Martin Buber's Theology and Religious Education." *Religious Education* 54 (1959): 5–17.

————. "Martin Buber's Challenge to Jewish Philosophy." *Judaism* 14 (1965): 267–76.

McDermott, John. "Martin Buber and Hans Urs von Balthasar." *Cross Currents* 13 (1963): 115–21.

Simon, Ernst. "Jewish Adult Education in Nazi Germany as Spiritual Resistance." *Leo Baeck Institute Year Book,* pp. 68–104. London: East and West Library, 1956.

————. "Martin Buber and German Jewry." *Leo Baeck Institute Year Book,* pp. 3–39. London: East and West Library, 1958.

Sloyan, Gerald, "Buber and the Significance of Jesus." *The Bridge* 3 (1958): 209–33.

Tillich, Paul. "Martin Buber and Christian Thought." *Commentary* 5 (1948): 515–21.

Wolf, Ernst. "Martin Buber and German Jewry: Prophet and Teacher to a Generation in Catastrophe." *Judaism* 1 (1952), 346–57.